ELIZABETH'S BRITAIN

1926 to 1986

ELIZABETH'S BRITAIN

1926 to 1986

Philip Ziegler

Country Life Books

Frontispiece
Her Majesty the Queen photographed at Buckingham Palace in
May 1985 by Karsh of Ottawa.

Front endpaper
The gold coach bearing the Queen to her Coronation has just left
Buckingham Palace and is approaching the Mall.

Back endpaper
The Queen and her family on the balcony of Buckingham Palace
after the Silver Jubilee service of thanksgiving at St Paul's
Cathedral and lunch at the Guildhall.

Published by Country Life Books,
an imprint of Newnes Books,
a division of The Hamlyn Publishing Group Limited,
Bridge House, 69 London Road,
Twickenham, Middlesex TW1 3SB, England
and distributed for them by
Hamlyn Distribution Services Limited,
Rushden, Northants, England.

First published 1986
ISBN 0 600 35872 0
Printed in Great Britain

Contents

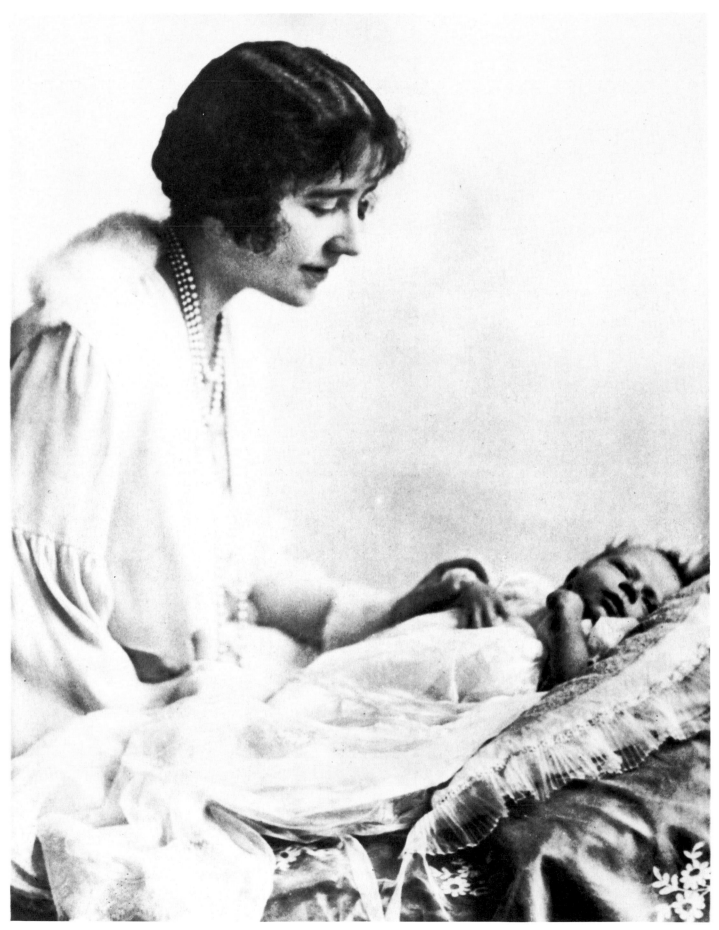

The Duchess of York with her infant daughter. When this photograph was taken it seemed only remotely possible that either Duchess or Princess would ever bear the title of Queen.

Prologue

Britain: April 1926

WEDNESDAY, April 21, shortly before dawn on a chill spring morning. A few hours earlier there had been a crowd gathered in Bruton Street, Mayfair, but the cold and drizzle had long driven away all but a handful of dejected reporters. Inside the house the home secretary, Sir William Joynson-Hicks, waited dutifully outside the bedroom in which the Duchess of York was about to have her first child. At twenty minutes to three his vigil was over. Princess Elizabeth Alexandra Mary had been safely born. 'Such a relief and joy', wrote Queen Mary in her diary.

The news spread rapidly. By early afternoon several hundred well-wishers had congregated in Bruton Street and King George V and Queen Mary were cheered enthusiastically when they arrived to inspect their new grandchild. The news had come too late for the morning press but it was broadcast by the British Broadcasting Company, soon to become a Corporation, from its station 2LO, and was hailed in triumphant headlines by the evening papers. The fuss, indeed, seemed somewhat disproportionate to the significance of the birth of a daughter to a younger son,

The christening of Princess Elizabeth on 29 May 1926

7

The Duke and Duchess of York, later King George VI and Queen Elizabeth, leave their home 17 Bruton Street on a tour that was to take them eventually to Australia and New Zealand and separate them from their baby daughter for six out of the first fourteen months of her life. A cluster of servants watch the departure from the first floor.

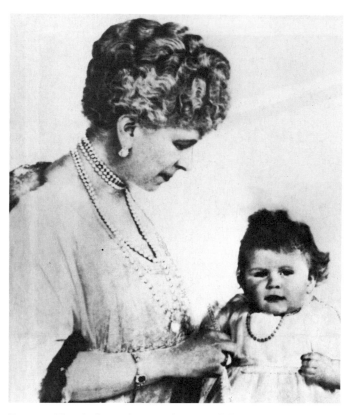

Princess Elizabeth, at the age of one, with her grandmother Queen Mary. She was to find Queen Mary an alarming figure and it was some time before she fully appreciated the warm affection that lay behind her grandmother's cool and dauntingly dignified exterior.

especially since the Princess Royal had already provided the King and Queen with their first grandchild. The Duchess of York, however, had established herself as a favourite with the British public. It was true that the child stood little chance of succeeding to the throne – the Prince of Wales was still only in his early thirties, and even if he failed in his duty to marry and produce an heir, the Yorks could be expected in due course to have a son who would displace his sister in the line of succession. For the moment, however, only the Prince of Wales and her father stood between the new baby and the throne. Princess Elizabeth was a person of considerable importance and royalist Britain was quick to celebrate her coming.

THE BRITISH people had plenty of other things to think about at that moment. April and May of 1926 were eventful months in Britain. Influenza and foot-and-mouth disease were ravaging the country in their different ways and there was a scare about dirty meat alleged to be on sale at unhygienic country butchers. Only a week before the birth the Australian cricketers had arrived unseasonably early; three days after it 92,000 watched Bolton Wanderers beat Manchester City 1-0 in the Cup Final at Wembley stadium. Unlike the meat, the match was clean. The women were also in the news. Miss Gibson shot Mussolini in the nose – she was said to be suffering from 'religious mania', which seemed as good a reason as any for shooting Mussolini. Lady Dorothy Miles returned from a visit to Liberia,

The Cup Final at Wembley in 1926. A crowd estimated at 92,000 watched Bolton Wanderers beat Manchester City 1-0. In the picture a Bolton back and a Manchester forward battle for possession of the ball.

The Women's Guild of Empire processes through London, 15,000 strong, in protest against the current wave of strikes and lock-outs. The redoubtable lady bearing the flag is Mrs Lionel Gibb, a champion horsewoman and looking every inch of it.

FRED and ADELE ASTAIRE.

Stage Photo Co.

Fred and Adele Astaire at the time they were appearing in Lady Be Good *at the Empire.*

during which she had had a brush with cannibals and trodden where – as she tirelessly assured every journalist she could induce to listen – no white woman had set foot before. Doris Neaves, aged nineteen, was found drunk in charge of a car in Baker Street – fears were expressed in court that late nights and cocktails were undermining the morality of modern youth. More healthily, the Women's Guild of Empire marched through London 15,000 strong in protest against strikes and lock-outs.

There was a rich variety of entertainment. At Stratford the plays had to be performed in a cinema because the Memorial Theatre had burnt down, but there was Little Tich at the Alhambra and Fred and Adele Astaire were starring in *Lady Be Good* at the Empire. Paul Whiteman's band from the United States was playing at the Kit Kat Club while Gershwin's *Rhapsody in Blue* could be heard at the Hotel Metropole. Scouts arrived from all over Europe for London's 'Great Rover Moot'. Processions of cars blocked the roads to Brighton and Portsmouth during the Easter bank holiday and police in Yorkshire pursued car thieves in a hectic chase that at times worked up to speeds of almost forty miles an hour. Imperial Airways demonstrated that there was another way by offering fifteen-minute flights from Croydon in their new Handley Page airliner.

And then, on 3 May, the general strike began.

THE LONG and embittered miners' strike of 1926 and the general strike that briefly grew out of it were manifestations of a deep discontent that consumed a great part of the British people. Between 1914 and 1918 the men had gone off in their millions to fight for King and country. They had endured hideous dangers and privations and had comforted themselves in their travail with the belief that their struggle would end in a return to – if not a land fit for heroes – then at least a better, fairer Britain. They had been disappointed. Nothing seemed to have changed, or where it had changed change was often for the worse. In war a sense of unity had sprung up, now the unity was shown to be spurious, Disraeli's 'two nations' were divided as starkly as ever.

To some women it seemed that the division was not so much between rich and poor as between male and female. They had been awarded the vote, but could not exercise it until the age of thirty; a woman of twenty-nine was assumed to be less responsible than a man of twenty-one. Though they could not serve either God or mammon – as exemplified by the Church of England and the Stock Exchange – most careers were now in theory open to them, but in practice their prospects for promotion in almost all of them were bleak indeed. Matrimony, house-keeping and child-bearing were felt by most men to be the proper function of the female, yet the massacres on the Western Front meant that there were many fewer men than women, so even this recourse was often denied them. The very fact that the new Princess would be overtaken in the line of succession by a younger brother seemed to demonstrate that at the heart of the body politic women remained the weaker, if not the inferior, species.

Though Welshman might differ from Scot, Scot from Englishman, race was not yet a serious divisive factor. Of the forty-four million-odd inhabitants of the British Isles almost all were white and of British birth. There were some quarter of a million Jews but though many of these practised a separate faith they seemed to most of their fellow citizens to be little if at all less British than their Gentile neighbours. There were Chinese settlements in Liverpool, Swansea and the East End; a scattering of black faces in the larger seaports; but to all intents and purposes Britain was a homogeneous nation. A truer division was between town and country. Half the population lived in towns of 50,000 inhabitants or more; 80 per cent of the people were crowded into five million acres, 20 per cent sprawled over the remaining thirty-three million. It was an age of increasing mobility but most Britons still stayed at home; the country dweller looked on the city with alarmed suspicion; the city dweller repaid the compliment with a tolerant contempt.

But it was still the traditional criteria of money and privilege that divided Britain most fundamentally. The statistics were stark enough. In 1926 one per cent of the

Women were developing new skills and asserting their right to enter every walk of life. In business, however, their role was still almost always confined to the secretarial. Here Miss Dorothy Neave, a repertory actress from Southend-on-Sea, pokes apprehensively at her new-fangled electric typewriter – a machine with which she appears inadequately acquainted.

population enjoyed two-thirds of the national wealth; three-quarters of the population possessed less than £100, even if all they owned in the world was taken into account. In the previous two years a majority of manual workers had actually seen their anyway exiguous wages reduced; 400,000 miners, to name no others, suffered a sharp cut in their pay packets. Opportunities of escaping to more remunerative work were rare. Even if the jobs were there, the educational attainments and cast of mind of the average industrial worker made such displacement difficult if not impossible.

Now this under-privileged working class found itself threatened with the loss of even the little that it enjoyed. There were in fact more people in work in Britain than ever before in peacetime, many thousands more than a few years before, but there were still more than a million unemployed by the time that Princess Elizabeth was born and the figure had risen by another half million before the end of the year. Since 1921 unemployment benefit had been available to everyone, but the amounts were meagre and the cost in dignity was great.

It would be unfair to pin the blame for this unhappy situation solely on the government. Britain in 1926, as in 1986, was in painful transition between old industries and new; the manufacture of cotton goods, to mention only the most conspicuous example, became increasingly unprofitable; car manufacturing and the service industries were yet to experience their dramatic expansion. But the process was already far advanced.

Ironically, the general strike occurred in the middle of a period of steady if unspectacular recovery. For the recovery itself the government deserved some credit, but there was little in the composition of Baldwin's team of contented businessmen to suggest that much imagination or compassion could be expected if anything went wrong. When exports slumped, the only remedy that occurred to the massive Conservative majority was to cut wages. The miners led the opposition, with the rallying cry of: 'Not a penny off the pay, not a minute on the day.' On 1 May the owners closed the mines and declared a lock-out. With the possible exception of Churchill and Birkenhead the Conservative leaders shrank from confrontation; so too did the panjandrums of the trade-union movement; but the tide of events proved too strong. On 3 May the trade-union leaders approved a national strike.

WHAT AT the time appeared a crisis of potentially catastrophic dimensions that might destroy the fabric of the state can now be seen to have been little more than a tremor on the surface of a profoundly stable society. The memories that linger most clearly in the mind are not of the belligerent speeches, the occasional violence, the revolutionary gestures, but of the cricket match between the police and the strikers organised by the Chief Constable of Plymouth, the eagerness to compromise shown by the vast majority of the union leaders, the indignation with which George V turned on Lord Durham when that coal-owning magnifico

A charity ball aboard the SS Majestic *at Southampton in April 1926. In spite of the move towards convenience and comfort in male dress there would have been no question of wearing a dinner-jacket on such an occasion. Whether this contributed to the fixed gloom manifested by most of the guests must remain debatable.*

abused the miners – 'Try living on their wages!' shouted the King. It took as divisive an emergency as this to prove how coherent the country still was; only extremism could demonstrate the underlying moderation of the British people.

Every so often some great event demands the total attention of the nation. The Suez crisis was one such, the national strike another. Yet within a few weeks the normal preoccupations of the average citizen renewed their potency: would Australia surrender the Ashes? what horse would win the Derby? what had happened to Agatha Christie? The latter's sensational disappearance in December 1926 drove politics and economics from the headlines. Except when the strike was actually in progress, indeed, it seemed as if nothing was likely seriously to ruffle the tranquillity of the people. The Irish question, it was believed, had been finally resolved. Nearly three-quarters of the Irish electorate had supported the treaty which had set up the independent North; the armed bands of Sinn Fein had been crushed in the civil war that had followed the granting of independence. In Europe there were economic troubles enough, but no hint of serious conflict. A major war with any country in the world seemed inconceivable.

The British were a patriotic race – fond of parades, saluting the flag, standing stiffly to attention when the national anthem was played – but they were not belligerent. They liked the idea of Empire – or Commonwealth of Nations as they now had to learn to call the curious amalgam of virtually independent Canada,

Back to work. Miners at Clipston pit in Nottinghamshire line up for the first wages paid out since their long and embittered strike began. The last relic of the General Strike was over.

A queue of unemployed waiting outside a labour exchange in 1924. There were in fact more people employed in Britain than ever before in peacetime but the total of unemployed still rose inexorably and was to pass a million by the time that Princess Elizabeth was born.

The general strike of 1926. Undergraduates help handle mailbags from the Continent on the quayside at Dover.

A tank patrols an East End street during the general strike. This somewhat alarming manifestation of military might was by no means typical of the period – the army on the whole kept a low profile. Certainly the passers-by seem more interested than concerned.

Australia, New Zealand and South Africa with the old-style colonies – but they did not want to have to fight for it. Nor did they expect to have to do so. India was giving trouble, but India always had given trouble. It was only seven years since General Dyer had shot down nearly 400 Indians at Amritsar; the British on the whole felt that he had gone a bit too far but that authority had to be maintained. The Indians, like any other coloured race, were patently incapable of governing themselves; but it did not seem at all likely that the British would have to fight to maintain their supremacy.

Fear God, Honour the King! God, however, did not figure largely in the national consciousness. It was more than fifty years since Matthew Arnold had heard the 'melancholy, long, withdrawing roar' that marked the ebbing of the Sea of Faith, and still the tide flowed out. There were eight million confirmed members of the Church of England of whom nearly three million were regular communicants, 2.5 million baptised Roman Catholic, two million members of the Free Churches, yet every year the numbers dwindled, church-going declined. Sabbitarianism faded as Sunday newspapers began to appear in the most respectable households; even divorce was beginning to seem acceptable since two years earlier Josiah Wedgwood, guilty party in a divorce action, had taken his place in the cabinet. Religion was not a spent force, but it had lost much of its potency.

The Church of England was very much part of the British establishment, as exemplified by the Very Reverend C.A. Alington, headmaster of Eton. Here he parades his bailiwick on the Fourth of June, traditionally Eton's greatest annual feast. He is accompanied by his daughter, who was later to marry the young Viscount Dunglass and become successively Countess of Home, Lady Douglas-Home and Lady Home – and all with only one husband.

Jacob Epstein, the sculptor, inspecting the memorial to W.H. Hudson which was unveiled in Hyde Park in 1925. It was greeted with some derision and daubed with green paint by vandals who felt its modernism to be out of place in a London park (or anywhere else for that matter).

The British were a patriotic race – fond of parades and saluting the flag. The habit extended to the schoolchildren, here on the march at the Hugh Middleton school in Clerkenwell.

Oxford Circus, looking north from Regent Street.

As ever, the British viewed any innovation with suspicious distaste. When Epstein's statue of Rima had been unveiled in Hyde Park the year before it had been daubed with green paint and greeted with derision – 'Take this horror out of the Park!' pleaded the *Daily Mail*. Eliot had published *The Waste Land* and Joyce *Ulysses* four years before, yet the general public knew and cared little for them, had hardly heard of Henry Moore or Ben Nicholson. Yet, almost without noticing, the country had embarked upon the greatest revolution of its history. Old landmarks were vanishing; even as the King and Queen visited the baby Princess Elizabeth the crash of tumbling masonry a few hundred yards away showed that another chunk of Nash's Quadrant at Piccadilly had gone for ever. New forces were emerging. The motor car, first an eccentricity, then a luxury, was fast becoming a commonplace. Mass-production had arrived; the first Baby Austin had come off the assembly line in 1924. Car registrations doubled in five years, to nearly half a million.

Radio had begun to operate four years before when the British Broadcasting Company was set up under the rigid and Calvinistic Reith. The moral tone was

Charlie Chaplin, the most widely loved actor the world has ever known, in his characteristic costume.

By the time the British Broadcasting Corporation was set up in 1926 radio was already established as a vastly important medium. Here passengers on a train bound for the 1923 Grand National at Aintree listen in a wireless saloon set up for the journey.

Piccadilly, London, traditionally the hub of the British Empire, on a summer night in 1926. The scene was painted by Maurice Greiffenhagen.

Dejection and apathy were stamped on the figures in this Labour party poster. There were more than a million unemployed on the day Princess Elizabeth was born, by the end of 1926 there were half as many again.

Informality in male dress, though growing, rarely extended beyond the bounds set by this sporting character. Note the length and looseness of the trousers.

high; the sartorial tone as well – announcers were required to wear dinner-jackets when they read the news. Distant voices crackled through earphones, distant music too; by the time the Corporation was set up in 1926 it was clear that a vastly powerful new medium was gathering force. Two months before Elizabeth was born J.L. Baird achieved a breakthrough that led to television.

The cinema too was on the march, undermining the traditional music-hall and threatening even the role of the pub as the favourite resort of the Briton in search of entertainment. Thirty million people a week flocked to the films of Chaplin and Harold Lloyd, Garbo and Douglas Fairbanks Senior. When Valentino died in 1926 a multitude mourned. Talking pictures were still a little time away – a disastrous attempt to film *Der Rosenkavalier* led the critics to conclude sadly, if unsurprisingly, that opera was improved by sound.

Apart from the demands of war, half the population had never travelled more than fifty miles from their homes. Yet the age of mobility was around the corner. In 1926 Southern Railways alone took just over two million passengers to the Continent. Greyhound

Early automation at the petrol pumps. For the 1/- (5p) which the lucky motorists were requested to put into the slot, they could expect to get the best part of a gallon.

Breasts and hips were to be deplored and, if possible, concealed. Rubens would have marvelled at the androgynous drain-pipes whom Marshall and Snelgrove selected to model their dancing 'Directoire' cami-knickers.

Motors of Bristol began an omnibus service to London; the fare was £1 return, the buses reached 40 mph on the flat. Telephones became less of a rarity, the half-millionth telephone was installed in London in July, the three-thousandth telephone box made available. The popular press flashed news around the country. Less than half British families took a daily paper; no newspaper sought seriously to reflect the opinions of the masses, but Northcliffe had broken the pattern of the nineteenth century and created the modern press, with sensationalist headlines, extensive sports coverage, crisp and simplified news reports.

It was the age of jazz, with the American influence predominant. 'Swanee' and 'Bye Bye Blackbird' were the hits of the day; Gershwin flourished and Irving Berlin, Cole Porter and Jerome Kern. Fashion reflected the same trend towards informality and liberation; hemlines went up; black woollen stockings gave way to flesh-coloured silk; hair was cut shorter; the rich Rubens-esque figure was out, androgynous sylphs were all the rage. Men yielded less readily to the spirit of the age, but at every level of society grudging concessions were made to convenience and comfort. The shepherds in Cumberland, the housewives in South Wales, knew little and cared less about the fashions of the metropolis, but they were aware of them. The great, levelling force of modern communications had begun its work.

In every age, in every country, any time is one of transition. Any year can be portrayed by the determined historian as a gateway from the past to the future, from light to darkness (or, if it suits the argument better, from darkness to light). Yet it does not seem extravagant to maintain that the time of Princess Elizabeth's birth was one of peculiar uncertainty. If in 1866 or 1906 the average Briton had been asked to predict the shape of his country sixty years on he would have done so with some confidence, basing his prophecy on the situation he saw around him. In 1926 he would not have been so sure. Vast changes lay ahead, but what they might be he did not know. Few indeed would have predicted the microchip and the nuclear power-station, the supermarket and the Chinese take-away, but that something strange would happen now seemed certain. In 1926 the British were waking up to the possibilities of the future. They were not sure they liked the look of it.

Demonstrating the 'twist' – a dance that bore no relationship to its more tempestuous namesake of the 1960s. This earlier version was invented by M. Camille de Rhynal, President of the International Dancing Federation, and was said to have charmed Mrs Stanley Baldwin when performed before her and her husband at Aix-les-Bains.

Princess Elizabeth at the age of ten with one of the first of what was to be an interminable sequence of royal corgis. The dog, named Dookie, has apparently just been bitten on its snout by a passing mongrel of republican sympathies. The Princess is consoling her unfortunate pet, who was presumably more used to biting than being bit.

Chapter One

Depression and Recovery

1926 to 1936

THE FIRST ten years of Princess Elizabeth's life were passed in the dawning awareness, first that she might possibly, then that she would probably become Queen. Her sister, Margaret Rose, was born at Glamis Castle in 1929, and no young prince appeared to take over the burden of succession. The Prince of Wales seemed bent on remaining a bachelor. Elizabeth acted as a bridesmaid at the wedding of the Duke of Kent and it was noticed that she got particularly loud cheers along the way. When she did not accompany her parents on a visit to Edinburgh, to marked public disappointment, her mother wrote: 'It almost frightens me that the people should love her so much. I suppose that it is a good thing, and I hope she will be worthy of it, poor little darling.'

Though she was a serious and conscientious child, the burdens of approaching glory were not allowed to weigh heavily upon her. Her upbringing was sensible and unassuming, her nanny and governess instructed to stand no nonsense, still less to inculcate it in their

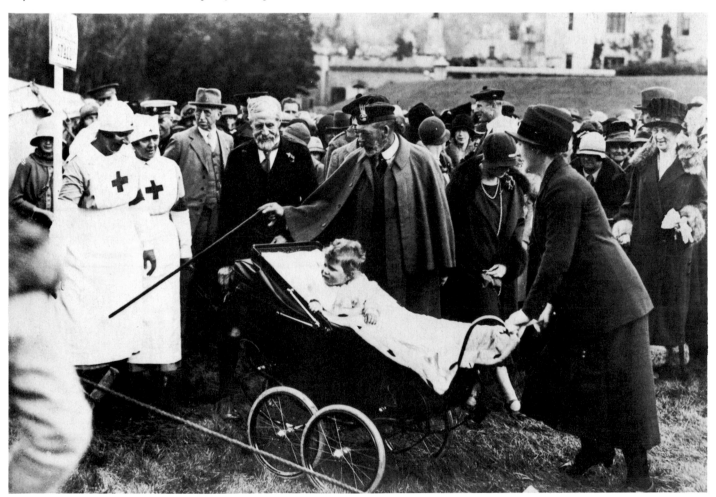

Princess Elizabeth in her pram is accompanied by her grandfather, King George V, at a fête in the grounds of Balmoral in the summer of 1927.

charge. Pets abounded – the first corgi came to her home at 145 Piccadilly in 1933. Friends were more difficult. Inevitably it was a lonely and, by the standards of other children, formal existence. When their governess, the egregious Crawfie, took the Princesses by underground to Tottenham Court Road and then to tea in the YWCA, they were spotted, mobbed, and the break for freedom ended in ignominious rescue by a royal car.

She was terrified of George V and still more of Queen Mary, about whom the divinity that doth hedge a queen clustered with particular density. The children were required to curtsey to their grandmother when they first met her in the morning; if Queen Mary stayed away from home in the 1930s two pages took it in turns to sit outside her bedroom door. George V, massive, bearded, formidable, nevertheless had a warmth and geniality that his wife lacked. Almost by mistake, certainly not by contrivance, he won the love of his people. His Christmas broadcast, heard for the first time in 1932, became a national event: the rich, resonant voice, the direct and patently sincere simplicity. The least self-publicising of kings, he achieved a public image unknown to any of his predecessors.

The Silver Jubilee of May 1935 gave the people the chance to show their loyalty. What might have been arrogantly chauvinistic or an empty parade of splendour was turned by their enthusiasm into a personal

The two Princesses photographed in Oxford Street on their way to the underground station for their first ride in a tube train. The expedition ended in disorder when they were identified, mobbed and had to be rescued by a royal car.

The Duke of Kent married Princess Marina of Greece in 1934. Princess Elizabeth and Lady Mary Cambridge acted as bridesmaids and look pretty cross about it. Prince and Princess Nicholas of Greece stand with the King and Queen beside the bridal couple.

The nation rejoiced at the Silver Jubilee of 1935. Milecote Street in South East London had certainly been at particular pains to show its loyalty but it was by no means untypical of the rest of the capital, indeed of the rest of the country.

The royal family arrive at the west door of St Paul's Cathedral for the jubilee service of thanksgiving in May 1935. King George V and Queen Mary stand in the centre of the picture with behind them the Lord Chamberlain followed by the Prince of Wales and the Duke and Duchess of York with the two Princesses. The Duke of Gloucester is to the right of the Duke of York and the Duke of Kent to the left.

During the service in St Paul's Cathedral to mark the jubilee the King and Queen kneel in front of the altar with their family ranged in the rows behind them.

A year after the Silver Jubilee George V was dead. 'People who had never seen the King,' wrote the left-wing intellectual Kingsley Martin, 'and only heard his voice on the wireless talked about him as if he were a personal friend or a near relation.' There is no questioning the grief on the faces of these schoolchildren.

tribute to a man they had grown to love. There were fireworks, decorations, floodlit buildings (a daring novelty); the magistrates of Southport joined in the fun by allowing children under fourteen to see 'adults only' films; but what came through was the affection of the crowd. It was 'For He's a Jolly Good Fellow', not 'God Save the King' that was most often heard. 'I'd no idea they felt like that about me,' said the King in wonder. His broadcast on 6 May caught the flavour both of the occasion and of his personality:

How can I express what is in my heart? I can only say to you, my very, very dear people, that the Queen and I thank you from the depths of our hearts for all the loyalty and – may I say so? – the love with which this day and always you have surrounded us. I dedicate myself anew to your service, for all the years that may still be given me . . .

Less than a year was given him. Early in 1936 the sombre bulletin came from the Palace: 'The King's life is moving peacefully towards its close.' The BBC cancelled its programmes; the music stopped in the restaurants and dance halls around the country; the nation waited. 'How is the Empire?' were said to be his dying words. Some prefer 'Bugger Bognor!' – a rebuff to a courtier who suggested he would soon be convalescing

Here pictured, the lying in state at Westminster Hall.

A detail from Thomas Dugdale's 'The Arrival of the Jarrow Marchers in London' provides a vigorous commentary on the social gulf between rich and poor. But could any couple have been quite as unmoved by the spectacle below them as these languid butterflies?

*Above anything else, the British when they relaxed did like to be
beside the seaside. This splendid picture by Charles Cundall shows
a bank holiday crowd at Brighton in 1933. The congestion at
Blackpool might have been greater but the spirit would have been
much the same.*

Stanley Baldwin, the Conservative leader, addressing electors in the City in the Cannon-Street hotel. His celebrated slogan 'Safety First' is much in evidence but was not enough to prevent Labour winning the greatest number of seats in the 1929 election.

in that salubrious resort; others allege that the 'Empire' in question was a music-hall. Certainly George V shunned grandiloquence, but no one who knew him doubted that the welfare of his people would always have been to the forefront of his mind.

'No one who talked to his neighbour on a bus,' wrote that left-wing intellectual, Kingsley Martin, 'to the charwoman washing the steps or to a sightseer standing at the street corner, could doubt the almost universal feeling of loss . . . People who had never seen the King and only heard his voice on the wireless talked about him as if he were a personal friend or a near relation.'

For Princess Elizabeth it was the death of a beloved if somewhat alarming grandfather; it was the passing of a monarch – 'Ought we to play?' she asked anxiously, when grooming her toy horse; and it was another step on the path that led inexorably towards the throne. Shades of the prison-house – or the palace rather – began to close upon the growing girl. Elizabeth now stood second in the line of succession and the public more and more accepted that she was probably a future monarch. As the coffin of the late King was carried into Westminster Hall the Maltese Cross of the Imperial Crown tumbled into the gutter. 'Christ, what's going to happen next?' enquired the startled Edward VIII. It was a question to which he was soon to give the answer, and already those near the throne were beginning to suspect that the answer might not be one acceptable to the people of Britain. 'There goes the hope of England!' a man in the crowd had called out as the Duke and Duchess of York with their children left Buckingham Palace during the Jubilee celebrations. Not many people would have echoed the cry in 1935; now every month that passed lent fresh volume to the swelling chorus.

THE COUNTRY over which Edward VIII was briefly to rule seemed in far better shape than had been likely a few years before. The period had started well; once the miners' strike had petered out towards the end of 1926, the last years of the decade had been ones of prosperity. It was as if Britain had finally overcome the economic problems that had plagued it since the war. At the general election of 1929 the country split on the lines that were to become so familiar over the next half century – Conservative and Labour roughly equal, with the Liberals a bad third. The Conservatives won more votes but the electoral system – devised in 1911 and taking no account of the drift of population from north to south or from city centre to suburb – gave Labour more seats. The Liberals, with five million votes against some eight million for each of the major parties, won only fifty-nine seats, less than ten per cent of the House of Commons for nearly a quarter of the votes.

With the largest number of votes the Conservative leader, Stanley Baldwin, might reasonably have tried to cobble together a coalition with the Liberals. Instead he told the King that it would be 'unsporting' to keep Labour out, and George V invited Ramsay Mac-Donald to form a minority government. Administrations that cannot command a majority in the House of Commons have little chance to adopt strong, let alone extremist, policies. MacDonald's cabinet considered abandoning the use of court dress but faltered even at this trivial hurdle – though the commissioner of works, George Lansbury, with much daring wore a dinner-jacket for his first formal appearance at the Palace. No socialist monuments marked the Labour government's existence; the provision of facilities for open-air bathing in the Serpentine in Hyde Park was indeed probably the most memorable of its achievements.

*Labour ministers visit Buckingham Palace after their electoral victory. Ramsay Macdonald, the
incoming prime minister, is on the left, with beside him J.H. Thomas, the lord privy seal,
Arthur Henderson, the foreign secretary, and J.R. Clynes, the home secretary.*

*A national government was formed in August 1931. Here the
prime minister, Ramsay Macdonald, leads a group of his
ministers down the steps into the garden at 10 Downing Street.
J.H. Thomas is immediately behind him, then come Lord Reading
and Stanley Baldwin. Philip Snowden, another survivor from the
Labour cabinet, supports himself with a stick. At the top, from
left to right, stand Herbert Samuel, Neville Chamberlain, Samuel
Hoare, Philip Cunliffe-Lister and (in the hat) Lord Sankey.*

Then, in October 1929, everything went wrong. The
Wall Street crash in New York, which wiped out vast
fortunes overnight and destroyed the savings of a generation, did not directly harm many British investors,
but the knock-on effects were catastrophic. American
money largely disappeared from the world markets; the
producers of raw materials could no longer sell them or
afford to buy British goods. Exports slumped, unemployment soared – to two million in July 1930 and 2.5
million six months later. The Labour government had
as little conception how this crisis should be tackled as
did the Conservative opposition; the only minister with
ideas on the subject, Sir Oswald Mosley, left the ministry in despair to found his own party. Strict financial
orthodoxy was the shibboleth to which the Labour
chancellor, Snowden, clung hopefully: order, disci-
pline, a balanced budget. With the support, some
would say under the control of the Bank of England, he
refused to countenance anything that might stimulate
the economy or pump fresh money into the system.

In the summer of 1931 came financial collapse in
Europe: Germany was ravaged by hyper-inflation; the
gold reserves were draining from London; the bankers
of France and the United States insisted on still more
austere measures if they were to come to the rescue.
The balanced budget was now more than ever the first
priority of the chancellor of the exchequer. Backed by
MacDonald he insisted that an essential element in any
package must be a cut of 10 per cent in unemployment
benefit. Nine cabinet ministers out of twenty threatened resignation rather than accept such a harsh
imposition; the TUC categorically rejected the cuts. A
minority government could not stand the defection of
nearly half its members; a Liberal/Conservative coalition seemed an unpromising alternative. It was the

Liberal, Herbert Samuel, who put forward the proposal for a national government with MacDonald as prime minister as a temporary measure to deal with the emergency. George V eagerly supported the idea and pressed MacDonald to go along with it. MacDonald rashly assumed that those of his colleagues who had accepted the need for cuts would support the coalition or at least abstain from opposing it. On 24 August 1931 the national government was formed. MacDonald transformed himself by this one act into the most hated figure of the left.

To most of the nation he seemed a saviour rather than a villain. Only two weeks before, Noel Coward's patriotic extravaganza *Cavalcade* had burst upon London's West End. Its celebrated final toast: 'Let's couple the future of England with the past of England' and 'Let's drink to the hope that some day this country of ours, which we love so much, will find dignity and greatness and peace again,' provoked a frisson of excitement in even the most sophisticated. The national government, it was fondly believed, might find the path to dignity and greatness and peace. 'Thank God For Him,' was Garvin's headline tribute to MacDonald in the *Observer*, and the nation thanked God for him.

The national government did what it was supposed to do – it checked the run on the pound. It achieved this aim by imposing pay cuts on everyone over whose income it exercised control and many over whom it had no hold except one of conscience: the King for instance, asked that his Civil List be cut by £50,000 and gave up his shooting at Windsor. The Prince of Wales chipped in £10,000; the Duke of York sold his hunters. Every

state employee had his pay cut by an average of 10 per cent, but the disparities were striking; the police got away with 5 per cent, the teachers lost three times as much. In the Royal Navy the ratings on the lower deck suffered severely compared with the officers. Discontent was so serious that the men of the Atlantic Fleet mutinied at their base at Invergordon. Such behaviour on the part of Britain's senior and traditionally most cherished Service sent a shiver of horror down the spine of the middle classes, who remembered the prominent role that the Russian navy had played in the Bolshevik revolution. The Admiralty hurriedly changed its tune and rescinded the more unreasonable of the cuts.

Encouraged by such excesses, the run on the pound resumed. Ramsay MacDonald, having saved the nation once, found that he had to do so all over again. On 19 September the Bank of England reported that foreign credits were exhausted. In such circumstances one must conceive the inconceivable. The government's response was to suspend the gold standard. The pound, thus left to fend for itself, fell heavily against foreign currencies; from $4.83 to the pound to an average of about $3.40. There it remained and to everyone's surprise things seemed otherwise much the same. 'A few days before,' as A.J.P. Taylor has put it, 'a managed currency had seemed as wicked as family planning. Now, like contraception, it became a commonplace.'

The country liked it, or perhaps more accurately, the country could think of no safe alternative. The national government went to the country and asked for 'a doctor's mandate', ministers appealing to the electorate

Noel Coward's Cavalcade *was one of the theatrical successes of the time and its celebrated toast to the restored greatness of Britain stirred popular sentiment. This scene is from C.B. Cochran's production at Drury Lane.*

The national government won an overwhelming victory in the election of 1931 and the massacre of the Labour leaders left the way open for youngsters like Clement Attlee and Stafford Cripps to win early prominence. Here Attlee is shaking hands with a butterfly-collared Arthur Greenwood.

to ask no questions but to put its trust in their ability to set the economy straight. The trust was granted. The Labour party, bereft of its most alluring leaders and judged by the country to have run away in the face of crisis, lost two million votes. The government won 554 out of 615 seats, 14.5 million out of 21.6 million votes – the largest number of seats and votes won by any administration in British history. Every member of the former Labour cabinet who had stuck to the sinking ship, except George Lansbury, went down with the wreck and lost his seat, leaving the way clear for youngsters like Clement Attlee and Stafford Cripps to climb towards the top.

The national government's solution for the economic problems was renewed restraint: higher taxes, stringent curbs on spending. As motor-car registrations multiplied, so the miles of new roads built or planned dwindled to almost nothing. Neither the problem nor the solution were unique to Britain; within four years of the crash of 1929 world trade fell by almost a half; by

Unemployment and poverty caused much suffering in the 1930s. Here the famous aviators Jim and Amy Mollison (formerly Amy Johnson) attend a coffee stall designed for those with no financial resources. The queue of unemployed seem remarkably unmoved by this somewhat patronising visitation.

1933 there were thirty million unemployed in the industrialised countries. The United States had recourse to the New Deal, Germany to fascism; the national government stuck to the mixture as before. It worked after a fashion, but the price in suffering was fearful. Unemployment rose to a peak of just under three million in January 1933. Nobody starved, but crushing poverty was added to the burdens of frustration and humiliation involved in being out of a job. The Means Test was imposed – after the unemployed had exhausted their insurance stamps they were handed over to a Public Assistance Committee which enquired, with what often seemed indecent relish, into every detail of a household's income and expenditure. Whole industries disappeared – doomed, perhaps, anyway to die by attrition, but now extinguished almost overnight. The great 300-mile march of the Jarrow shipbuilders – victims of a one-business town that had lost its business – did not take place till 1936, yet the genesis of Jarrow's misery lay four or five years before.

The unemployed of Jarrow found that they were marching from a still destitute north to a south to which prosperity had returned. The worst was over by 1934. Britain, Neville Chamberlain exultantly proclaimed, had finished with *Bleak House* and could now start on *Great Expectations* (he can hardly have remembered what happened to Pip's expectations in the end). Income tax was reduced, the cuts in unemployment benefit restored. Building was booming and a new programme of slum clearances was launched. Rearma-

ment was lending a stimulus to industry. Half-hearted efforts were made to direct investment to those parts of the country that were still economically depressed but it was the flow of population to the areas where jobs were plentiful that did most to reduce the figures.

MacDonald's time was over; he had become no more than a magnificent shell, hated by the opposition, despised by his colleagues. 'The Boneless Wonder,' Churchill had called him, and though the insult was unfair it had enough truth in it to stick. His last public appearance as prime minister was at the Jubilee; then he resigned to make way for Baldwin, who had in fact dominated the coalition from the start. A successful businessman, cautious, lacklustre, safe, Baldwin was helped immeasurably in the management of his party by the inveterate opposition of the press Lords, Beaverbrook and Rothermere. Their campaign against him – rooted, in Kipling's memorable phrase, in their quest for 'power without responsibility – the prerogative of the harlot throughout the ages' – proved, if proof were needed, that the new popular press could reinforce a national mood but never redirect it. When Baldwin went to the country in 1935 he did so as unquestioned master of a ministry which was still 'national' in name but in fact was emphatically and almost exclusively Conservative.

The election showed that not much had changed. The Conservatives held their vote, the Socialists regained some part of their dissident following that had retreated into abstention four years before. The

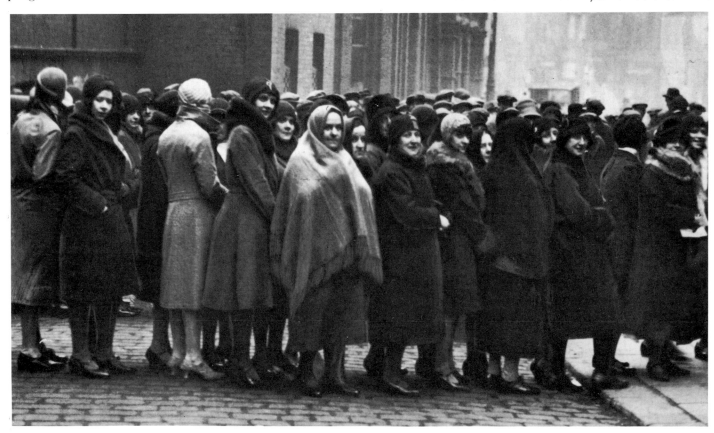

One of the industries worst affected by the depression was that of cotton. Unemployed women machine operators queue outside the Labour Exchange at Oldham in Lancashire but have little hope of finding a job.

Ship-building was another casualty. The great Jarrow march to London (above) was the most dramatic demonstration of a misery that was nationwide. (Top) A group of marchers take a break to refresh themselves and Paddy, the mascot of the march.

By the mid 1930s the worst of the depression was over and the building trade was booming. These suburban semi detached villas are typical of many thousands that sprang up about this time.

By the time of the 1935 general election the government, though still officially 'national', was led by Baldwin and was predominantly Conservative. It is a fair bet that this Chelsea Pensioner, leaving Holy Trinity School for Boys in Chelsea after recording his vote, has given his support to the national government.

national government still enjoyed an overwhelming majority: 432 seats to a mere 154. Though no one would then have thought it possible, it was to be the last election till 1945. By the time that Britain went to the polls again, it would be a different world.

THE NATIONAL strike had seemed at the time a cataclysm from which the country might never recover; the great depression brought misery to hundreds of thousands, discomfort at least to millions. And yet it is doubtful whether Britain's evolution in the decade after Princess Elizabeth's birth was altered substantially by either of these phenomena. The economic and social condition of the country was changing radically, to take account as much of the progress of the other nations of the world as of events in Britain itself. The great march was on: from steam to petrol engines, from heavy metals to plastics. Coal-mining, which in 1924 had earned three times as much as any other industry, had had its lead whittled away to a mere 20 per cent by 1935; a third of the labour force left the mines between the two wars. Faced with fierce competition, the cotton industry withered, falling from third to eleventh place. In terms of output, agriculture throve, but fewer men grew more crops; the advance of technology drove 10,000 men a year from the land.

The new sources of employment were the manufacturers of cars and electrical equipment, the hotels, cinemas and dance-halls, the civil service and accountancy, the building trade. By 1939 a third of the nation's

New industries were expanding to take the place of the dying mastodons of the past. The mass production of motor cars grew by the day. This picture was taken in the upholstery and trimming shop of Morris Motors at Cowley, Oxford.

Electrical equipment too was a rapidly growing sector of industry. This four-valve radio-gramophone was the very latest thing on show at Radio Olympia in September 1931. The cheapest model cost sixteen guineas.

Large blocks of flats were becoming a common feature of the landscape. They were usually built for private ownership but it is interesting to find these fifteen-storey buildings being put forward early in 1936 as a substitute for slum areas in St Pancras. Evidently it was only the war that saved the British cities from a premature rash of tower blocks.

Advertising burgeoned, and endless care that previously had gone into the quality of a product was now lavished on its packaging and promotion. Actresses and society beauties were hired to extol the merits of rival brands of soap or scent. This advertisement proclaimed '9 out of 10 film stars use Lux Toilet Soap' – a claim that must have been singularly hard to prove or disprove.

houses had been built since the First World War, large blocks of flats for the first time were becoming a common feature of the landscape.

The scientific skills of the nation had rarely been more impressively deployed. In 1928 Alexander Fleming discovered penicillin; in the following years it was the turn of James Chadwick with the neutron, Blackett established the existence of the positive electron, Cockcroft took the crucial step towards the splitting of the atom, the giant figure of the New Zealander Rutherford presided over Cambridge physics. The disastrous gap between invention and commercial exploitation which was to mar Britain's post-1945 performance was not yet apparent. If Britain did not lead the world in technological advance, it was at least well to the fore.

It was the decaying industries, the soup-kitchens, dole-queues, hunger marches, that provide the popular image of the 1930s. Yet for the lucky three-quarters of the population it was a period of new and burgeoning prosperity. The working population enjoyed unprecedented wealth and spent it lavishly. In 1935 the nation consumed twenty-three million barrels of beer, eleven million hundredweight of oranges. New prosperity created new forms of consumer demand. Clothes mass-produced by Montagu Burton and the Fifty Shilling Taylors spread elegance to the lower and lower-middle

classes; Lyons' teashops offered roast beef, Yorkshire pudding, two veg and a sweet for a mere 1/- (5p). Woolworths, with its proud boast 'Nothing over 6d' (2·5p), brought a wide range of manufactured products within reach of the smallest income (though the definition of 6d was sometimes stretched – spectacles costing 6d for the frame and 6d for each lens). The 'stop-me-and-buy-one' salesman peddled (and pedalled – since bicycles were the usual conveyance) his ice-cream in areas where no ice-cream had been seen before. At the other end of the culinary scale, André Simon founded the Wine and Food Society.

The fires of demand were eagerly fed by the manufacturers. Hire-purchase became a commonplace in the 1930s, though still conducted in a shame-faced manner; a leading firm in the business guaranteed that its deliveries would be made in unmarked vans. Advertising blossomed: electric-lit signs blazing in the provincial cities as well as London, aeroplanes scrawling smoke messages across the skies, newspapers crowded with puffs for patent medicines, cosmetics, sweets and cigarettes.

Advertising, indeed, was becoming the life-blood of the press. More readers meant more advertising at higher rates; the circulation war was on. The popular papers bought new readers, with gifts and prizes. The *Daily Express* distributed 10,000 pairs of silk stockings,

This Woolworths, with its proud boast that it sold nothing that cost more than sixpence (2.5p) and triumphantly art deco façade, was typical of many such stores that brought a wide range of manufactured goods within reach of the lowest earners.

the *Express*, *Mail* and *News Chronicle* respectively presented their presumably gratified readers with 124,000, 120,000 and 65,000 sets of the works of Dickens. Each new reader cost the *Daily Herald* £1, the *Daily Express* 8s.3d. (41p). But the papers were more fun to read as well. In the *Daily Express* Lord Beaverbrook, who as a Canadian was improperly disrespectful of the British class system, sought to create a paper that would appeal to readers of every social level. In the *Daily Herald* Hannen Swaffer pioneered what was in effect Britain's first gossip column. Sales of both *Express* and *Herald* rose above two million; the *Express* stayed there.

But journalism was only one of the ways by which new ideas were spread abroad. The radio was the most significant single force of the age. New sets were licensed at an average rate of half a million a year; by 1939 nine households out of ten could tune in to the BBC. What most of them listened to was the popular music: the Savoy Orpheans, Henry Hall with 'Bye-Bye Blackbird' or 'Twilight on Missouri'. The demand for light music seemed insatiable – whether it was Tauber's soupy rendering of 'You Are My Heart's Delight', Gracie Fields's more energetic 'Sally – Pride of our Alley' or Al Jolson's 'Sonny Boy', which in 1928 sold twelve million records in four months. It was the triumph of a new classless culture. But the BBC did

more than propagate jazz and sentimental crooners. In 1927 Henry Wood broadcast his first concert on 2LO. Within a few years no day passed without classical music being made available to audiences which had previously hardly been aware of its existence. Many did not care to listen, but many did. Drama too took to the air. In the same year as Wood's first concert, Reginald Berkeley's *The White Chateau* was heard by twelve million listeners. It was the first full-length play written for radio – a story of war in the trenches. The BBC made much of the novelty of the occasion, the audience was advised to do its listening in a darkened room.

Radio was the great leveller: as nothing had done before it provided entertainment accessible and acceptable to the rich man in his castle or the poor man at the gate, to country dweller and townsman, to man and woman, to old and young. Perhaps most significant of all, by its news bulletins and programmes designed to educate or instruct, it created an informed population. Whether the average Britons understood the issues of the day is an open question (whether the exceptional Britons understood them either is another) but at least they knew what they were. Class differences, regional differences, all the sectarian groupings survived, but radio was the first force that seriously sapped their strength.

It was an age of dawning awareness, of a mobility

At the National Radio Exhibition at Olympia in 1933 young ladies on the Lissen stand demonstrate how to assemble wireless kits. Do-it-yourself was enjoying an early vogue. By 1939 nine households out of ten could tune in to the BBC.

which was physical as well as intellectual. New possibilities opened up, a restlessness affected large sections of the population which had previously seen no reason to peer beyond the boundaries of their parish. The car was the most conspicuous single instrument of the new *Wanderlust*. Every year hundreds of thousands of new, cheap cars poured on to the roads of the British Isles; by 1939 almost two million had been licensed. In 1930 the old 20 mph speed limit, long ignored in practice, was formally abolished. For four alarming years there was neither speed limit nor driving test. Deaths on the road in 1934 were as numerous as those in 1964, when six times as many cars were in circulation. Then Britain began to come to terms with its killer-toy. A 30 mph speed limit was introduced in built-up areas; driving tests became compulsory; one-way streets, roundabouts, even bypasses began to appear; Belisha beacons sprouted to protect the passage of the pedestrian.

The tram, with its rails and inflexible itinerary, became unfashionable. By 1939 its numbers had been halved, but for the war it would quickly have vanished altogether. In its place came the bus, covering the ever-growing suburbs and venturing out into the countryside beyond. The car and the bus transformed the face of Britain, bringing the road-house and ribbon development to a hitherto virgin land. To the week-ender and holiday-maker they were a boon, but the price was high; C.E.M. Joad said of his contemporaries that they found Britain a land of beauty and left it a land of beauty spots.

The train was still the staple of travel, performing with a regularity that cannot be matched half a century later, venturing to innumerable now vanished rural stations, running at speeds that have not been greatly improved today. In 1932 the Flying Scotsman did the journey from London to Edinburgh in 7 hours 27 minutes and almost always arrived on time. For those whose travelling was more ambitious, the great liners provided facilities at every level, from frugal comfort to the grandest of luxury. The latest miracle of British technology, the 72,000-ton *Queen Mary*, was launched in 1934.

But already the more far-sighted believed that, like the mastodon and the dinosaur, the liner's days were numbered. Travel by air was still adventurous, but it

The motor bus took the place of the tram and opened up the countryside. This bus, on a Norwich road, would look very much the same today. The arch survived till 1981 but was then demolished.

In 1930 the old 20 mph speed limit was abolished. For a few years it was a free-for-all and the total of deaths on the road soared alarmingly. A national campaign for a speed limit was organised and two of its stalwart adherents, with a supporting cast of schoolchildren, are here in action.

The tram, with its inflexible route and expensive infrastructure, was falling out of favour by the time this photograph was taken in 1936. But for the war it would have vanished by the early 1940s; as it was, it lingered on for another twenty years.

The Queen Mary, *latest and greatest of Cunard's liners built for the Atlantic crossing, prepares to leave Southampton for her trials in the Firth of Clyde on 15 April 1936. To the right the former flagship of the Cunard fleet, the* Berengaria, *is edging her way out of the Ocean Dock.*

In the 1920s travel by air was still for the intrepid. Amy Johnson was a national heroine. In 1930 she flew solo to Australia. Here she is standing by her aircraft at an early stage in her journey.

was beginning to be recognised as a practicable alternative. Lindbergh had made the first non-stop flight across the Atlantic the year after Princess Elizabeth was born; in a few years Amy Johnson took over – in Britain's eyes at least – as the most celebrated aviator of them all. In 1930 she flew solo to Australia. She was not the first person to do so, nor even the fastest, but she caught the attention of the nation and returned to a prize of £10,000 and a triumphal progress along the Strand and Fleet Street. For those who believed that man should not venture beyond his proper element, the destruction of the airship R101 with the death of forty-eight of its fifty-four travellers provided grisly evidence to support their view. But such setbacks could not check the great advance; in 1931 an airmail service was inaugurated between Croydon and Australia (still taking nearly three weeks to complete the journey); by the mid 1930s there were commercial flights from London to most of the countries of Europe and the Empire.

Few people availed themselves of such rarified delights, but holidays away from home ceased to be a

The great ocean-going liners provided the grandest of accommodation and every luxury that the plutocratic traveller could require. This is the first-class smoking room of the Queen Mary, *which was launched in 1934.*

The R101 was the greatest of the rigid airships built in Britain between the wars. In October 1930, with a distinguished company aboard, it crashed and burnt out, killing forty-eight out of the fifty-four people aboard.

TO PARIS WHILE YOU READ YOUR PAPER

& HOME AGAIN
IN TIME FOR DINNER!

**NEARLY 1,700 PERSONS FLY
BETWEEN LONDON & PARIS
EVERY WEEK—**
WHY DON'T YOU?

The luxury of Imperial Airways' air liners is proverbial. Pullman-like comfort, meals, attentive stewards, lavatories and luggage space. For you the chops of the Channel look like ripples and you arrive in Paris fresh and unfatigued, having spent no more time in the air than it takes to run in your car from London to lunch with your cousins in the country. Air travel is not expensive and it is very delightful—try it!

**LONDON to PARIS from £4 : 15 : 0
RETURN £7 : 12 : 0**

IMPERIAL AIRWAYS
THE GREATEST AIR SERVICE IN THE WORLD

THERE ARE FIVE
SERVICES A DAY
BETWEEN LONDON
AND PARIS

Bookings from Imperial Airways Ltd., AIRWAY TERMINUS, VICTORIA, LONDON, S.W.1.
Telephone : VICtoria 2211 (Day and Night), or principal travel agents

By the mid 1930s there were regular commercial passenger flights to many European destinations. Imperial Airways offered a flight to Paris for £7.12.0 return (£7.60) and made their aircraft look as much like a train as possible.

Mail began to be carried by air from the end of the 1920s. Here the Argosy *is being loaded up with mailbags at Croydon airport. The aircraft could carry a large load of letters, including some in the small compartment in the nose of the aircraft. This photograph was taken in 1929, two years later an airmail service to Australia was inaugurated.*

middle-class prerogative. Fifteen million people took an annual holiday, mainly in the traditional coastal resorts – Margate, Southend, and above all Blackpool. On Bank Holiday Monday in August 1937, 425 special trains ran to Blackpool; it was claimed that more than five million visitors savoured its delights. In the same year Butlin's opened its first holiday camp at Skegness; by 1939 more than half a million people a year subjected themselves to the rigours of that relentlessly jovial institution.

The spending power and higher expectations generated by the new industries were reflected dramatically in the cinemas built throughout the 1930s. Vast fantasy palaces with architectural features culled from every style known to man and some not yet invented sprang up in all the cities and large towns; fortunes were lavished on the spectacular theatre organs which rose majestically into the auditorium, bathed in polychrome illumination, and regaled the waiting public with 'In a Monastery Garden' or selections from *Chu Chin Chow*. The investment was amply justified, repaid by huge and ever-growing audiences.

In 1928 Al Jolson in *The Jazz Singer* heralded the age of sound. Colour too became increasingly the fashion, Warner Brothers as early as 1929 announcing that they wanted no more black-and-white. The British cinema achieved something of a breakthrough with Charles Laughton in *The Private Life of Henry VIII*, *Pygmalion* with Leslie Howard, the comedies of Will Hay and George Formby, the excellent documentaries of John Grierson, but the multitude which each week visited the cinema paid mainly to see American imports: Fred Astaire, the Marx Brothers, Shirley Temple, Deanna Durbin, garnished with the cartoons of Felix the Cat, Popeye the Sailorman and Mickey Mouse.

The theatre had no such innovations, whether technical or aesthetic. It was the age of musical comedy

The first Butlin's opened at Skegness in 1937 and within two years half a million visitors a year were experiencing the bracing delights of this chain of holiday camps. Early morning exercises were a feature of the day's activities – note the propriety of the dress.

The train was still the most heavily patronised means of transport. These bank-holiday crowds at Waterloo station in August 1938 could have been duplicated all over the country. 425 special trains ran to Blackpool alone.

British cinema achieved something of a breakthrough with the spectacular The Private Life of Henry VIII. *Here Charles Laughton as the King demonstrates the Tudor technique for dealing with a chicken while hungrily inspecting a promising-looking boar's head.*

Noel Coward's Private Lives *was one of the greatest (and most enduring) of the theatrical successes of the period. Here Coward grapples with Gertrude Lawrence on the floor while the young Laurence Olivier and Adrienne Allen look on in some dismay.*

Enormous new cinemas, cathedrals of contemporary culture, sprang up in all the major cities and large towns. They were built in every style known to man and some as yet unknown. The Granada, Tooting, opened at the end of 1931, was conceived in Gothic style, though the connoisseur will detect flourishes from other civilisations.

The King and Queen attended the cup final of 1928 between Huddersfield Town and Blackburn Rovers at Wembley Stadium. A crowd of 90,000 saw Blackburn win the Cup. Wilson of Huddersfield is here shown heading the ball.

British public were in no mood for the *avant garde*: T.S. Eliot's *Murder in the Cathedral* took place in a church and so might be respectable, but *The Family Reunion* was greeted with suspicion and some alarm. Deep in the Sussex countryside John Christie in 1934 opened an opera-house at Glyndebourne; an operation which anyone of any sense could have told him was doomed to rapid failure.

The British public eschewed intellectual adventure as much in literature as in drama; P.G. Wodehouse and Agatha Christie were the mainstay of the reading classes; sturdy realists like A.J. Cronin and J.B. Priestley far outsold the more exacting novels of Virginia Woolf (it was also an age of initials – the P.G.s, A.J.s and J.B.s, whether among cricketers or novelists, outnumbered the homelier Christian name). A flowering of left-wing novelists and poets was becoming visible but political commitment and social content were still exceptional. Propriety was highly prized; when Lawrence sought to publish *Lady Chatterley's Lover* in 1928 he had to satisfy himself with a limited, private edition, which was passed furtively from hand to hand swathed in an untitled dust jacket.

Britain was becoming a nation of sports-watchers. Football was the national passion. The cup final was first played at Wembley in 1923 and soon became a hallowed feature of the annual calendar; when Blackburn Rovers beat Huddersfield Town in 1928 the King and Queen were among the 90,000 who watched, though not among the unruly mob that stampeded on

shading into operetta: Ivor Novello gathering lilacs in the spring again; Webster Booth and Anne Ziegler spinning out their Ruritanian idylls in aimiable if unmemorable melodies; Noel Coward with *Bitter Sweet*. And then, by way of plays, there was Noel Coward again with *Private Lives* and R.C. Sherriff's *Journey's End*, another emotional reminder of war in the trenches. The

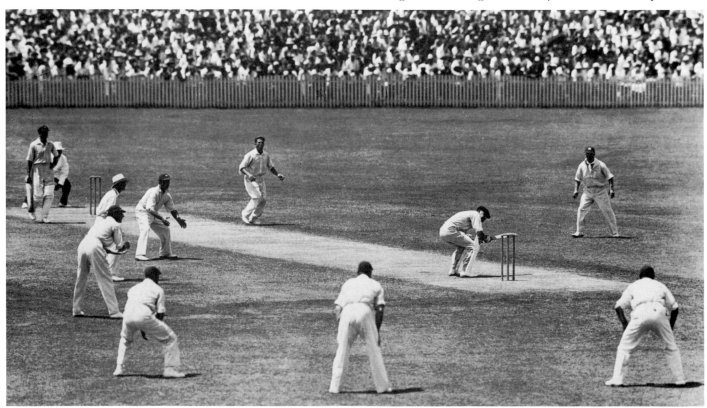

Cricket or warfare? 1933 saw the 'body line' tour, in which the English fast bowlers – Harold Larwood in particular – shattered the Australian batting with a fusillade of short, bouncing and very fast balls pitched on or outside the leg stump. Here Woodfull ducks under a bouncer from Larwood; he was not always so successful.

to the pitch. The English were still the acknowledged masters in the game they had invented. When in 1929 Spain became the first foreign side to beat them – by 4-3 in a heatwave in Madrid – a feeling of outrage swept the nation. A fearful revenge was taken two years later when England won 7-1 in deep Highbury mud. Subsequently England sometimes lost away, but never at home. A new dimension was added to the game when football joined horse racing and the dogs as a means of gambling; in the 1930s the football pools waxed spectacularly, enriching a few punters and, more consistently, the shrewd entrepreneurs who had detected the latent craving for excitement and the chance of winning a fortune overnight.

Cricket raised almost equal passions and Hobbs and Sutcliffe, Woolley and Hendren, later Hammond, Hutton and Verity were heroes in every schoolboy pantheon. In 1932 passions ran too high when England countered Bradman's apparent invincibility by unleashing Larwood bowling bumping balls of terrifying speed to a packed leg-side field. The Australians went down like ninepins, their wickets usually but too often their players as well. Accusations of unsportsmanlike behaviour and cowardice were liberally exchanged and the structure of the Commonwealth itself seemed in danger. Then it all died down and things went on much as they had before.

It was an era when Britain still won at games – though the occasions seemed to come at ever more infrequent intervals. In 1933 England took the Davis

Another British sporting hero was Henry Cotton. In 1934 he won the Open at Sandwich and thus, though only fleetingly, broke the dominance of the American golfers. Here he is driving off from the first tee.

Cup for the first time in twenty-one years, Fred Perry winning the decisive match to gain victory over France. The following year Henry Cotton broke the dominance of the American golfers by winning the Open at Sandwich. Tennis and golf were no longer a preserve of the upper middle classes; every year more and more people not merely exulted in British victories or mourned

Fred Perry was the hero of British tennis. In 1933 when England took the Davis Cup for the first time in twenty-one years, it was Perry who won the decisive match to gain victory over France. Here he is playing at Wimbledon the following year.

British defeats, but played the games themselves.

In 1936 a new sport was invented. The National Trust set up a branch to preserve country houses in peril of destruction or decay. The British aristocracy had long been strikingly liberal about allowing the casual passer-by access to its stately homes. Now it began to be perceived that such houses were part of a precious heritage, and even that they could be exploited economically to help support their upkeep. Opening to the public was still remote from the minds of the country-house dweller of the 1930s, but the first steps had been taken.

In every field there were more experiences shared at every level of society, more common interests, enthusiasms, dislikes. People dressed more like each other every year. The top hat vanished except for ceremonial occasions and freakish sub-groups such as undertakers and Etonians; the bowler hat was preserved by factory foremen and city workers; the cloth cap by the industrial proletariat; but the classless trilby was the symbol of the age. Every suit still had a waistcoat and braces but the loose-fitting 'Oxford bags' and the polo-necked sweater were spearheads of a new and comfortable informality. Men could now wear wrist-watches without being dismissed as common or effete; a daring novelty, the zip-fastener, was well established by 1934. Women's fashions spread more rapidly from class to

Cheap mass-produced clothing brought fashion within the grasp of the middle-classes. In this group of office workers leaving Unilever House the smartly dressed girl at the top of the steps probably spent little more on her clothes than her dowdier and older colleagues below.

Students needed little encouragement to dress up. This rag, for the benefit of the Berkshire Hospital, was organised by the undergraduates of Reading, the only new university to open between the wars.

William Temple was the outstanding churchman of his day. When this photograph was taken in 1935 he was Archbishop of York and on his way to Washington; later he became Archbishop of Canterbury. He was the leader of the reformist wing of the Church of England and a man of notable liberality.

class and area to area; cheap mass-produced clothing ensured that, though standards of cut and material might differ widely, to the untutored eye the fashion-conscious of every income group could look surprisingly alike.

The tendency was towards a new classless society but progress was painfully slow and impeded by an educational system which seemed designed to perpetuate inequalities rather than relieve them. In 1934 only four in every thousand pupils at an elementary school could hope to have any higher education, less than one in a thousand went to Oxford or Cambridge. Since there were some 5.5 million boys and girls at elementary school this meant that the senior universities were not wholly without representation from the lower classes, but the influence of public and grammar school was predominant. It was the grammar schools that provided the significant bridge between the classes and proved themselves the most intellectually and socially dynamic educational force. Higher education expanded little – only one new university, that of Reading, opened between the wars.

The Church of England was on the whole a force for egalitarianism and the rights of the working man. William Temple, Archbishop of York from 1929, was the leader of the politically reformist body within the church and by far the most celebrated churchman of his generation. He had to deal with a mainly conservative ecclesiastical hierarchy and a laity which looked with suspicion on clerical progressiveness. In 1928 the House of Commons refused to sanction changes to the prayer book which the church itself requested, on the

'Oxford bags' could attain almost grotesque bagginess. One suspects that this particular subject was well aware of the effect his appearance caused and was inclined to relish it.

The upper classes knew their place, which was on top. The arrogant self-assurance of this couple at a race meeting at Lingfield is the fruit of generations of unquestioned superiority.

grounds that the revisions were tainted with papistry. In the 1930s as the 1980s, churchmen who questioned conventional theology attracted disproportionate attention; in 1930 Bishop Barnes of Birmingham shocked millions when he refused to state categorically that Jesus was God.

Religion could still make news. Early in 1936 newspaper vans scurried all over London bearing the flaming banner: 'Is there an After-Life? See Tomorrow's *Evening Standard.*' The Oxford Group Movement, later re-christened Moral Rearmament, gained much *réclame* with its well-connected right-wing clientele, its slick American-inspired presentation and its titillating 'sharing of sins' by confession. But such is the frivolity of mankind that the antics of the vicar of Stiffkey attracted more public interest than any of the doings of Archbishop Temple, Bishop Barnes, or even the Oxford Movement's Frank Buchman. The Reverend Harold Davidson was charged with immoral practices and eventually defrocked – his defence being made more difficult by photographs showing him naked with female acquaintances. He sought to right what he felt to be an injustice, first by appearances in cinemas at which he expounded upon his wrongs, then by sitting in a barrel on Blackpool beach. More than 3,000 people paid sixpence a head to see him. As a final demonstration of his innocence he appeared among the lions of a travelling menagerie. No David he, the lions mauled him fatally. A large crowd attended his funeral and fought to secure handfuls of soil from the grave.

The lower classes for the most part knew their place too – which was on their knees scrubbing the steps. These Lambeth slums seemed as immutable a part of the British way of life as any aristocratic enclave.

In 1933 J.B. Priestley published his *English Journey*, which for the social historian must be one of the most significant works of literature of the age. Priestley found the two Englands that Disraeli had described in the nineteenth century – the England of rich and poor, squire and peasant, landlord and tenant, employer and employed – but also a new England, amorphous, inchoate, a land of filling stations and dance-halls, cinemas and roadhouses, Woolworths and country clubs, a restless England taking its values from the United States, indifferent to its past, careless of its future.

This is the image of the decade that comes foremost to the mind. Britain between 1926 and 1936 was a curiously uncertain land; alarming in some ways yet also filled with hope; rooting up its ancient landmarks yet preserving the most important of its standards; looking eagerly for new sensations yet not wholly discontented with what it had. The monarchy, that institution which more than any other encapsulated the standards and values of the past, had been battered and degraded yet had survived. In the young Princess Elizabeth it had found a figurehead which seemed to suggest a way to a brighter, more certain future. Not everyone believed that this was the path that the country was going to follow. To some pessimists it seemed that its fibre had been fatally weakened, its determination sapped by easy living and gratification of its every appetite. The test was soon to come. In the next few years the institutions and the character of the nation were to be tested with unique severity.

Harold Davidson, the ill-fated vicar of Stiffkey, was charged with immoral practices and defrocked. He drew attention to what he felt to be an injustice by sitting in a barrel on Blackpool beach sandwiched between a fasting girl and a flea circus, and charging sixpence (2.5p) to look at him. Later he was eaten by a lion.

A very different street scene. A luxurious car, with chauffeur in attendance, waits outside one of Bond Street's elegant shops. The car's owner could well spend in a morning's shopping what the woman scrubbing the steps would have to keep her family on for a year or more.

King George VI and Queen Elizabeth with their daughters, Princess Elizabeth and Princess Margaret, at Buckingham Palace after the Coronation ceremony on 12 May 1937. Princess Elizabeth, now the heir-presumptive, was the star of the show.

Chapter Two

In the Shadow of War

1936 to 1939

THE CORONATION of King Edward VIII was to take place on 12 May 1937. To the ten-year-old Princess Elizabeth it seemed likely to be a grand and exciting occasion, but not one that would mark any dramatic change in her existence. Secluded on the top floor of the family home at 145 Piccadilly she knew little or nothing of the fearful pother that was disturbing first those closest to the throne, then the inner circle of the well-informed, finally the nation.

She would have been an insensitive child, however, if she had not suspected that something was going wrong, that her parents were peculiarly preoccupied and anxious. Since long before Edward VIII's accession but

now with growing force, those whose task it was to serve the crown doubted whether he would ever make an adequate, let alone a distinguished monarch. He had good qualities: charm and a quick if facile brain, courage, generosity. When he went among the unemployed miners of South Wales and said in dismay: 'Something will be done for you' and 'I am going to help you,' he spoke in sincere distress. But if he had thought for even a moment he would have known that there was little he could do; if he had been even slightly aware of his own temperament he would have recognised that the impulse to act would anyway not survive for long once the immediate stimulus was out of sight.

During a visit to South Wales in 1936, Edward VIII went among the unemployed miners. Dismayed at their distress, he blurted out 'Something will be done for you'. It was not.

Edward VIII was idle and capricious; the gratification of his pleasures was more important to him than the performance of no doubt tedious royal duties; when he argued with the royal private secretary, Sir Frederick Ponsonby, that it would be right for him to come down from the pedestal to the level of his people, he spoke not from any serious democratic purpose but because he was disinclined to bother with formality or sacrifice his golf, his cocktails or his entourage of raffish friends.

Wallis Simpson saved Britain from an unworthy monarch. A smart, attractive, wise-cracking American, already divorced and with a second marriage nearing the rocks, she was supremely unsuitable as a future Queen. Edward VIII doted on her, depended on her, and was unable to conceive that he could live without her. In October 1936 she formally petitioned for divorce from her current husband. A decree nisi was granted in time enough to ensure that the King could have married her shortly before his coronation on 12 May 1937. Scandal, always grumbling underground, now gathered strength. First the affair was whispered about in London, then taken up by the foreign press. Claud Cockburn's mail-order journal, *The Week*, was the first paper in the British Isles to talk openly of the romance, then the *Yorkshire Post* broke the story and suddenly it was in the forefront of everybody's mind.

It is a bold historian who states with confidence that 'The people felt this', 'The country felt that'. 'We are the people of England, that never have spoken yet,' wrote Chesterton, and the people of England were no more communicative in 1936 than at any other time. Such indications as there are, however, suggest that the popular reaction was at first strongly in favour of the King. That he should be allowed to marry the woman he loved seemed mere justice. But the mood did not endure for long. 'Hit won't do, 'Arold,' J.H. Thomas told Harold Nicolson. 'I tell you straight. I know the people of this country. I *know* them. They 'ate 'aving no private life at Court.' At a meeting in a church hall in Islington only ten people out of an audience of 400 rose to their feet when the national anthem was played. At best, Edward VIII would rule over a deeply divided nation.

The King was not without supporters. The *Daily Mail* and the *Daily Express* were his champions. The non-conformist *News Chronicle* more surprisingly advocated a morganatic marriage which would leave Mrs Simpson wife but not queen. Churchill headed a little gang of 'cavaliers' who were disposed to stand by their monarch right or wrong. But such views could not prevail against the obstinate opposition of the government and the religious leaders, backed as it was by articulate middle-class opinion. On 16 November Edward VIII dined with Queen Mary. She was sympathetic, the King noted, but: 'To my mother the Monarchy was something sacred and the Sovereign a personage apart. The word "duty" fell between us.' The King's duty, as his mother saw it, was to renounce Mrs Simpson. Failing that, he must renounce the throne. He did his best to escape from the bleak alternatives, but in the end accepted their inevitability.

The Prince of Wales at a nightclub, with Wallis Simpson seated on his left. It is perhaps not too extravagant to detect in his wistful air of isolation evidence of the frailty that was to destroy him as a monarch.

Public opinion was at first on the side of King Edward VIII in the abdication crisis. Soon it changed, but a little band of loyalists remained fervently attached to the cause – Winston Churchill and some of the press Lords being prominent among his supporters.

King George VI, as Duke of York, riding on a roundabout. The picture aptly exemplifies both the spirit of duty which led him to do disagreeable things and the shyness which made them even more intolerable. He is clearly hating every minute of his adventure.

The Crystal Palace burnt to the ground on 1 December 1936 in one of the most spectacular conflagrations ever seen in peace-time London. Designed by Paxton, the Palace was originally erected in Hyde Park for the Great Exhibition of 1851 and was moved to Sydenham three years later. Demolition was completed in 1941 when it was feared the ruin might help guide German bombers to central London.

The British genius for making money out of its royal family was shown at the time of the abdication as well as on more happy occasions. Records of the abdication speech are still to be found, but are now considerable rarities.

On 1 December 1936 the Crystal Palace burnt to the ground in one of the most spectacular conflagrations ever seen in peace-time London. There was no shortage of gloomy prophets who saw in such a disaster a portent that spelt ill for the monarchy. The King duly obliged them. At 1.52 pm on 10 December 1936 the royal assent was given to the Act of Abdication. Forced to choose between his country and the woman he loved, Edward VIII, now Duke of Windsor, had opted for the latter. Princess Elizabeth, puzzled by the noisy, cheering crowds outside the house, asked a footman what was going on. Given the news, she rushed upstairs to share it with her younger sister. 'Does that mean that you will have to be the next Queen?' demanded Princess Margaret. 'Yes, some day.' 'Poor you!' commented Margaret.

'The Yorks will do it very well,' said Queen Mary firmly after the abdication. Not everyone would have agreed. The future King George VI had existed too long in his brother's shadow; he was a shy, diffident man, stammering when required to speak in public, painfully conscious of his inadequacies. His integrity, his decency, his determination, his unshakeable common sense were not so immediately apparent as his lack

of panache and colour. He took over a throne that had been tarnished, some felt irreparably weakened. Dalton and Attlee were not alone among the Labour leaders in believing that the monarchy could never recover its prestige, and there were Tories too who feared the same. At the end of 1936 republicanism was probably stronger among the British people than at any other moment in the twentieth century. Yet it was never more than a transient mood, and even then felt only by a small minority. 'Sir', Baldwin told the King, 'if I may say so, you need have no fear for the future. The whole country is behind you with a deep and understanding sympathy.' When James Maxton proposed in the House of Commons that the abdication should be followed by the creation of a republic, he was defeated by 403 votes to five. Baldwin's words, the Commons' votes, exaggerated the solidarity of the monarchists. There were doubts: those who felt that a royal family which could produce a king like Edward VIII was hardly worth preserving; others who believed that the wrong king was now on the throne. But the doubters dwindled rapidly; the King and his family grew rapidly in popularity; the wraith of Edward VIII was soon exorcised. By the time of the coronation it seemed

Crowds cluster outside 145 Piccadilly on the morning of 11 December 1936, hoping to catch a glimpse of King George VI who had acceded to the throne the previous day after his brother's abdication.

The Coronation of 12 May 1937 was designed above all to emphasise that a happy and united family were again on the throne. Here the King and Queen flank Princess Elizabeth and Princess Margaret Rose with Queen Mary in the centre on one of their many appearances on the balcony of Buckingham Palace.

Crowds of people waited all night to get a good view of the Coronation procession as it moved between the Palace and Westminster Abbey. Here a group of resolutely cheerful women while away the hours of darkness in Trafalgar Square.

Many shops, hotels and public buildings were lavishly decorated for the Coronation, but few if any can have been at greater pains to commemorate the occasion than Selfridges in Oxford Street.

almost as if the succession of George VI to the throne had been expected and wished for all along.

Each recent coronation seems in retrospect to have struck a particular note, to have been addressed towards a particular end. Elizabeth's own coronation was to be inspired by a theme of regeneration, the birth of a new epoch, the second Elizabethan age. Her father's ceremony was more concerned with consolidation, rebuilding after the ravages of the past. At its heart was the family; the central image was that of the King and Queen flanked by their daughters.

No pains were spared to make it clear that George VI's coronation was as much of an occasion as had been planned for his brother. More than 200,000 visitors were expected from abroad, including the Crown Prince of Denmark, Prince Chichibu from Japan, Mr Litvinoff from Russia and Miss Sheila Martin from Wagga Wagga, selected as the 'best representative of Australian girlhood'. The traditional excesses were perpetrated; the chief exhibit at the Ideal Home Exhibition was a 'coronation piano', a white baby-grand with red and blue keys. It was an event for the whole nation, not just the capital. In Hastings the coronation sports meeting included an event in which couples of mixed sex, wearing ordinary clothes over bathing-dresses, had to undress and put on each others' clothes; in a mining village celebration was economically combined with political vendetta when an effigy of Ramsay MacDonald was burnt on the coronation bonfire. The first television service had been opened by Leslie Mitchell in November 1936 and 60,000 viewers were able to watch the procession, Ipswich being the most distant spot receiving the transmission. But it was London which drew the crowds. Half a million people spent a night in the rain to watch the last rehearsal; 50,000 besieged the Palace the day before the ceremony.

Whether she liked it or not – and, on the whole, it was not – Princess Elizabeth was the star of the show. A machine rigged on a roof in Whitehall recorded that, while the carriage containing the King and Queen drew cheers registering eighty-three decibels, the one containing Queen Mary and the two Princesses scored eighty-five. Elizabeth was commemorated by Princess Elizabeth Island in Antarctica and a six-cent stamp in Newfoundland; her waxen effigy appeared on a pony in Madame Tussauds and her portrait in implausible colour on the front page of *Time*. She was now heir-presumptive to the throne – 'presumptive' because it was still theoretically possible that her father would have a male child, but full heir in all but name.

Her parents still did their best to give her the upbringing of a normal child. A Girl-Guide company and a Brownie pack were established at the Palace, Elizabeth's patrol being organised by her cousin, Patricia Mountbatten. But there was no question of her attending a school; a series of private tutors provided her education, with company of her own age apart from that offered by the Guides found in dancing-classes and a few other such activities in which she was allowed to

A Girl-Guide company and Brownie pack were organised at Buckingham Palace and the two Princesses became enthusiastic members. Here they stand with their mother in the quadrangle at Windsor Castle on the occasion of a Girl-Guide rally in 1938.

meet the children of courtiers and other carefully selected members of the royal circle. Queen Mary took a vigorous interest in her grand-daughter's education, insisting on the learning of much poetry by heart; history, geography and French because of their relevance to her future life; genealogy for much the same reason; but with little emphasis on mathematics or other such unmonarchical subjects. Whenever possible her parents took her with them on their travels around the realm; in 1939 she accompanied them to the West Country in the royal yacht, the *Victoria and Albert*. A visit to the naval college at Dartmouth was part of the itinerary, and her cousin Prince Philip of Greece among the cadets that she met there. She was only thirteen, he eighteen, but she was never to look at another man.

'How disappointing,' observed the twelve-year-old Princess Elizabeth when told that because of the Munich agreement, there would be no war. It was a child's reaction, signifying nothing, but it contrasted strikingly with the feelings of most of the people over whom she was to rule. By the time of Munich in 1938 the inevitability of war had become apparent to most thinking British, but it was a conclusion reached with sadness and only after strongly pacifist inclinations had

A photograph taken at the Dartmouth Naval College on 22 July 1939, which must be the first showing Princess Elizabeth with her future husband. Prince Philip, in a cap, is standing in the second row, beside his uncle Lord Louis Mountbatten. 'After all,' wrote Mountbatten to the Prince of Wales many years later, 'Mummy never seriously thought of anyone else after the Dartmouth encounter when she was 13!'

Women in paper 'gas-masks' led a march to Trafalgar Square in May 1936 for a great peace-meeting to be addressed by, among others, the veteran suffragette Sylvia Pankhurst. The banner carried by the lady on the right shows a fine combination of estimable if not necessarily compatible objectives.

been duly overcome. It was five years since the Oxford Union had voted by 275 to 153 that 'This House will in no circumstance fight for its King and Country' – a resolution made more poignant by the fact that within a few years more than three-quarters of the members would be doing the very thing that they had condemned so vociferously in 1933. They voted as they did in full sincerity, for pacifism was a rallying cry for the young intellectuals of the age and seemed even as if it might sweep the country.

In October 1934 Dick Sheppard, Vicar of St Martin-in-the-Fields, invited people to write on a postcard: 'I renounce war and never again will I support or sanction another, and I will do all in my power to persuade others to do the same.' The following year a peace ballot won the support of an amazing 11.5 million people, by far the most impressive private referendum ever organised. The movement transcended the bounds of any political party but was still generally linked with socialism; in East Fulham in 1933 the pro-armaments Tory saw a conservative majority of 14,000 turned into a win of 5,000 for a Socialist who believed in immediate and total disarmament. The result was not representative of the nation's

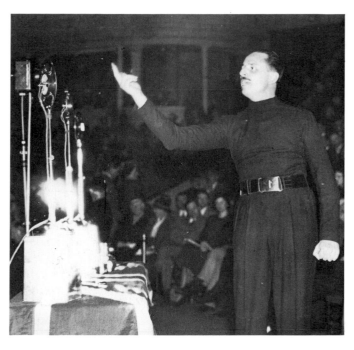

Sir Oswald Mosley, leader of the British Union of Fascists, addressing a rally of 10,000 of his followers in the Albert Hall. He called upon the people to 'give all and dare all for England'.

On 4 July 1937 Mosley addressed a meeting of his followers in Trafalgar Square. Anti-fascists rallied to oppose him and are here shown giving the clenched fist salute as they tried to form a barrier in his path. The luckless police, as usual, were caught between the two.

considered view. Baldwin trimmed his sails to the prevailing wind, fought the 1935 election on a platform of peace and support for the League of Nations, and won the day for the Conservatives. But more strongly than for many years before or after there was a national revulsion, idealistic if not always rational or clear-headed, against the system that accepted war as an instrument of policy and exalted the virtues of those who had died fighting for their country while neglecting the plight of those who were still alive. Auden summed it up in his bitter lines:

> Let us honour if we can
> The vertical man
> Though we value none
> But the horizontal one.

Of all the political parties the Communists were the most active in favour of disarmanent and the outlawing of war. By the year of Princess Elizabeth's birth, membership of the party had risen to over 10,000 but since then it had slumped and only in the mid 1930s did it begin to recapture its former following. Keynes told Kingsley Martin that the Communists were 'the nearest things we have to the typical nervous nonconformist English gentlemen who went to the Crusades, made the Reformation, fought the Great Rebellion.' Philby, Burgess, Maclean, perhaps hardly fitted this description but to them the party offered authority, adventure and a genuine idealistic appeal. They, and many others like them, espoused it eagerly.

Another phenomenon of the 1930s at the other end of the political spectrum, the British Fascists, offered an oddly similar appeal. After Mosley abandoned the Labour party in despair, he founded in 1932 the British Union of Fascists. It throve, supported by Lord Rothermere and other well-meaning enthusiasts who felt that Britain's social problems could never be solved by the established parties. By 1934 there were 400 branches, 20,000 members. Then the ugly side of the movement became more evident; the brutal beating-up of political opponents, provocative marches through London's East End, fierce confrontations with Communist counter-marchers. Above all, Mosley became associated with a strident anti-Semitism which appealed to a small, sick minority but shocked the average Briton.

It was Hitler's increasingly overt persecution of the Jews that rallied opinion against him and opened the way for rearmament. A government that could behave like that to a section of its own people, the British felt instinctively, could not be trusted in international relations. A flood of Jewish refugees both enriched the intellectual life of the country and opened people's eyes to the realities of life in Germany. Not all of these displaced people were immediately made welcome, but when Freud came to London he was granted British citizenship the following day and the membership roll of the Royal Society, which had never previously left the Society's premises, was taken to his house for him to sign.

For several years before the war Jewish refugees from Germany or German-dominated Europe flooded into Britain. Here a group of refugee children wait at Liverpool St station in July 1939.

In 1936 HITLER marched into the Rhineland, Mussolini over-ran Abyssinia, the Rome-Berlin-Tokyo axis was formed, civil war began in Spain. It was the last of these which meant most to the British people. The government adopted a position of formal neutrality, the right somewhat hesitantly found virtues in the cause of Franco, the left more ardently supported the legal government. It was a cruel and bloody war, but whatever view was taken of it by the British, all shades of opinion were dismayed by the cynical opportunism with which the fascist regimes pledged themselves to non-intervention and then threw their powers fiercely into Franco's support. It was another step in the slow and painful preparation of the British people for the inevitability of war.

After the coronation Baldwin retired to make way for Neville Chamberlain, grey, desiccated, almost insufferably conscientious, a supremely competent chairman of committee presiding over a cabinet of committee members. Churchill was isolated, the country still reluctant to heed his call for rearmament, dismissing him as an alarmist or, worse still, a warmonger who was preoccupied above all by his own aggrandisement. Those who criticise Baldwin and Chamberlain for failing to rearm and seeking to appease the dictators, should remember that the country would not have supported a more bellicose policy. The energetic pacifism of the church, the left wing, the idealistic young, was matched by the apathy of most of the rest of the population. Britain was waking up to its danger, but the process was proving a protracted one.

In March 1938 Hitler incorporated Austria into the German Reich. Now it was the turn of Czechoslovakia. The situation was not wholly one of black and white; there were three million Germans within Czechoslovakia and they had some grounds for complaint about their treatment. Nevertheless there could be no doubt who was the aggressor and who the victim. Chamberlain saw this as clearly as anyone but he felt that the cause was not worth a European war. He brought pressure on the Czechs to hand over large tracts of territory to their German neighbour and, thus, render what was left of their country defenceless. Yet it seemed that even this might not be enough to satisfy Hitler's demands.

In September 1938 Britain believed that it was on the brink of war. It was a fearsome prospect. Working

Rearmament was slow in coming but gathered pace as the war approached. This photograph was taken inside the big guns' shop in a Royal Ordnance factory of the ministry of supply.

Neville Chamberlain returns to Britain from Munich brandishing the scrap of paper that guaranteed 'peace with honour . . . peace for our time.' Many people later denounced the Munich settlement but at the time it was welcomed with overwhelming relief and satisfaction.

from an exaggerated estimate of the damage done by German bombers in the First World War, multiplying by several times to allow for improved explosives, miscalculating the size of the German air force, the authorities had arrived at extravagant fears about the likely effectiveness of attack from the air. They foresaw an immediate, all-out assault on the great cities, London in particular: 600,000 dead; twice as many injured; panic-stricken mobs fleeing the devastated areas; looting; famine; the breakdown of law and order. More than thirty-eight million gas masks were distributed – whether they would work, or against what gases they might prove effective was anybody's guess, but the sight of wardens demonstrating these obscene, black pig's snouts was enough to frighten the children and the nervous. All forty-four of the anti-aircraft guns that Britain then boasted were deployed; barrage balloons – some forty of them – flew over London. Trenches were dug in the London parks; though it is hard to see what protection they would have offered against the sort of attack the authorities anticipated. The people braced themselves for disaster. They were prepared to accept it as a grim necessity. The prime minister was not. 'How horrible, fantastic, incredible it is,' said Chamberlain, 'that we should be digging trenches and trying on gas masks here because of a quarrel in a far-away country between people of whom we know nothing.'

On 28 September an apprehensive House of Commons heard the prime minister describe the melancholy history of the past few weeks. His speech was interrupted when a message was brought to him. Hitler had agreed to a meeting at Munich. The House was exultant; Chamberlain no less so when he returned two days later, bearing 'peace with honour. I believe that it is peace for our time.' Whether or not he meant what he said, the British people were eager to accept his judg-

ment. Of all those who were later to denounce appeasement and condemn the Munich settlement as ignoble, even treacherous, few indeed did so at the time. The nation felt a vast relief. A *Punch* cartoon showed John Bull comfortably relaxing, remarking as 'War Scare' flew out of the window: 'Thank God that's gone!' Chamberlain dolls were offered for sale, and sugared umbrellas – the utilitarian tool which he carried everywhere and which had been exalted to the role of prime minister's trade mark. The *Daily Telegraph* compared Chamberlain to Gladstone while Godfrey Winn did even better and linked the prime minister with God, proclaiming that there was 'no sacrilege, no bathos, in coupling the two names.'

The euphoria was short-lived. The collapse of the rump of Czechoslovakia in the face of German pressure dispelled whatever illusions still persisted. Poland seemed certain to be the next victim and, at the end of March 1939, Chamberlain guaranteed that Britain would go to war to protect its independence. It was another far-away country, of whose people the British knew still less than they did of the Czechoslovakians, but this time the country was united in the belief that a line must be drawn. The time bought by the Munich settlement was used in a feverish programme of rearmament; the clouds of war carried a silver lining of increased economic activity and a sharp fall in unemployment.

The most notable difference between Britain in 1914 and in 1939 was that the people now knew more or less what was going on. Sixty-seven per cent of adults read a daily paper; total circulation had risen from 4.5 million a quarter of a century before to 10.5 million. The British were literate; borrowing from public libraries

Conscription, which had been resisted by the Labour and Liberal parties in 1938, finally came into effect in 1939. It initially affected men between the ages of eighteen and forty-one. Here a group of potential recruits read the text of Neville Chamberlain's statement on the subject.

had risen fifty-fold between the wars to more than 200 million books a year. The BBC provided a service of news and comment unmatched in any other country. The people in no sense *wanted* to fight, the massacres of the First World War were less than twenty years behind, but they were satisfied that their leaders had done all that – perhaps even more than – could reasonably be expected to avert disaster. They were alarmed by German aggressiveness, sickened by all they knew of the brutal anti-semitism and intolerance of the Nazi regime. They had not finally abandoned the hope that Hitler might be checked without recourse to war, but they knew that the hope was a faint one. They were resigned to the inevitability of what was likely to prove a fierce and protracted conflict.

At dawn of 1 September 1939 the Germans invaded Poland. The British and French honoured their pledge and delivered an ultimatum threatening war unless hostilities ceased and a withdrawal begun. At 11 am on 3 September the ultimatum expired. In the sad, flat tones that the people had come to expect from him, Chamberlain told the country that it was now at war. Australia, New Zealand and Canada unhesitatingly followed suit; South Africa wavered but in the end came into line. Ireland opted for neutrality. Chamberlain had scarcely finished speaking before the air-raid sirens wailed their announcement of impending destruction. The Londoners, who had expected nothing else, took shelter in their trenches, their tin huts, under the stairs or in the cellars. Half an hour later, looking slightly sheepish, they filed out again. Armageddon, it seemed, would be a little late in coming. No bomb was to fall on Britain in 1939. The 'phoney war' had begun.

At 11 am on 3 September the Anglo-French ultimatum expired and Neville Chamberlain announced that the country was at war. A newsboy on the Thames Embankment carried a placard with the news. Air-raid sirens had already sounded to warn Londoners of an impending raid but no bomb was to fall on Britain in 1939.

It was at one time proposed that the royal Princesses should be evacuated to Canada but the idea was dropped: 'The children can't go without me,' said the Queen firmly. 'I can't leave the King and of course the King won't go.' The Princesses settled at Windsor, where they are shown preparing to work on their garden plots.

Chapter Three

A People at War

1939 to 1945

WHEN ONE has braced oneself for a supreme test of courage and endurance and in the event nothing is required, one feels relieved, a little foolish, curiously even disappointed. Such was the mood of Britain at the end of 1939. Poland had been obliterated, which was very sad, but it was a long way away and not many people had known exactly where it was until the maps in the newspapers brought it home to everyone (the war, in fact, was to provide an extended geography lesson – remote corners of the world suddenly becoming as familiar as Surrey or Yorkshire, then disappearing back into obscurity). Otherwise nothing much seemed to be happening. The term 'phoney war' was not adopted by the British until long after it was over; at the time it was known, if by any term, as 'the bore war' or 'the funny war'. But in fact, after the first few weeks people ceased to find it funny. This was what contemporary war must be like, concluded the British: inconvenient certainly, dangerous for a few, but not something which impinged forcibly on the life of the average civilian.

Chamberlain's government did little to dispel this comfortable illusion. Churchill and Eden were brought in but these were the only changes; the Socialists and Liberals remained outside; in no way did the administration seem qualified or even concerned to wage total war. When it was proposed to Kingsley Wood, the air minister, that the RAF should shower incendiary

Plans were made to evacuate four million children from the inner cities but not more than a third of them actually moved and most of these came back. A group of evacuees are here boarding the train at Euston.

bombs on German forests he protested in outrage: 'Are you aware it is private property? Why, you will be asking me to bomb Essen next!' At the end of 1939 only one Briton in five conceived it possible that the war would last as long as three years.

Restrictions on lighting did as much as anything to remind the British that they were at war. Street lighting was extinguished on 1 September, windows heavily draped in black, and the use of car headlights banned. The immediate result was a dramatic increase in accidents; deaths on the road in October were double what they had been in the same month the year before. By the end of 1939 a fifth of the inhabitants of the British Isles has suffered some sort of accident as a result of the blackout; in the same period not a single soldier had been seriously injured by enemy action, seventy-nine airmen were casualities and 586 sailors. The perils of the streets provided a strong incentive to stay at home, but familiarity soon restored confidence and social life resumed, cinemas and theatres began once more to remain open at night, the pubs and night-clubs flourished.

It became compulsory to carry a gas mask (a regulation enforced with little fervour); some children were issued with models in the form of Mickey Mouse masks, presumably to convince them that war was just a game. The same was not true of evacuation which – both for

The black-out was the cause of many accidents and injuries. A prudent precaution taken by some male pedestrians was to wear their white shirt-tails outside their trousers. These doubly wary walkers also encourage their female companions to walk slightly behind them, thus providing a useful buffer if need arises.

those who left the supposedly threatened cities and for those who remained there – provided war's heaviest impact. Plans had been made to evacuate four million children, teachers and mothers of under-fives, but not many more than a third of these actually moved. This was enough, however, to cause acute social and logistic problems. Many of the children came from slum areas,

'Put out that light,' or more often 'Put out that ----ing light' became a common cry. The problem of ensuring that no light escaped through the windows varied in scale but was essentially the same, whether in a terraced house in Bath (above) or on the great staircase of Easton Neston in Northamptonshire (right).

Gas masks had to be carried everywhere – though on inspection the case was often found to be empty or to contain sandwiches. The photograph shows five-year-olds during gas-mask drill at a school near Windsor. Whether the boy in front is trying to help his friend or to expose him to the threatening gas must be uncertain.

and their sedate middle-class hosts were appalled by the lice, bed-wetting and bad language which were now unleashed on them. The city children were no less dismayed by the quiet, the tedium and the dispiriting propriety of their new surroundings. Their education posed problems, but even more difficult was the education of those who stayed behind. With teachers dispersed and schools requisitioned or closed for lack of shelters, a million children were left to run wild. The problem gradually solved itself as the city parents, concluding that the bombers were never coming, called their children home. Cambridge, for instance, expected 24,000 evacuees, received 6,700 and had only 3,650 by November 1939. By mid 1940 the figure was a mere 1,624.

There was more permanent dispersal too. The treasures of the National Gallery went into a slate quarry in North Wales, the ministry of food to Colwyn Bay, Queen Mary and her household to stay with the Duke of Beaufort at Badminton. The government at one time planned to send East End children to safety across the Atlantic, but shortage of shipping and the resistance of parents meant that few actually left. Many more children from the richer classes went at their family's expense. It was at one time suggested that the two Princesses might join the exodus, but the King and Queen had little doubt that their children should share the dangers and privations of the British people. 'The children can't go without me,' said the Queen firmly. 'I can't leave the King, and of course the King won't go.' The Princesses went to Windsor, where they continued their schooling, knitted scarves, gathered firewood, collected scrap metal and pursued the other traditional occupations of the diligent child in a country at war.

Mr E.W. Mills of Hextable in Kent invented a gas-proof perambulator which is here being demonstrated. It was approved by the local authorities but did not find popular favour.

greatest. If one word more than any other could be applied to Britain at war, almost as much during the first tentative months as when the fury was at its height, it was mobility. As in an ant-hill which has been violently disturbed, everyone seemed to be on the move, some purposefully as duty called, some merely for the sake of motion. In September 1939 alone between a quarter and a third of the population travelled from one place to another; during the war sixty million changes of address were registered among a civilian population of something over forty million. In spite of the surface calm of early 1940 the nation was in monstrous flux. Nor was the surface calm to last.

IN APRIL 1940 Germany attacked neutral Norway. The campaign ended the first phase of the Second World War. 'Hitler has missed the bus,' proclaimed Chamberlain, in the most disastrous of his usually ill-fated attempts to prove that he possessed the common touch. The military fiasco that followed eroded his support. In one of the most dramatic debates the House of Commons has ever known, a Conservative revolt reduced his majority to an unmanageable level. The King would have liked Halifax to have succeeded, but the Labour opposition was not prepared to serve under

Winston Churchill became prime minister in 1940 and at once showed that man and task were miraculously well-suited. Given half a chance he would have been in the firing line himself, as is shown by this picture of him trying out a tommy-gun with US troops in Britain.

German citizens were rounded up *en masse* and moved to the Isle of Man; many of them were Jewish refugees from fascism and the work of national importance on which some of them were engaged suffered severely before the red tape was cut and they were allowed to return to their new homes. During their internment they rubbed shoulders uneasily with the fascists detained under Defence Regulation 18B. Most of the latter, however, including their leader Mosley, were at liberty till May 1940. By August of that year 1,600 suspects were imprisoned without trial.

In theory every man between the ages of eighteen and forty-one was liable for conscription from the first day of war but arms, uniforms and accommodation were all in short supply and the call-up was applied selectively and slowly. This did not stop many thousands of would-be recruits presenting themselves hopefully wherever they felt the chance of employment was

Many of the schools in Britain's cities closed at the outbreak of war, but most of them were soon open again. Here parents and children are working together to pile sandbags around the main entrance to Manchester Grammar School.

a man of Munich. The only man who could command the support of every part of the House of Commons – grudging and suspicious though that support promised sometimes to be – was Winston Churchill. Almost for want of an alternative, the post was his. Only after he had taken power did it become clear that task and man were miraculously well suited. He gauged the national mood and articulated it with magnificent eloquence. 'I have nothing to offer,' he told the British, 'but blood, toil, tears and sweat.' 'What is our aim?' he asked. 'Victory . . . victory at all costs, victory in spite of all terror; victory, however long and hard the road may be . . . Come, then, let us go forward together with our united strength . . .'

The national government that Churchill set up early in 1940 lasted without major changes until the end of the war. Attlee as his dry, efficient, socialist deputy; Eden for foreign affairs; Ernest Bevin to keep the unions in order; the austere and intellectually formidable Stafford Cripps – these were the stars of the team that waged and eventually won the war. Churchill was his own minister of defence. His administration concentrated more power in a smaller number of hands than had ever been known in Britain. The inner war cabinet, from which even the three Service ministers were excluded, was the supreme fount of authority; the only body of remotely comparable importance was the chiefs of staff and in this forum too Churchill took the chair on most of the more significant occasions.

With the acquiescence of the Tory majority, Britain became the most fully controlled and socialised country on earth, to a degree beyond anything achieved by the planners of Soviet Russia. Every aspect of national life was regimented; nothing was so trivial that it did not become a cause for official concern. By the end of the war the government absorbed 60 per cent of all production; a third of personal expenditure was on items covered by schemes of rationing. Parliamentary life went on – one member of parliament returning from France in June 1940 was amazed to be told that a committee was busily considering plans for uniting the West Indian islands in a federal unit within the Commonwealth – but the effective control of parliament over the administration was diluted if not abolished. Britain was a dictatorship, sustained by the participation of all the major political parties and the support of the vast majority of the people.

This is not to say that Churchill's leadership was unchallenged. Aneurin Bevan played a vigorous Fox to Churchill's Pitt. The government lost four by-elections

British soldiers leave for France shortly after the declaration of war. They might have looked less cheerful if they had known how soon and in what circumstances they were to come home again.

in 1942. But such critics as Emanuel Shinwell and Lord Winterton – 'Arsenic and Old Lace' as they were unkindly dubbed – could not be taken seriously as potential replacements and the prime minister had only to confront the House on an issue of confidence for opposition to crumble. The only man who could ever have been contemplated as a rival was Stafford Cripps. Churchill disliked him. After a long flight over the desert he is said to have remarked: 'Miles and miles of arid austerity. How Stafford would like it!' But he never doubted Cripps's formidable intelligence and ability. If the Socialist leader had chosen to oppose Churchill he would have presented a serious threat; instead he entered the government and made a contribution of signal importance to the winning of the war.

Churchill was the voice of the nation and the focal point of that nation's loyalty and patriotic fervour. So completely did he monopolise the limelight that the King, who might have been expected to become more than ever the symbol of British unity, instead played a relatively minor role. If an alternative voice to Churchill's had to be found, it would probably have belonged to J.B. Priestley, whose affable yet inspiring broadcasts had some of the power of the prime minister's speeches yet with a more homespun and demotic flavour providing comfort to a harassed people.

Inspiration was badly needed, for with the fall of France and the evacuation from Dunkirk in June 1940 Britain found herself alone. Wars are not won by evacuations and there was no escaping the fact that the army had been defeated and largely disarmed. It had survived however. The people's reaction was one of vast relief and a curious satisfaction at their isolation. 'Now we know where we are, no more bloody allies,' a tug-keeper shouted to A.P. Herbert. Churchill once more

Two air-raid wardens manning an observation post on the south bank of the Thames opposite the Palace of Westminster. London was bombed seriously for the first time on 7 September 1940.

spoke for the nation when he proclaimed defiantly: 'We shall fight on the beaches, we shall fight on the landing grounds, we shall fight in the fields and in the streets, we shall fight in the hills; we shall never surrender.'

The need to fight seemed imminent. German invasion was never as real a threat as it then appeared, but the country believed the enemy was coming and prepared accordingly. The coasts were the primary concern, but the possibility of airborne assault made everywhere a potential battlefield. Landing sites were blocked and the countryside defended by squat pillboxes designed to control every strategic point. Church bells were reserved to warn against invasion. If the enemy landed he would be confounded by the discovery that sign-posts and street names had been removed and identifying details scraped from war memorials. Railway stations were rendered anonymous or allowed

A veteran sergeant in the Home Guard. The photograph must have been taken in 1941 or later, since in 1940 he would have been lucky to have been given even a pike to polish. From his wife's equanimity one can assume she has reason to know the tommy-gun is unloaded.

A group of airmen cadge a lift home in the tractor which is towing their aircraft to the hangar. A member of the WAAF (Women's Auxiliary Air Force) is at the wheel.

only to advertise in tiny placards invisible from the air, indeed from a passing train. In anticipation of the hijacking of the BBC or at least its wavelengths, the news readers were required to announce themselves by name. Frank Phillips, Bruce Belfrage, Stuart Hibberd, Alvar Liddell became celebrities. 'Here is the nine o'clock news and this is ---- reading it,' became the best known sentence in the British Isles.

The idea of a civilian army to police the coasts and guard against parachute attack was launched by Eden in May 1940. Within twenty-four hours a quarter of a million local defence volunteers had come forward. 'Dad's Army', armed with pikes and pitchforks, composed of schoolboys and old-age pensioners, was a gift to the satirists but in fact provided a useful adjunct to the regular forces. Its members would have been massacred by the German army in full battle, but in their proper role of sentry and skirmisher could have proved invaluable. By the summer of 1943 there were 1.75 million of them, armed, uniformed and, up to a point, well organised. The Germans were sufficiently irritated by the existence of the Home Guard, as Churchill had rechristened it, to denounce its members as terrorists who would be executed when captured. The Home Guards took it as a compliment and resolved to die first.

Before the Germans could invade England they had to conquer the air. The Battle of Britain was fought with gallantry and skill by a small band of fighter pilots against an enemy who was more experienced, more numerous and often better armed. The British had great advantages – proximity to their own airfields, so that they could remain longer in combat; the fact that a pilot shot down but uninjured could soon be back in the air; the technical excellence of the Spitfire – but the Germans should still have won. They almost did. If they had continued their strategy of battering the British airfields, they might have done so. At the end of August, however, a cargo of bombs was jettisoned over central London. Churchill ordered a retaliatory raid on Berlin. Piqued, Hitler commanded that the weight of

From 7 September to 2 November 1940 London was bombed every night, and the first phase of the blitz continued until mid-May 1941. Thomas Wallis's store in Holborn was set on fire and burnt out on 17 April.

The provincial cities did not escape the bombing. The worst hit were Bristol, Coventry,
Clydebank and Birmingham where, on 25 October 1941, 2,170 people died. Here, soldiers begin
to clear up the damage in this badly scarred city.

the German attack should be switched to the cities. Battle of Britain became blitz. The Royal Air Force was reprieved. 'After shooting Niagara,' Churchill described it, 'we had now to struggle in the rapids.'

From 7 September to 2 November 1940 London was bombed every night. Stepney was the first target and the East End bore the brunt of the attack. Many trekked out each night to Epping Forest or other remote areas; others forced their way into the underground stations and, at first against official opposition, established a troglodytic settlement along corridors and platforms. 'Everyone is worried about the feeling in the East End,' wrote Harold Nicolson in his diary: 'There is much bitterness . . .' Fortunately for national unity the West End and the more prosperous suburbs were battered too. The hotels, night-clubs, pubs and cinemas defiantly continued to serve their customers; the Windmill Theatre's proud boast was, 'We never closed.' In March 1941 the fashionable Café de Paris was hit and many young officers on leave killed as they danced to the music of 'Snakehips' Johnson. The worst and final night of the London Blitz came on 10-11 May 1941. The Thames was at low ebb, the fires ran riot. The House of Commons was gutted; the Tower, Law Courts, Mint badly damaged; 200,000 books burnt at the British Museum. At least 1,436 people died.

The provincial cities did not escape. On 14 October an attack on Coventry marked a new phase of the battle. The damage was far more intense in this much

Pubs, cinemas and night-clubs defiantly stayed open and continued to serve their customers even when the blitz was at its worst. For troops in London it was a desirable relief from a bleak existence – military boots must have been a bit hard on the dancing partners but, after all, there was a war on.

smaller target. A third of the city's houses were destroyed, six out of seven telephone lines put out of action, all the main railway lines and most streets blocked. A new word entered the vocabulary; in November Bristol was 'coventrated'. The smaller the city the more shattering the impact. On 25 October 2,170 people died in Birmingham, four times as many as in Coventry; while Birmingham was badly scarred, Coventry was truly devastated. Clydebank had the

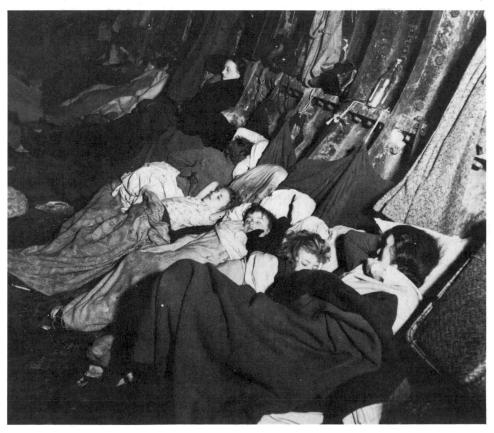

In spite of initial opposition from the authorities, Londoners took over the underground stations as a refuge against the bomber. Disused sections of track, platforms and stairs were all taken over by a squatter population who often established cherished territorial claims to their own little patch.

Queen Elizabeth with the two Princesses at Windsor, in July 1941, posed decoratively in front of a profusely blooming mock orange.

The royal family grouped around the fireplace towards the end of the war. Princess Elizabeth is diligently knitting; another popular wartime activity, as a result of which serving men and women were deluged with a flood of ill-made balaclava helmets and mis-shapen mittens.

The Houses of Parliament were hit and the House of Commons gutted on the worst night of the blitz, 10-11 May 1941. A group of visitors is inspecting the damage.

On 14 October 1940 Coventry was attacked and the centre of the city almost obliterated. A third of the houses were destroyed. Most conspicuous victim was the fourteenth-century cathedral. A new verb, to 'coventrate', was added to the language.

One of London's most fashionable night spots was the Café de Paris. In March 1941 it was hit and many young officers on leave were killed as they danced to the music of 'Snakehips' Johnson.

painful honour of being the most seriously damaged town; all but 7,000 of its 12,000 houses were damaged, 35,000 out of its 47,000 inhabitants left homeless.

The evacuation schemes, which had been reversed at the end of 1939, were now reactivated. Statistically, 1.25 million people left the cities, many more abandoned their homes for the night. After a heavy raid on Plymouth, 50,000 trekked out each evening into the surrounding countryside. Yet many more stayed behind: because their work made it necessary; because they could not bear to abandon their husbands, friends or homes; because they were damned if any German was going to make them change their way of life. Gradually the anti-aircraft and night fighter defences improved, a ceiling of barrage-balloons – the comfortable, portly 'blimps' – lent a largely spurious air of security to the scene. Light, corrugated steel shelters had been distributed in their millions, christened 'Andersons' after Sir John Anderson who was responsible for their conception. More deep shelters were made available; 'British restaurants' were opened to give cheap and adequate, if monotonous fare to those who could not feed themselves. The peril from the air was never conquered, but Britain learnt to live with the blitz.

The purpose of the blitz was to weaken the morale of the people and to destroy, or at least seriously impair, the industrial capacity of the country. On both counts it failed. It produced much hardship and bloodshed. In the first phase of 1940 and 1941 it caused 43,000 deaths; by the end of the war the total was 60,000 with a further 86,000 seriously injured. For every person killed, thirty-five houses were destroyed or damaged. Nearly half a million homes were rendered uninhabit-

Winston Churchill in the cabinet war-room in 10 Downing Street. If aerial attack seemed likely he retreated to starker quarters in the bomb-proof headquarters far below the cabinet offices.

able during the war. The suffering was great and the people sometimes near despair. There were occasions on which Churchill or the King met with apathy or even hostility when they visited the bombed areas. But these were the exceptions: defiance, cheerfulness, indomitable determination were far more frequently encountered. 'Britain can take it' was not an empty propagandist's slogan but a fair representation of the nation's mood. And Britain kept making it too. Industry was amazingly little affected. Five days after the devastation of Coventry something close to full production had been resumed. Improvisation, flexibility, the readiness to forget the rule book and work for long hours in appalling conditions, ensured that the vital production of weapons and materials for the war was never seriously interrupted.

IN SEPTEMBER 1940 Buckingham Palace was hit by a bomb and the chapel destroyed. 'I'm glad we've been bombed,' said the Queen. 'It makes me feel I can look the East End in the face.' The royal family committed themselves to the needs of war with a zeal and conscientiousness which won new respect from their subjects. The food at the royal homes was notoriously scanty, the baths shallow, the temperature frigid. The King practised shooting with a revolver in the grounds and, if occasion arose, had every intention of dying in the ruins of his palace. The death in a flying accident of his brother, the Duke of Kent, in August 1942 showed that the tradition by which members of the royal family fought and sometimes died for their country was alive as it had ever been.

Princess Elizabeth repeatedly pleaded to be allowed to play her part, but she was considered too young to join any of the Services until the war was almost over.

The Home Guard, 'Dad's Army' as it came affectionately to be known, may have seemed a bit of a joke to many people but it also did a valuable job in relieving the regular army of some of its duties. Here the 25th Battalion demonstrates the art of camouflage. The fearsome weapon in the centre is a type of mortar known, after its inventor, as a Blacker Bombard.

Liverpool, as a great port and departure point for many Atlantic convoys, was an obvious target. Whole streets were destroyed and traffic in the centre of the city suspended for many hours.

Children playing on piles of debris in the East End of London, wearing what are presumably toy tin hats. Once the blitz proper got under way most of them will probably have been evacuated to safer parts of the country.

Millions of Anderson shelters, named after Sir John Anderson, a member of the War Cabinet, were distributed throughout Britain. Made of light corrugated steel, they provided excellent protection against anything except a direct hit or very near miss. In the hands of an artist they could also perform a strikingly decorative role.

Queen Elizabeth talks to Air Vice-Marshal Harris outside the gates of Buckingham Palace
just before the Battle of Britain parade. 'Bomber' Harris is identified above all with the view
that the war could be won by bombardment from the air.

St Paul's escape from destruction, when so much around it was destroyed, was one of the war's more remarkable survival stories. One compensation for the blitz was the spectacular views of Wren's great church which were opened up by the bombing.

Winston Churchill was a regular visitor to the bombed areas, in this case not far from home at Tufton Street in Westminster.

One child who was not evacuated. A woman reserve worker lifts a little girl from the ruins of a building in Buckingham Gate.

For every one person killed hundreds were made homeless. It was the dislocation of daily life that made the blitz so intolerable for many victims. Here a family assembles what is left of its possessions after a bomb made its home uninhabitable.

The royal family shared the nation's sufferings. In September 1940 Buckingham Palace was hit by a bomb. 'I'm glad we've been bombed,' said the Queen. 'It makes me feel I can look the East End in the face.'

Business as usual in London's East End. Within a few hours of a bomb falling shopkeepers would be trading in their shattered buildings and factory workers doing what they could with the ruins of their assembly lines. This blitz picture, taken in 1940, must have been one of the last to show bananas and oranges offered for sale.

Her role was inevitably unobtrusive; her only moments of glory coming each year in the Windsor pantomime. She first starred as Prince Charming in *Cinderella* in 1941, and in 1943, in *Aladdin*, had the pleasure of knowing Prince Philip was in the audience. One of the few occasions on which she came to wider notice occurred in October 1940 when she broadcast with Derek McCulloch – 'Uncle Mac' – on Children's Hour. 'I can truthfully say to you all,' she declared, 'that we children at home are full of cheerfulness and courage. We are trying to do all we can to help our gallant sailors, soldiers and airmen, and we are trying, too, to bear our own share of the danger and sadness of war. We know, every one of us, that in the end all will be well.'

The end still seemed far away. In the summer of 1941 the blitz dwindled as Hitler switched his bombers to the eastern front and invaded Russia on 21 June. Russia, which had joined Germany in the assault on Poland in 1939, was suddenly hailed as Britain's gallant ally: 'If Hitler invaded Hell,' remarked Churchill drily, 'I would make at least a favourable reference to the Devil in the House of Commons.' The British were relieved, and unruffled by the antics of the indigenous Communist party. For at the outbreak of war the Communist leader, Harry Pollitt, following the party line, had inveighed against anyone who refused to fight against 'the Fascist beast'; a month later the party decided that an error had been made – this was just another war between two capitalist powers of almost equal turpitude. Now all signals went to green again and the war became once more a crusade.

But though the threat from the air was reduced, it was never removed. In the spring of 1941 the picturesque Baltic town of Lübeck was largely destroyed by fire-bombs. Hitler ordered in retaliation the so-called 'Baedeker raids'. Exeter, Bath, Norwich, York, Canterbury were each in turn assaulted; little of military importance being touched but some of the most beautiful buildings in Britain destroyed. It was yet one more example of the beastliness of war, and one that was going to be repeated a hundredfold on German soil.

The invasion of Russia had quickly been followed by the launching of the 'V for Victory' campaign; its musical expression the dot-dot-dot-dash at the start of Beethoven's Ninth Symphony; its most loved manifestation Churchill's celebrated two-finger V sign. It was a huge popular success, in occupied Europe as well as in Britain. Victory became more than a pious hope in December 1941 with the Japanese attack on Pearl Harbor and the United States's entry into the war. The immediate results were catastrophic: vast shipping losses in the Atlantic, the fall of Britain's South East Asian empire. Yet there was no doubt left about the final outcome. 'So we had won after all!' wrote Churchill gratefully.

Britain was now to become an armed camp as the Americans poured in to prepare for the Second Front. By 1944 there were nearly 1.5 million foreign troops in the British Isles – the majority American GIs. It would have been a miracle if they had been universally popular. 'Over-paid, over-sexed and over here,' was the bitter description; they were said to lure away British girls with their money, nylons and superior comforts; to

The traditional Windsor pantomime: Princess Elizabeth starring as Prince Charming in Cinderella *in 1941. The Queen appears to be giving her younger daughter tips on how to manipulate a fan. Her fur cape shows the temperature maintained within the royal residences in winter.*

With petrol in short supply, if available at all, the pony trap returned into its own as one of the staples of the British transport system. It is doubtful whether the two Princesses depended heavily on this vehicle for transport but it still played an important part in their lives.

By 1944 there were nearly 1.5 million foreign troops in the British Isles, the majority American GIs. That the negro troops made their mark was demonstrated by the crop of dusky children who were to be seen at schools all over the country in the years after the war.

corrupt British youth with chewing gum; to be noisy, braggart and drunken. Friction was rare, however; on the whole the Americans were welcomed with enthusiasm and remained as cherished friends. The negro troops provided an exotic touch; that they made a lasting mark was demonstrated by the crop of dusky

children who were to be seen at schools all over the country in the years after the war.

British civilians began to hope that for them the perils, if not the privations, were almost over. There were many incidents in 1943 but few big raids, the worst disaster occurring at Bethnal Green when a woman tripped on the staircase of the underground railway; her fall brought down others; a human cascade crashed down and 173 people were killed in the tangled pile of bodies at the bottom. Then in June 1944 came the first flying bomb, the V1, familiarly known as the doodle bug or buzzbomb. London was the target, the country between London and the coast an incidental victim. People learned to listen to the engine, sigh with relief if it puttered over to hit some other unfortunate, prepare to dive for cover if it cut out overhead. On 29 July when a buzzbomb narrowly missed Lords cricket ground, Jack Robertson hit the next ball for six. Over 6,000 people were killed but by September techniques for interception had improved, the menace was dwindling when the next horror struck. The V2s, rocket-propelled bombs, forty-five feet long, weighing four tons, began to fall on London. Against these there was no defence; only the erratic functioning of the rockets, their small numbers and the overrunning of the launch sites saved London from appalling destruction. The

One of the worst individual disasters in the war was not caused directly by enemy action. A woman tripped on the staircase of the underground railway at Bethnal Green and 173 people ended up crushed to death in the tangled pile of bodies at the bottom. Here a group of anxious local residents await news of the victims.

British Isles had been served notice that, for the purposes of defence, they were hardly islands any more.

THOSE GOODIES which the American servicemen so conspicuously enjoyed were remarkable only in contrast to the privations which the British were enduring. Shortage of shipping and concentration on war production meant that almost everything was in short supply and many goods disappeared altogether. Paradoxically, the average Briton was healthier and better nourished by the end of the war than at the beginning. What food was available was rationed with scrupulous fairness; milk, orange-juice, cod-liver oil were available to every child – in small quantities, certainly, but nevertheless enjoyed by many who would never have had the chance before 1939. The diet was monotonous and sometimes distasteful, but it was always adequate.

It seemed that the nation flourished mentally as well as physically. No one had time to worry. Psychiatric diseases dwindled; the suicide rate fell from 12.9 per hundred thousand in 1938 to 8.9 in 1944. The strains of unemployment disappeared together with their cause. After sharp inflation in the first year of war, the cost of living was stabilised by subsidies and price controls. Taxation was high and extended to many people who had not endured it before, but with so little

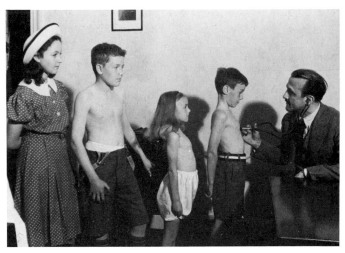

Far from suffering as a result of the war, the nation's health actually improved. Children in particular ate more nutritious, if not always more appetising, food and received far more medical attention than had been the case with most of them before 1939.

to spend money on poverty did not seem a particularly serious complaint. The disparity between rich and poor was less marked than at any other period of recorded history. Spending was denounced as a social evil; the 'Squanderbug' became the symbol of all that was self-indulgent and unpatriotic; 'Save for Victory' was the

A photograph taken from a roof top in Fleet Street shows a V1 rocket falling to earth half a mile or so away. This particular rocket fell near Drury Lane.

Garden gates and railings were removed for scrap and pots and pans collected for their aluminium content. The exercise was not of much practical use – the railings were often left to rust in vast heaps and to extract the aluminium from the kitchenware proved prohibitively expensive – but those who sacrificed their property felt that they were making a contribution to the war effort and the effect on morale was good.

Wartime shopping offered limited delights, though in January 1940 when this photograph was taken the grocers still had plentiful supplies. Butter, bacon and sugar had just been rationed, and the shop assistant is here snipping the relevant coupons from the customer's ration book. From the display it seems that this grocer over-stocked with tins of Christmas pudding and is now hoping to dispose of his pudding mountain as gifts to the troops.

order of the day, and Britain saved. It gave too. Binoculars and guns were surrendered for use by the Home Guard or other services. Pots and pans were collected for their aluminium content. Railings and ornamental gates were removed for scrap. Gifts were solicited to 'Buy a Spitfire' or some part of it; for 15s.0d. (75p) the donor could feel proudly responsible for the blast tube of a machine gun.

Austerity came slowly. The official doctrine was that if the working man ate less he would provide less, and Churchill for one believed that meat was the most important element in the labourer's diet. Rationing was therefore imposed with reluctance. Most consumer goods were still to be procured in early 1940, petrol too; in the spring of 1940 there were still twenty makes of car on the market. Rationing gradually spread to a wider and wider range of products but the initial allowances were generous. Bacon, ham, butter and sugar were rationed from January 1940, but the bacon ration, at eight ounces, was higher than the average

consumption. It was not till 1941 that real sacrifices were imposed. Jam, margarine, cheese, eggs and clothes were added to the list of rationed items; other less essential products became rarities; whisky, razorblades and real coffee were treasures doled out to favoured customers by the now all-powerful shopkeeper. The queue became an inescapable feature of national life; a black market began to grow up for those who were not prepared to share the privations of their fellow citizens. There were not many of them; on the whole the British grumbled, tried to get a little bit extra on the side, but made do manfully with what they had.

Britain at last adapted itself to a wartime economy. As the demands of the Armed Services took personnel away from the factories and the land the direction of labour became inevitable. It was in 1941 that women escaped from the home and domestic service; assembly lines which had never seen a female face were now operated entirely by women; the Land Girl became a feature of the countryside. At the end of the year, when

Wartime posters figured largely in the national consciousness. This healthy and ebullient Land Girl might have attracted anyone to the farm, though her harvesting technique seems a little unsophisticated even by the standards of the age. 'Is Your Journey Really Necessary?', like 'Dig for Victory' or 'Walls have Ears' became one of the catch phrases known to everyone in Britain.

The conscription of women was announced at the end of 1941, and by 10 January 1942, when this photograph was taken at the Westminster Labour Exchange, the registration of women was under way. By 1943 ninety per cent of single and eighty per cent of married women between the ages of eighteen and forty were in some way helping the war effort.

As the men left the factories to join the Services, assembly lines which had never before seen a female face were handed over entirely to women. These workers are rolling out the metal bands used in the construction of the hulls of bombers.

the call-up age for men was extended to fifty-one, the conscription of women was announced. By 1943, 90 per cent of single and 80 per cent of married women between the ages of eighteen and forty were in industry or the armed forces. Of all the social consequences of the war the conscription of women was the most striking and the most permanent; the once ubiquitous parlour-maids and cooks, essential elements of every middle-class home, disappeared in their hundreds of thousands and were never to return.

One place where women did not go was down the mines. Somebody had to, however. While 80,000 young miners joined the forces, others went into munitions factories. Coal production, which had been 227 million tons in 1938, was close to falling below 200 million tons. The government first offered conscripts the opportunity to choose the coal industry in preference to the Armed Services, then imposed a compulsory ballot to direct them down the mines. Christened the 'Bevin boys', a cross-section of young men who would never normally even have seen a coal mine now found themselves forced to work under-

ground. Their experiences help explain the sympathy which the British public has felt for the cause of the miners over the last forty years.

Britain had to grow more of its own food or starve. Four million additional acres were ploughed up in the first two years of the war. Golf-courses were sacrificed, the Great Park at Windsor turned into a gigantic field of wheat, tracts of the New Forest that had never been disturbed by man were now converted into grazing. There were still more than half a million cart horses at work at the end of the war but mechanization was on the march and the tractor becoming a commonplace. Every man became his own farmer, half a million new allotments were opened, the backyard chickens, or even pig, became a feature of city life.

By 1942 imports of food were at less than half their pre-war level. British agriculture could do something to fill the gap but many products were beyond its capacity. The 'points' system, by which consumers could use their coupons as they chose to buy a wide range of goods, was gradually extended to cover canned foods, rice, dried fruit, sago, condensed milk, cereals, syrup,

The Land Girl became a common feature of the countryside. Jobs which men had long considered to require more strength or skill than a mere woman could provide were mastered with embarrassing ease by the new recruits.

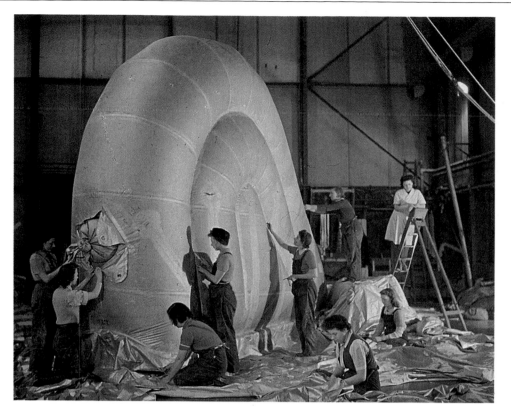

Women workers engaged in the manufacture of barrage balloons. By the end of the war whole factories were almost entirely run by women. Having once escaped from domestic labour they were never to be put back again.

Lord Woolton, businessman turned minister of food, addresses a contingent from the Women's Land Army. By the end of 1942, when this photograph was taken, imports of food were at less than half their pre-war level and four million additional acres of British soil had been ploughed up to help fill the gap.

treacle, biscuits and oatflakes. Soap and sweets were rationed. Stafford Cripps assumed the mantle of austerity and wore it with apparent relish. He vehemently denounced any kind of personal extravagance, removed what was left of the petrol allowance for private motorists, cut the clothes ration. Waste became a crime; fines were imposed for throwing away food; Lady Diana Cooper was prosecuted for feeding stale bread to her chickens.

The ministry of food, 50,000 strong under its powerful minister, Lord Woolton, urged the British public into new expedients to eke out its rations or make them more palatable. Spam, dried milk, dried eggs, the dingy grey 'national loaf', were nutritious enough but not immediately appealing. Turnip water could provide the baby with his vitamin C; young nettles could furnish an agreeable soup; horse flesh was an excellent substitute for beef or mutton; the rabbit became a cherished feature of the country menu. The ministry issued a series of recipes of remarkable ingenuity – for rissoles without beef, cakes without sugar, Christmas pudding without eggs. As tea and coffee became rarer a variety of indigenous leaves – raspberry, mulberry, black-currant – were advanced as substitutes. The rancid reek of home-grown and home-cured tobacco offered a new threat to the more sensitive nostril. The unctuous accents of Charles Hill, 'The Radio Doctor', seconded the efforts of the ministry: sugar was bad for

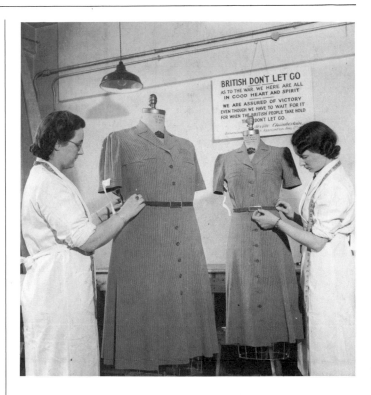

Clothes were austere and only available against a very limited ration of coupons. Here 'rational dresses' are being prepared at a London factory. The photograph was taken in May 1940; a few months later Chamberlain's exhortation would probably have been replaced by some Churchillian rhetoric.

The British resolutely continued to enjoy themselves, in spite of all pressures to the contrary. In July 1941 there was dancing in the open air on Plymouth Hoe, with a barrage balloon wallowing comfortably in the background.

you, grey bread much healthier than white, dandelions provided an excellent emetic and reinforced 'the natural grinding action of the stomach'.

As the war news grew better, so rationing grew more severe. The meat ration was reduced every year from 1941 to 1945. In May 1945 the bacon ration was cut from four ounces to three, the clothes ration made still more exiguous. If the average Briton had been told in September 1939 that more than five years later he would still be at war and that his material condition would still be deteriorating, he would have despaired. It would have seemed to him that such a life could not be worth living. Yet in fact morale was still generally high and people continued to enjoy life and to find ways to entertain and amuse themselves.

For many, indeed, the war opened doors on to a world whose existence had hardly been suspected before 1939. Of nothing was this more true than classical music. For those in the metropolis, Myra Hess's lunchtime piano recitals in the National Gallery possessed an almost sacred quality in their triumphant affirmation that, though Hitler might do his worst, the banner of culture and civilization still flew proudly over Trafalgar Square. But it was the carrying of music to the masses, whether in the factory or the barracks, that marked the most significant departure. The slightly

Silk stockings disappeared from the shops. An ingenious substitute was evolved in April 1940. Cream was smeared evenly over the bare leg and, with a dark brown eyebrow pencil, a line was then drawn up the back of the leg.

Vera Lynn, 'the Forces' Sweetheart', entertaining the troops in September 1940. Her raw, starkly sentimental rendering of 'We'll Meet Again' was the only indigenous tune which had anything approaching the potency of 'Tipperary' or the German 'Lili Marlene'.

seedy pianist playing Strauss waltzes in the works' canteen, the ENSA string quartet sawing away devotedly in a hangar on an East Anglian airfield, may not have been among the most distinguished practitioners of the art, but they gave pleasure, they aroused interest, they created a new enthusiasm which did not die with the ending of the war.

For the great majority, of course, music was to dance to or was expressed in popular songs. At first these were bellicose and chauvinistic: the braggart 'We're going to hang out the washing on the Siegfried Line' displayed the ill-founded confidence with which too many British contemplated the task ahead. Soon this was to change. The Second World War had no 'Tipperary', but the raw and starkly sentimental sound of Vera Lynn – the Forces' Sweetheart – singing 'We'll Meet Again' caught the longings of the age. So, too, did those bluebirds perpetually circling over the White Cliffs of Dover, or the ever-shining Harvest Moon. 'Lili Marlene', the only popular song with 'Tipperary's' enduring potency, was purloined from the Germans and was likely to be heard on either side of the line of battle.

Travelling only with difficulty, often cut off from friends or relatives, the British took refuge in books. Escapist literature was what was mostly called for, but escape often into a more secure and leisurely age – Jane

Austen was much in fashion, Trollope enjoyed a merited revival. There was no war poet to enjoy the renown of Julian Grenfell or Rupert Brooke, still less Owen or Sassoon, but Alun Lewis caught the imagination of the young with his *Raider's Dawn* and *Ha! Ha! Among the Trumpets* and might have achieved greatness if he had not died in Burma in 1944.

Preoccupation with the progress of the war ensured that more Britons than ever before read a daily paper. Even before the war the *Daily Mirror* had established itself as the voice of the working classes, now it reigned supreme with its advice to servicemen; the lively polemical column of that scourge of the authorities, William O'Connor, 'Cassandra'; and above all the strip cartoon 'Jane', the adventures of an antiseptic and curiously innocent beauty who lost her clothes twice a week to the delight of her millions of admirers. The *Daily Mirror* owed much of its popularity to its readiness, determination even, to challenge authority. Sometimes it seemed to the government that it was actively subversive, once it was almost banned, but it survived and in time proved itself one of the major educational forces of the age.

'Lili Marlene' was not the only contribution the Germans made to British morale. The Anglo-Irish William Joyce broadcast each night from Berlin to a

Newspaper reading became more widespread than ever before or since, never more so than on 6 June 1944 when crowds in Piccadilly Circus read the first news of the invasion in the early editions of the evening papers.

British audience reckoned at six million. His listeners christened him 'Lord Haw Haw', mocked his exaggeratedly languid diction, disbelieved his facts. His execution after the war was a poor recompense for the unwitting help he gave beleaguered Britain. But it was the BBC which did most to satisfy the needs of the people. If one image more than any other catches the flavour of wartime Britain it is a family group clustered around a box of brown bakelite and indeterminate timber, while the paterfamilias twirls the heavy black knobs in the hope of finding a crackle-free rendition of the nine o'clock news.

Even more than the nine o'clock news, however, ITMA – acronym of It's That Man Again – united the country, every age-group, every social class, in common laughter. 'That man' was Tommy Handley, and he created a fantasy world peopled by his own grotesque yet only-too-familiar characters. Mrs Mopp, Colonel Chinstrap, Funf the German spy, Mona Lott, entered the national pantheon; their catchwords: 'Don't forget the diver', 'I don't mind if I do', 'Can I do you now, Sir?' – were instantly recognised and appreciated wherever a wireless was to be found. If a real German spy had been arrested and interrogated he would only have had to reply 'This is Funf speaking' to be immediately absolved of suspicion.

Almost as popular was the Brains Trust. Julian Huxley – clear-headed, precise, omniscient on every

The wireless was the link that kept most Britons in touch with what was going on. Here a group of demolition workers listens to a speech of Churchill's in the Black Dog pub in Shoe Lane, EC4.

Tommy Handley – 'Mrs Handley's boy' – with three members of the ITMA team (Joan Harbin, Molly Weir and Tini Goss) in a nearby pub before they give a show in Wadhurst, Sussex. Surprisingly absent from the bar is another member of the team, Jack Train, among whose parts was the bibulous Colonel Chinstrap.

scientific subject and most others besides; the irritable and almost as irritating Professor Joad; bluff Commander Campbell with a tall traveller's tale to embellish every answer, could hold forth articulately and entertainingly on any subject. Their catch-phrases too entered the national consciousness: 'It depends what you mean by . . .' and 'When I was in . . .' were Joad and Campbell's favourite and much-loved preambles. These two programmes, and 'The Robinsons', first of what was to prove a momentous sequence of radio and television soap operas, did as much as any individual except Churchill to sustain the British in their tribulations.

Outside the home the pub continued to be the centre of social life. Spirits were rarities hoarded for favoured customers, the beer was watered, but there was usually a fire in winter, darts, cheerful conversation. 'Careless Talk Costs Lives' proclaimed the poster on the wall, but there was never any shortage of weird rumours: Hitler had been dead for years and his place taken by a double; the same was true of Stalin; most frequently of all, there was a new and fearful secret weapon which could win/lose the war in a matter of days.

Between twenty-five and thirty million people visited the cinema each week: the lights, the comparative warmth, the glamour and variety, provided a welcome relief from the frugal daily grind. To the government it offered an opportunity to make propaganda. The news

'Utility' fashions, designed by the royal couturier, Norman Hartnell, and demonstrated here in June 1943.

films, the documentaries, Noel Coward's story of a destroyer, *In Which We Serve* – based on the experiences of Lord Louis Mountbatten and HMS *Kelly* – even Laurence Olivier's extravagant *Henry V*, were all designed to stir up patriotic fervour. But the greatest of all popular successes dealt with another war. *Gone With The Wind* arrived in London in 1940 and ran continuously for four years. Almost everyone saw it once, some people ten or twenty times, and it set a standard for romantic spectaculars that has never been surpassed.

There were limits to what the people were prepared to give up. In spite of the discomfort and irregularity of public transport, many persisted in taking their holidays away from home. Horse racing continued – even in May 1940, 10,000 travelled by train to Ascot in a single day; Gordon Richards became the royal jockey in 1943. Epsom was taken over by the army but there was still racing at Newmarket; the Oval was turned into a prisoner-of-war camp, but cricket went on at Lords. Highbury was closed and football curtailed throughout the country, but the pools kept going.

To some it seemed that sex had become a national sport. The separation imposed on so many husbands and wives, the disappearance abroad of vast numbers of men, their replacement by glamorous and often opulent foreigners, ensured that sexual promiscuity increased. Syphilis became more common; the divorce rate soared. The church did little to check this decline;

indeed it cannot be said that it exercised much moral authority in any sphere. The Church of England's attitude towards the war was characteristically eclectic; ranging from the church militant, which prayed for victory and denounced the Germans as sinners whom it was the duty of good Christians to chastise, to the Church pacifist, which condemned the bombing of German cities and other particularly unpalatable features of the war.

No number of bellicose clerics or rousing propaganda films could prevent the British becoming increasingly weary as the war wore on into its fifth and then sixth year. Strikes, which had become a comparative rarity after Dunkirk, became more frequent again as the immediate danger passed. By the end of 1942 the pre-war average of days lost a month was being equalled or even exceeded. When real emergency threatened the people were as staunch as ever, but once victory seemed certain human nature ensured that those who had done so much to gain it should start to put their own preoccupations first, to look more jealously at their neighbour and to wonder what their situation would be when the fighting stopped.

The government fostered such speculations by commissioning plans for Britain after the war. The most ambitious was that by Sir William Beveridge, a blueprint for the welfare state, offering social security from the cradle to the grave. It was instantly and immensely

Any letters leaving the country were censored in case they gave away information that might be of value to the enemy. Recipients of letters from indiscreet correspondents could find themselves confronted by something resembling imperfectly manufactured confetti. Here work is going on inside the Postal Censorship Department for the North of England (exact locality censored).

To mark the second anniversary of the Battle of Britain the people of Stepney attend a service conducted by their rector, the Rev. Reginald French. The service, held in the open air, took place amidst the ruins of a blitzed school in the district.

popular; 635,000 people bought copies of it or its official summary and the expectations of the nation were fixed irrevocably on its proposals. The Beveridge report was published at the end of 1942; a ministry of town and country planning set up in 1943; in 1944 R.A. Butler's Education Act provided for the leaving age at school to be raised after the war first to fifteen, then to sixteen, with free education at grammar, technical and secondary modern schools.

Despite the rosy prospects, the national government became ever more unpopular. Significantly it was the Tory rather than the Labour element in the coalition which was most out of favour. A series of defeats in by-elections, by candidates standing for a variety of diverse groups or even just for themselves, made the seemingly impregnable Conservative majority seem suddenly vulnerable. The evolution of the political scene was portrayed in its most simple and dramatic form when the Marquess of Hartington, son of the Duke of Devonshire and defending what was generally held to be a family borough, was defeated by a swing of 10,000 votes in favour of the independent Socialist Charlie White, radical son of a village cobbler.

The people were beginning to seem more concerned about what would happen after the war than about winning the war itself. By the summer of 1944 it was universally felt that the fighting was as good as over. There were still battles to win, deaths to grieve, but the worst of the pressure was off. Holidays by the seaside became a possibility again. In September the blackout was relaxed, the Home Guard stood down in December, the last V1s and V2s fell in January 1945.

The exultation that swept the country when Germany surrendered on 8 May 1945 showed that the relaxation of the previous months had not gone very deep. Everywhere there were spontaneous and heartfelt celebrations; in London vast crowds roamed a miraculously flood-lit city, singing, cheering, dancing. Churchill's car was pushed from Downing Street to the House of Commons; hundreds of thousands of revellers milled down the Mall and in front of Buckingham Palace. Time and again the King and Queen with the Princesses appeared on the battered balcony in front of the boarded-up windows; time and again the crowd cheered its approval. With some hesitation, the two Princesses were allowed to sally out with a group of young officers to join in the celebrations. 'Poor darlings', wrote King George VI in his diary, 'they have never had any fun yet.'

So far as Princess Elizabeth was concerned, at least, her father's remark did less than justice to her resourcefulness and capacity to enjoy life. Certainly she had

Though prefabricated housing did not sprout in large quantities until after the war, a certain amount was already available in 1944. Here Mr and Mrs Hickman inspect the building that might become their home.

No 230873 Second Subaltern Elizabeth Windsor demonstrating some of the finer points of the internal combustion engine to her admiring mother.

VE Day, 8 May 1945. A mood of exultation swept the country at the news that Germany had finally surrendered. There was still Japan to defeat, but the war in Asia seemed very far away and only those with close friends or relatives involved in the fighting felt intimately involved.

been deprived of some of the traditional pleasures of a teenage princess, but this had been compensated for by the greater freedom and the informality which wartime conditions had made possible. Princess Elizabeth did not delude herself that she could ever live just like other girls of her own age, but she still wanted to share their lives as much as was possible. In 1944 she took a significant step in that direction when she persuaded her parents to let her join the ATS, the Auxiliary Territorial Service. As No.230873 Second Subaltern Elizabeth Alexandra Mary Windsor, she donned shapeless overalls and settled down to an intensive course in map-reading and the driving and maintenance of heavy vehicles. She was duly photographed, standing beside a lorry, with a diligent expression and a spanner or some similar utensil in her hand, oil-spattered, very evidently at work. The work was genuine, she applied herself conscientiously and won good reports, but there was still an element of play-acting about it. Even if the war had continued she would never have been allowed to exercise her new skills anywhere near a battlefield; when it ended, as was clearly going to happen soon, it was unlikely that the maintenance of heavy lorries would play any great part in her royal duties. She enjoyed the work, however, and it was a valuable experience, bringing her closer than anything

had done before to the way of life led by the vast majority of her future subjects.

Those subjects were now about to show that they felt the time for a change was overdue. Churchill had proposed that the wartime coalition should continue until the end of the war against Japan. The Socialists were unwilling to prolong it beyond October 1945. The advent of the atom bomb was in fact to mean that the Asian war ended before the October deadline but Churchill decided to opt for a July election. The political pattern, frozen since 1935, was about to be broken.

The Conservatives put their faith in tried methods and familiar faces; Churchill was their trump card; 'Vote National. Help him finish the Job!' their favourite slogan. Churchill's progresses around the country were triumphal; huge crowds cheered him ecstatically in Yorkshire, Lancashire, even Glasgow. There was an attempt to scare the electorate into believing that a Labour government would lead to a left-wing dictatorship – Professor Laski, the Socialist ideologue, was built up into a bogey-man seeking to create a bureaucratic Gestapo – but the emphasis was on sticking to the winning team. The pundits agreed that no more was needed; the only question was how large the Tory majority would be.

It is hard to understand why more attention was not

The royal family, with Winston Churchill, on the balcony of Buckingham Palace as the crowds surge up the Mall to celebrate VE Day. The boarded-up windows behind the balcony are a tacit reminder of the perils from which Britain has just emerged.

paid to the by-elections of the previous years. Rarely has an electorate been more misjudged. When the results were announced – three weeks after polling day because of the delays in collecting the Service vote from overseas – it was found that the huge Conservative majority had disappeared in an equally massive victory for Labour. Out of 640 seats, Labour won 393, the Tories 213, Liberals twelve and various Independents twenty-two. Thirteen Conservative ministers were out, including Harold Macmillan and Churchill's protégé, Brendan Bracken. As always, the composition of the House of Commons exaggerated the electoral swing. The Conservatives had gained nearly 40 per cent of the votes, against Labour's 48 per cent. It was estimated that they still had well over four million supporters among the manual workers. But the victory had been a decisive one.

Once it was achieved everyone realised that it had been inevitable. Many factors were put forward to explain the phenomenon: the activities of the army education corps, believed by the Tories to be a covert left-wing striking force; the proselytising of the *Daily*

Mirror and *Picture Post*; the preaching of the church, whose leaders – notably Archbishop Temple – had lain stress on the need for a more egalitarian society and the evils of unbridled capitalism. No doubt all these helped, but no doubt also the British voter would have worked it out for himself without any guidance. The root of the matter lay in a sentence: the British wanted radical reform and did not trust the Tories to give it to them. The Tories did not even always trust themselves. 'I'd have voted Labour myself, if I hadn't been a Tory candidate,' remarked one young would-be member, and his comment explains the curious sense of relief that mitigated the Conservatives' disappointment. Even Churchill was understanding. His doctor, Lord Moran, spoke to him of the nation's ingratitude. 'Oh no, I wouldn't call it that,' replied Churchill. 'They have had a very bad time.'

The Labour government of 1945 came to power with a mandate for radical reform and an immense fund of goodwill, even among its opponents. The British people had indeed had a very bad time. Now it was up to the government to make things better.

The Labour party celebrates its sensational victory in the general election of 1945. Clement Attlee stands on the platform before his exultant supporters. Before the election the only question had been the size of the Conservative majority; now Labour had an overall majority of almost 150 seats.

One of the official engagement portraits by Dorothy Wilding. The announcement was made in June 1947 but nobody was taken by surprise.

Chapter Four

The Years of Austerity

1945 to 1952

SHORTLY AFTER the new Labour government took office, a photograph appeared showing George VI among his ministers, looking very much as he had used to appear when Churchill rather than Attlee had been prime minister. The picture did much to console the more apprehensive of his subjects, who had believed that the accession to power of the wild men of the left would mean revolution, with the Red Flag replacing the Union Jack and the tumbrils set up on Horseguards' Parade. The King, in fact, was more apprehensive than the photograph indicated. His cousin, Louis Mountbatten, reassured him that the inexperience of his new ministers would give him greater authority than he had ever enjoyed when Chamberlain or Churchill was prime minister. Mountbatten was proved right; though Attlee subsequently claimed credit for the idea, it seems that it was the King who first suggested that Bevin should go to the foreign office and Dalton to the exchequer rather than the other way round; the Labour ministers paid as much attention to the monarch as had their Tory predecessors.

'The royal firm' – as George VI sometimes referred to it – was back at work again. Quite what its functions were was harder to decide. Clearly it was not there to govern the country. The right to be consulted, to encourage and to warn, was how Bagehot had described the extent of the royal prerogative in the nineteenth century, and it certainly had not increased since then. Though a few residual and ill-defined powers could still theoretically be exercised, the monarch in the last resort was there to do what his ministers told him. Apart from this, he fulfilled, with reasonable cheapness, those formal and largely ornamental duties which would otherwise have had to be carried out by an elected head of state. He provided, though this was of little significance in 1945, a tourist attraction far surpassing in its potency any art collection or noble church. The monarchy, therefore, was justifiable on economic grounds. But it was more than this. The royal family was a symbol – of stability, security, continuity; the preservation of traditional values. It provided a defence against extremism, the erosion of family life,

King George VI with members of the 1945 Labour cabinet in the gardens of Buckingham Palace. (From left) Morrison, Attlee, the King, Greenwood, Bevin, Alexander.

Princess Elizabeth with King George VI in July 1946. By the time that this photograph was taken, the Princess's wish to marry her distant cousin Prince Philip of Greece must already have been preoccupying both father and daughter.

the disintegration of society. As well as providing for the romantic the delights of pageantry and soap opera, it gave the conservative an assurance that prudence, industry, decency, were still qualities to be admired and cherished. Since the typical Briton was both romantic and conservative, it was not surprising that the royal family enjoyed vast popularity. Republicanism, which might briefly have seemed a threat at the time of the abdication crisis, had now withered to its habitual proportions as a hobby of a tiny and unrepresentative fringe. Support for the monarchy was less whole-hearted on the left than on the right, but the difference was small, almost insignificant.

It was thanks in particular to Princess Elizabeth that the royal family moved back into the centre of public attention. The marriages and romantic involvements of its princes and princesses have always proved fascinating to the British people; when that princess is young, attractive and heir to the throne the appeal becomes irresistible. For several years there had been speculation that Princess Elizabeth would marry her cousin, Prince Philip of Greece. The King and Queen had known for a long time that this was her desire but had argued for delay, so as to give their daughter time to grow up, look around a little, meet some other eligible men. By the summer of 1946 the situation had become

In the first six months of 1947 the press office at Buckingham Palace refused to admit that there was any question of an engagement between Princess Elizabeth and Prince Philip of Greece; the British public declined to be deceived. One of the very few photographs of them together at this period shows the couple at the wedding of the Princess's Lady-in-waiting.

almost untenable. In September an official statement was issued denying newspaper rumours of an engagement. No one was deceived.

It was in part at least to escape the pressure of public attention that the King and Queen decided to take their daughters with them on a tour of South Africa in the winter of 1946-47. The timing was unfortunate. Britain was enduring austerity more harsh than anything experienced during the war and was about to suffer the coldest and longest winter of the generation. Less than a third of the people thought the visit desirable; 32 per cent believed it to be an expensive and unnecessary junket. The King and his ministers stuck to their plans, however, and Princess Elizabeth celebrated her twenty-first birthday 6,000 miles from home. In a broadcast on that day she reiterated the creed that was to guide her through life:

I declare before you all that my whole life, whether it be long or short, shall be devoted to your service and the service of our great Imperial Commonwealth to which we all belong. But I shall not have the strength to carry out this resolution unless you join in it with me, as I now invite you to do; I know that your support will be unfailingly given. God bless all of you who are willing to share it.

The engagement between Princess Elizabeth and Prince Philip was officially announced in June 1947. The initial response was not wholly enthusiastic. A surprising number of Britons objected to Prince Philip

The King and Queen, followed by Princess Elizabeth and Princess Margaret, leave St Paul's Cathedral after the thanksgiving service in May 1945.

The royal tour of South Africa, taken in part at least to escape public attention over the putative engagement of Princess Elizabeth. Another relationship throve during the visit: Princess Margaret stands to the left beside the Queen, Group Captain Peter Townsend to the right.

Princess Elizabeth celebrated her twenty-first birthday 6,000 miles from home, and broadcast to the British people from South Africa. 'I declare before you,' she said, 'that my whole life, long or short, shall be devoted to your service and the service of our great Imperial Commonwealth to which we all belong.'

on grounds of race; they were not clear whether he was Greek or German but he was certainly foreign, upbringing and service in the Royal Navy notwithstanding. Not many were as extreme as the forty-year-old bank clerk from Wimbledon who grumbled, 'With Attlee and Bevin being Jews, England will soon be ruled by a lot of foreigners,' but a vague disquietude existed. There was disapproval too among those who saw extravagance in the preparations for the wedding, or who resented the 300 extra clothing coupons allotted to the bride for her wedding dress. The Camden Town First Branch of the Amalgamated Society of Woodworkers struck a gloomy note: 'It wishes to remind you that any banqueting and display of wealth will be an insult to the British people at the present time. Furthermore, should you declare the wedding day a public holiday you will have a word beforehand with the London Master Builders Association to ensure that we are paid for it.'

As happens invariably with great royal occasions, all qualifications were forgotten as the day approached. The royal engagement, said Churchill, was 'a flash of colour on the hard road we have to travel.' To a provincial newspaper it was 'England's answer to *Oklahoma*,' the sensationally successful American musical that had brought a blaze of exuberant light into a grey and shabby London. Such an analogy does less than justice to the affection that the public lavished on

*Princess Elizabeth and her husband, who had been created Duke of Edinburgh the day before,
passing through Parliament Square in the Bridal Coach on their return to Buckingham Palace
from the wedding ceremony in Westminster Abbey.*

It was bad luck that the royal tour of South Africa in 1946-47 should have coincided with one of the bleakest and longest of British winters – photographs like this one of the two Princesses in summer dresses were not always well received at home. The visit was a success, however.

*An engagement photograph taken in Buckingham Palace, showing both Prince Philip and
the King in naval uniform.*

Telephone boxes make a convenient grandstand for enthusiasts determined to get a good view of the procession to the Abbey. These intrepid royalty-watchers were planning to spend the night on their exposed and uncomfortable eyrie.

this young, attractive and obviously loving couple. The wedding was celebrated with a glamour and pageantry that had not been seen in Britain since 1939, yet remained an intimate affair. It was a family wedding, yet the family was extended to include the British people; in London the usual crowds thronged the route; all over the country everyday occupations were abandoned as people clustered around the radio to follow and, in their own way, to share in the ceremony.

With the royal marriage the monarchy gained a new and incomparably brighter focus of attention. The King was in no way forgotten – his ever-conscientious attention to duty alone made this impossible – but Elizabeth was the future: hopeful sign of a brighter, more successful Britain. That future seemed assured when at the end of 1948 Prince Charles was born, eventual heir to the throne that his mother would soon occupy. A large crowd outside the Palace cheered and sang for two hours until, late at night, they were

Prince Charles was christened by the Archbishop of Canterbury at Buckingham Palace on 15 December 1948. Princess Elizabeth and her son are flanked by the Dowager Marchioness of Milford Haven (the Duke of Edinburgh's grandmother) and Queen Mary. Behind, from left to right, stand Patricia Brabourne (now Countess Mountbatten of Burma), the Duke of Edinburgh, King George VI, the Hon David Bowes-Lyon (brother to the Queen), the Earl of Athlone (standing proxy as god-father for the King of Norway) and Princess Margaret.

persuaded to go away and let the new mother get some sleep. It was an occasion for rejoicing and for speculation about the country he would one day reign over.

'WE ARE the masters now!' proclaimed Hartley Shawcross triumphantly in the House of Commons. The new majority party was indeed very different from its predecessor, yet it was by no means alarming in its composition; forty-six of its members had been to Oxford or Cambridge; for every two of the new members who were horny-handed, three, it was said, were horny-spectacled. When the House met and Churchill entered the chamber, what was left of the Conservative party sang 'For He's a Jolly Good Fellow'. The Socialists retaliated with 'The Red Flag' (few knew the words). It sounded revolutionary, yet when the Speaker drily commented that he had hoped he was to preside over a debating chamber, not a musical production, the House laughed and settled down to work.

Clement Attlee, the new prime minister. 'A sheep in sheep's clothing,' jeered Churchill, but he soon proved himself tough, indomitable and fully in command.

Ernest Bevin, foreign secretary in the new administration, was one of Labour's big three and some would say the most outstanding success in an outstanding government. Here he shakes hands with his opponent, Brigadier Smyth VC, after holding Wandsworth Central for Labour in the 1945 election.

Stafford Cripps, third in Labour's great triumvirate and president of the board of trade in the new government. Behind him hangs a poster which brings home starkly the facts of Britain's disastrous economic plight.

In 1946 the coal industry was nationalised. A veteran of the industry surveys the proof of this dramatic change.

Nor did the new government show much sympathy for the extreme left. Its leader, Clement Attlee, was treated by some with derision – 'a sheep in sheep's clothing', said Churchill; 'his light shone best under a bushel,' contributed Aneurin Bevan – yet he was tough, indomitable and fully in command. Cripps, Dalton, Bevin and Herbert Morrison were the most powerful members of his cabinet; three out of this big five had been to public schools and none was extravagantly radical. It was a business-like, high-principled and capable administration; pledged certainly to a potent measure of reform but unlikely to preside over the total disintegration of the social system.

The main problem of the new government was that the voter believed he had fought long and hard for victory and that it was now time he enjoyed a fair share of the fruits. Yet the most obvious fruits were bitter indeed: mountainous debts, ruined cities, shortages of every kind of goods and materials. There were no rewards to be distributed; all ministers could do was show that what little was available was distributed fairly and that the foundations were being laid for a better future. They did so with energy; between 1945 and 1950 inclusive the government passed 398 acts, involving 9,421 pages of legislation.

Nationalisation was its favoured weapon. The Bank of England, airways and the coal industry were nationalised in 1946; cable and wireless communications in 1947; gas, electricity and public transport in 1948. Not merely did this ensure that a far larger part of the wealth of the nation would in future be administered by the people's representatives and, it was hoped, in the people's interests, but it was also believed that it would raise the standards of efficiency and avoid industrial disputes. As a young official at the ministry of fuel and power, one Harold Wilson, wrote enthusiastically: 'It seems an inescapable fact that the men will not make their fullest effort under private ownership, but will make greater efforts when they know they are serving no private interest or profit-making agency but producing for the service of the community.' It was not to be long before Mr Wilson was given cause to wonder whether his assessment of human nature had not been a little naive. In the meantime the nationalisation programme went through with much huffing and puffing from the opposition but little passionate conviction in the injustice of the government's cause. It was not till it came to the Iron and Steel Act of 1949 that the Tories rallied their forces to fight the legislation to the last ditch and, if possible, beyond it.

The same was true of most of the other major pieces of legislation introduced by the Labour government. The opposition knew that the new policies were supported by the bulk of the electorate and was cautious about opposing them tooth and nail. Such was the National Insurance Act, which brought the whole population into a grand scheme covering them from conception to the grave, with special attention paid to unemployment, maternity, retirement, and the other vicissitudes to which flesh is prone.

Princess Elizabeth on her wedding day. Three hundred extra clothing coupons had been allotted to the bride for her wedding dress, and though some egalitarians claimed that this was unjust, most people felt the extravagance was very much in order.

The flesh was looked after still more effectively when the National Health Service was established in 1948. The idea that everyone, rich and poor alike, should have free access to doctors, dentists and the hospitals, met with relatively little opposition on grounds of principle but much indignant protest from the medical practitioners, who said that the scheme would put an intolerable burden on them and would never work. However, 90 per cent of the doctors joined the scheme. Within two months 93 per cent of the population had signed on as patients. Britain, Aneurin Bevan proclaimed, had taken the moral leadership of the world.

The middle classes espoused the Health Service with enthusiasm and by so doing helped to make it successful. They viewed state education with greater doubts and, by their hesitation, imperilled its development. The new government baulked at abolishing the public schools and, though developing free secondary education and encouraging local councils to espouse the cause of comprehensive schooling, did little to challenge the standing of the grammar schools. The increase in the leaving age from fourteen to fifteen in 1947 and the influx of new entrants produced by the post-war baby boom, were to place an increasingly oppressive burden on the system in the 1950s. The explosive growth of Britain's universities was to come later; the undergraduate population swelled rapidly after the war, but mainly by expansion of the existing institutions. The 4,000 pre-war undergraduates at

The Trade Disputes Act of 1947 put much greater power into the hands of the trade unions. Here Arthur Horner, the leader of the mineworkers and a prominent communist, is addressing the Trades Union Congress at Southport in September 1947.

The Cambridge Union in November 1948. The motion being debated is 'that this house would welcome a reunification of Ireland'. It was supported by the former Premier of Ireland, Eamon de Valera who is here shown speaking, but the motion was defeated by 542 votes to 236.

Oxford soon almost doubled to become a full 7,000.

The need for new towns was more to the forefront of the government's thinking than new universities. The concept of artificially created urban centres, self-contained, with their own light industry, strategically placed to link up with the network of road and rail, was not entirely new. Letchworth in 1903 and Welwyn in 1920 were early examples. The New Towns Act of 1946 planned to create twenty such centres, with populations of between 30,000 and 60,000. The most ambitious was the new city of Milton Keynes, intended to grow to 250,000 by the year 2000. The idea had many attractions but proved alarmingly expensive and was to contribute to the depopulation and blight of the existing inner cities over the next thirty years.

The House of Lords could have offered stubborn resistance to this flood of legislation, but wisely concluded that it would be ill advised to thwart what was clearly the popular will. The Tories would have been pleased radically to rethink the role of the upper house when an all-party conference was convened in 1948 but Labour were resolved to reduce its powers to almost nothing and negotiations soon broke down. The only result was that its power to delay legislation sent to it by the House of Commons was further limited. The government struck another blow for democracy when it abolished the double votes still enjoyed by university graduates and certain businessmen, and introduced voting by post. The universities, in particular, had

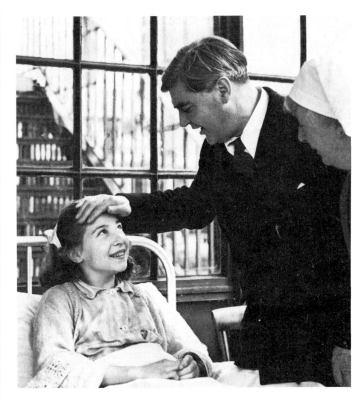

The National Health Service was established in 1948, perhaps the proudest monument of Labour's 1945 government. Here the minister of health and architect of the scheme, Aneurin Bevan, tours the 400-bed Park Hospital at Davyhulme in Lancashire, on the first day of the new regime.

Some Labour ministers deluded themselves that British labour would not resort to strikes if 'their own kind' were in power. More than 2,000 cleaning ladies from Whitehall offices demonstrate that they feel no obligation to remain acquiescent, even in the heartland of the government.

returned a series of distinguished and independent-minded members over the generations – their loss was regretted though few denied that the reform was a proper one.

One of the most significant pieces of legislation was the Trade Disputes Act of 1947. It was the ministers' assumption that organised labour, once 'its own government' was in power, would work with the system rather than against it. The power of the unions was therefore increased and civil servants were allowed to join them. Fortunately for the government the trade union leaders – Arthur Deakin and William Lawther in particular – were deeply conservative and determined to keep their rank-and-file in order. Even so, the number of days lost through strikes was never much less than 1.5 million a year, and though the figures were generally better under Labour than the Tories, the difference was hardly significant. Bosses, it seemed, were still bosses, whether they owed their loyalties to their shareholders or to Whitehall, and whatever the political colour of the ruling party.

Hugh Dalton was determined to use his budgets not only to manage the economy but as an instrument to further social reform. He sought to level the gap between rich and poor and to introduce a more egalitarian society by maintaining very high levels of tax on the higher incomes while exempting many of the lower paid from paying any tax at all, and by imposing fierce death duties that made it difficult to pass on the great estates from generation to generation. He had some

success. By 1948 the standard of living of the average working-class family had risen by 10 per cent since 1938, while that of the salaried earner had dropped by 20 per cent. Cripps' wealth tax, attacking not merely the incomes but the fortunes of the rich, was a still more radical move in the same direction. If Labour had remained another decade in office, a permanent redistribution of the nation's wealth might have been brought about; as it was the wealth tax was a once-only measure and the rich were left in a position from which they would bounce back once a more sympathetic government came to power.

The chancellor was handicapped by the fact that he had inherited a virtually bankrupt exchequer. During the war Britain had gone deeply into debt. Its expenditure abroad was now five times what it had been in 1939, while its exports were less than half. The terms of trade had deteriorated, so that 20 per cent more goods had to be exported to pay for the same amount of imports. In 1946 it seemed likely that Britain would spend £750 million more than she earned. American aid provided the only possible short-term solution, yet with the end of the war aid was cut off. Maynard Keynes visited Washington on behalf of the government and succeeded in negotiating a loan on generous terms and an equally liberal settlement of wartime debts, but this did no more than buy time. It remained to make use of it.

With the help of some ferocious cuts in defence spending it seemed that the national books might still

Shortages of labour, building materials and money meant that the desperately needed programme of school building and renovations was slow in starting. A few show-piece buildings were erected, however, among them Barclay Secondary Modern School at Stevenage in Hertfordshire.

be balanced, but such a happy outcome assumed a certainty of continued peace. The attitude of the Russians soon cast this into doubt and Winston Churchill's speech in Fulton, Missouri, which proclaimed that an Iron Curtain had descended, cutting Europe into two hostile camps, did no more than make public what ministers had already accepted as a fact. Thoughts of disarmament had to be set aside. As if the international scene were not already bleak enough, the winter of 1946-47 was the wettest and coldest of the century. There were fourteen-foot snow drifts in Essex; racing and football were largely suspended; passengers by rail marooned for days on end; the fireman on the 6.23 am from Huddersfield to Bradford was stunned by an icicle. By the beginning of February two million were out of work. When the thaw finally came it brought disastrous floods; an area as big as Kent was covered. By the end of the winter 30,000 cattle and a third of Britain's hill sheep had perished.

In 1947 the economic problems multiplied, and the lot of the average Briton became ever more depressing. Bread rationing, never found necessary in wartime, had been imposed the year before; now the private petrol ration was abolished, the meat ration cut, bacon halved. Even the humble potato was for the first time restricted. Recourse was had to desperate remedies in the search for nutritious food that would not cost dollars. An attempt was made to popularise whale-meat – 'rich and tasty,' said the ministry of food, 'just like a beef-steak', but the consumer knew better. Nor

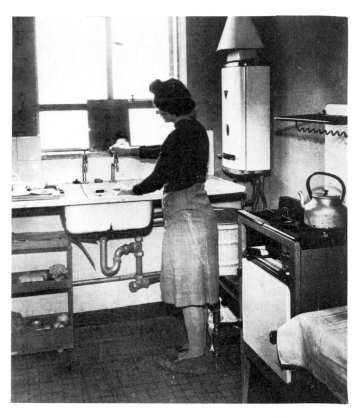

Housing was painfully inadequate for the needs of the nation. A lucky few got flats in the new council blocks. This flat in Chelsea was built in 1948 and was considered luxurious, with three bedrooms, living-room, kitchen and bathroom. The rent was 16/6d (82.5p) a week.

Almost everything was difficult to come by. This queue, outside a shop in Streatham, is for a consignment of carpets and rugs from the Continent. More customers were outside the shop than carpets were inside it two hours before the doors even opened.

The winter of 1916-47 was one of the hardest in living memory and tested an already dispirited Britain to the uttermost. Here a group of pedestrians cautiously pick their way across the frozen furrows of a provincial high street.

The frost and snow gave way to floods in the spring of 1947. At Plympton, in Devon, only the tips of the tombstones showed above the water and there were eighteen inches of water in the church. The Rev. J.C. Mitchell gloomily surveys the scene as a flotsam of hymn books floats around him.

was there conspicuous enthusiasm for snoek, a type of barracuda, which even the minister agreed was tasteless and which was eventually disposed of in bulk to feed the cats.

It was the Americans who came to the rescue again. Marshall Aid, the scheme by which the United States committed its resources to the rebuilding of Europe's economy, was dismissed by some as no more than self-interest on the part of the benefactor. To Warsaw Radio it represented an attempt to impose 'slavery and unemployment' on the Europeans. To most people, however, then and now, it was an act of unparalleled generosity, enlightened self-interest, perhaps, but enlightened beyond the normal wont of governments. The crisis stimulated a move towards European unity; both better to confront the Russian threat and to repair the shattered Continent. The OEEC – Organisation for European Economic Cooperation – was set up in 1948; NATO – the North Atlantic Treaty Organisation – a year later, and the Council of Europe in 1949. Britain was a member of all these bodies but shrank from closer commitments.'It's no good . . . the Durham miners won't wear it,' said Herbert Morrison, when it was suggested Britain might join the Coal and Steel Community, and the supposed inhibitions of the Durham miner, or for that matter the Norfolk farmer or the Scottish fisherman, were to bedevil British foreign policy for the next thirty years.

Marshall Aid provided an admirable crutch, but the patient still had to make a full recovery. If Britain was to continue to live even at its present meagre standard of living, it had to export enough to pay its way. It

Food was in shorter supply in 1947 than ever it had been in wartime. Queues were omnipresent, even for the once despised horse flesh. The fact that the meat was billed as 'passed for human consumption' can hardly have pleased the attendant dogs.

gained a remarkable measure of success. The pre-war volume of exports had been recovered by the end of 1947. Three years later, with the help of a judicious devaluation in 1949 which took the dollar from 4.03 to 2.80 to the pound, they had risen by two-thirds above that level. Motor-cars, tractors, electrical equipment, machine-tools, chemicals were providing the growth on which national prosperity depended. By 1948, 220,000 motor-cars, three-quarters of the country's production, were being sent abroad. In 1950 a surplus of £300 million had been recorded and Britain had recaptured 26 per cent of the world market for manufactured goods. It was all too soon to be seen that the triumph was ephemeral: Germany was only just beginning to re-emerge as an exporter, Japanese competition was still a remote and fanciful chimera. Wages were soaring – from a base of 100 in 1938 to 180 or so by the end of the war and 229 by the beginning of 1950 – yet productivity was only creeping upwards. The Korean War of 1950-53 was to force up the price of raw materials and turn a healthy surplus into a markedly more unhealthy deficit. For the moment, however, the British could legitimately congratulate themselves on having recaptured their position near the top of the world's trading ladder.

Difficult though it is to quantify the profits and losses which the Empire had produced for Britain, the existence of this vast captive market and carefully controlled source of raw materials was undoubtedly a defence against the hazards of international trade. In 1947 the government took a giant step towards dismantling the system when it gave independence to India and

On the occasion of India's independence, celebrations at India House in London included two students singing 'Salutation to the Motherland' in Hindustani, prior to the unfurling of the Indian flag.

Pakistan. The hand-over was marred by the communal massacres that followed partition, but Britain could legitimately take pride in what was hailed as an act of generous statesmanship. It was enhanced by the decision of both countries to remain within the Commonwealth, an example followed by Ceylon the following year, but not by Burma, which chose to go it alone.

By 1948 the non-white element in the Commonwealth's population had risen to 90 per cent. The cosy circle of nations whose people were drawn from common stock, worshipped the same god, accepted the same political and social dogmas, had gone for ever. When India became a republic within the Commonwealth in 1949 another cohesive element vanished. The monarch was now only a symbol of unity, whose value was as yet unproven. In the meantime the economic value of what was left of the old Empire became daily more uncertain. In 1948 Malaya, one of the richest of the remaining colonies, fell prey to civil disorders which were to last for more than ten years and take an army of more than 100,000 to resolve. This was only the first of a series of campaigns that were to mark the twilight of British imperialism.

AND WHILE all this was going on, with many vicissitudes and some painful relapses into austerity, the British people were slowly getting back to normal. Demobilisation was the first hurdle, which was taken too slowly for those who found themselves waiting impatiently with no war to fight and precious few duties to perform, but alarmingly fast for those who had to provide homes and jobs for the returning heroes. No one complained, however, that the process was not conducted with exemplary fairness; first in, first out was the general principle and no amount of string pulling could pervert it. The five million members of the armed forces at the end of the war had sunk to one million by 1947. Conscription however still existed; annually between 150,000 and 170,000 young men were recruited for National Service, the majority serving in Germany or elsewhere overseas.

In a country where hardly a single house had been built for six years, every kind of material was in short supply, and half a million homes had been destroyed or damaged, it was inevitable that many people would have nowhere to live or would have to put up with cramped and uncomfortable quarters. By the time Labour left office over a million houses would have been built, but the programme got off to a slow start and supply never got near to meeting demand. It was the age of the squatter, starting with the innumerable military buildings that were standing idle around the country, and spreading to any empty accommodation. September 1946 saw the 'Great Sunday Squat', when the homeless from all over London moved into a vacant block of flats in Kensington. The fashion spread, and there were unpleasant scenes as the police and local authorities sought to drive the homeless from their illicit lodgings.

The housing shortage was accentuated by the back-

The New Towns Act of 1946 provided for the creation of twenty new urban centres. Of these much the most ambitious was Milton Keynes, intended to have 250,000 inhabitants by the year 2000. This photograph shows the main shopping centre.

Lord and Lady Mountbatten are mobbed on India's first day of independence, 21 August 1947, as they drive in state to the Council House in Delhi, through scenes of jubilation and good will towards Britain.

In 1947 Tesco introduced the first turnstiles to the British shopper; Sainsbury's introduced self-service two or three years later. The shopping revolution was under way.

log of marrying and breeding left by the long wartime
separations. In the three years from 1945-8 there were
11 per cent more marriages and a third more births
than in the corresponding three years before the war.
Returning servicemen could perhaps put up with a
camp-bed in their parents' house, but the situation was
different when wives and babies were involved. The
influx to the cities made matters even worse. Despite
the shortage of petrol and machinery, the desperate
need for food and loss of labour had meant that Britain's farms became progressively more mechanised
throughout the war. Now the process grew even faster.
The army of lumbering and splendid cart-horses that
embellished the countryside began to dwindle at star-
tling speed, the need for manual labour followed suit.
The young countryman returning from the wars cast a
dismayed glance at his family home and headed for the
city where prosperity and bright lights were to be found
– the bright lights might illuminate a slum tenement
but at least there still seemed a better prospect of
improvement in the end.

The cities to which they flocked were only slowly
changing their patterns of existence. Britain was still a
country of corner shops, every urban mass a web of
villages which each supported its post office, its grocer,
its stationer. But signs of evolution were to be seen. In
1947 Tesco introduced the first turnstiles to the British
shopper, Sainsbury's began the transition to self-service
in 1950. The conservative shopper viewed such depar-
tures with doubt and some disdain but the more perceptive small shopkeeper began to wonder how he
would fare if the new giants used the economics of size
to undercut their local rivals.

*The returning servicemen were enthusiastically welcomed home, but
this did not necessarily mean that a job, or still less a house, was
waiting for them.*

*Demobilisation was the first hurdle, a difficult task carried out with efficiency and fairness.
An officer is fitted for his 'demob suit' at the clothing depot in Olympia.*

A Labour government did not put an end to many of the snobberies and absurdities of pre-war Britain. Here in the spring of 1949, a group of debutantes learn how to curtsey at the Josephine Bradley School of Dancing in South Kensington.

The idea of an exhibition on the South Bank of the Thames was conceived even before the war was over and was often nearly abandoned in the next few years as the cost soared and Britain's economic difficulties became more apparent. Those responsible stuck to their guns, however, and the Festival of Britain of 1951 was finally deemed a triumphant success.

Mechanical gadgets became more common, but three years after the war the electric refrigerator was still a comparative rarity. This flat in Paddington, completed in 1948, was considered the last word in luxury, with hot and cold running water, central heating and power points throughout as well as the fitted refrigerator here being proudly displayed.

Travel by air began to be a commonplace, though this view of the main departure lounge at London Airport suggests that traffic was still on a relatively modest scale.

At the end of the war fewer houses enjoyed the use of mechanical gadgets than in 1939, but as production switched from arms to consumer goods the position began rapidly to change. By 1948, 86 per cent of houses had an electric iron, 40 per cent a vacuum cleaner. Yet the potential for growth was enormous. The refrigerator and the washing machine were still unusual, the deep freeze and the dishwasher almost unknown on a domestic scale. Other new technological marvels began to appear. The ballpoint pen first appeared in 1947, a rarity held to possess almost miraculous powers and selling at a hefty £1.14s.10d (£1.74p) or something close to £15 at current prices. Equally miraculous was the first long-playing gramophone record in 1950; half enchanted and half dismayed, the British public saw its collections of heavy and fragile discs transformed into museum pieces.

The desperate shortage of foreign currency meant that tourism was almost impossible. Travel abroad was confined to the official and the businessman, and for both these categories rapid movement was desirable. At the beginning of 1946 London's airport at Heathrow entered service and later that year the first regular air service to New York by other than a seaplane was inaugurated. It was still a luxury, costing the equivalent of almost £800 at current prices for a single ticket, and the journey took eighteen hours with fuelling stops at Shannon and Gander, but notice had been served that the days of the ocean liner were numbered for other than pleasure cruising. The ocean liners appeared undisturbed; the *Queen Elizabeth* and *Queen Mary* were soon back in full service and rarely had a vacant cabin and in 1947 Princess Elizabeth launched a new liner, the *Caronia*, to relieve the pressure on the pre-war veterans.

Thus confined to their native shores, the British amused themselves in much the same ways as they had before the war. Television was still in its infancy and the cinema continued to reign as the most popular source of entertainment. At least 1500 million seats a year were occupied in the 5,000 cinemas. American productions still dominated, but the British film industry was making a bold attempt to capture pre-eminence in its own field. Michael Balcon's Ealing Studios enjoyed a stirring period of success; in 1949 alone they produced *Whisky Galore*, *Kind Hearts and Coronets* and *Passport to Pimlico*, all classics of their kind which were still to be much loved and often shown thirty-five years later. Yet it was *The Third Man*, with its haunting 'Harry Lime Theme' and portrait of a sleazy, battered Europe, which most vividly caught the feeling of the age.

With *Oklahoma* and *Annie Get Your Gun* the American musical revealed to a British public starved for warmth and colour that the theatre was still vigorously alive. Endless queues gathered to watch the performances in London, the music seemed to issue from every radio

It was the age of the cinema, with huge queues forming to watch anything of merit (and much of none). These hopeful crowds are outside the Odeon, Leicester Square.

Derby week: a scene on Epsom Downs showing the extraordinary mixture of race-meeting and carnival which gives this great occasion its special quality.

The King and Queen with Princess Margaret leave the aeroplane after saying goodbye to Princess Elizabeth and the Duke of Edinburgh as the young couple flew off on what should have been a tour of East Africa, Australia and New Zealand. The Princess was never to see her father alive again; when she returned to London it would be as Queen.

Kind Hearts and Coronets *was perhaps the finest of a crop of great comedies from the Ealing studios. Alec Guinness played eight parts and here is involved in six of them simultaneously, with Valerie Hobson (Mrs John Profumo) the only outsider.*

The Third Man, *with its haunting 'Harry Lime Theme' and portrait of a sleazy battered Europe, vividly caught the feeling of the age. Here the director, Carol Reed, works out a scene in the Vienna sewers.*

Sound radio still ruled the air. Daphne Oxenford is the reader in this edition of 'Listen With Mother,' with special effects (a trotting horse, perhaps?) provided by George Dixon.

Stanley Matthews, the 'Wizard of Dribble', at work in the cup final of 1953. Playing at outside right for Blackpool, he coolly steers the ball past Bolton's centre half. Blackpool triumphed to win the cup.

Donald Bradman, greatest of Australian batsmen and the most efficient run-making machine cricket has ever known, leading out the Australian team in the 1946 tour of England. Australia won the Ashes.

Bruce Woodcock was the white hope of British boxing. Matched against the Americans, he was just another of the courageous but second-rate 'horizontal heavyweights'. Here he is taking a count during his fight with the American Joe Baksi in April 1947.

The 'New Look', English-style, from a parade of Simon Massey's collection of suits, coats and dresses. Stafford Cripps deplored the long skirts and extravagantly flowing lines, but nobody paid any attention.

and gramophone in the country. The radio for the most part, however, concentrated on more homespun talent. ITMA survived the war, though it never again enjoyed such complete supremacy, and *Much-Binding-in-the-Marsh*, with Richard Murdoch and Kenneth Horne, was almost equally popular. The parish-pump domesticity of *Mrs Dale's Diary* engaged passionate loyalties, as also, from the beginning of 1951, did the antics of those country folk from Ambridge, the Archers and their fellow villagers, whose idyll was to enjoy apparently eternal popularity.

But the BBC was capable of sterner stuff. The Third Programme was launched in 1946. Nine out of ten British homes possessed a radio and one in a hundred of these was believed to tune in to the Third Programme with some regularity – by no means an inconsiderable audience for the diet of classical music and instructive talks that was regularly fed them. The other 99 per cent of listeners continued to relish *Music While You Work*, *Family Favourites*, Victor Silvester and his Ballroom Orchestra. The family's favourite, if not taken from one of the American musicals, was as likely as not to be 'Open the Door, Richard!' or 'I Wonder Who's Kissing Her Now'; songs of which neither the tune nor the words justified their triumphant popularity.

British football still seemed all-conquering. In 1947 the British team defeated a side drawn from the rest of Europe by six goals to one. In the peak season of 1948-9, forty-one million attended league matches; in 1951 almost 100,000 spectators watched the *amateur* cup final at Wembley. But the more perceptive observers had doubts about the future. The heroes of the English side were players who had made their names before the war: the giant goalkeeper, Frank Swift; Tommy Lawton; the arch-wizard Stanley Matthews. Other countries were getting better, England and the other British sides at the best standing still.

The British at play. Dancing in night-clubs, restaurants or dance-halls was one of the most general of diversions.

The same was still more true of England's cricketers. The Australian team, led by Donald Bradman, won the Ashes in 1946 and four years later it was the turn of the West Indies. Ramadhin and Valentine bemused the British batsmen; the three Ws – Worrell, Walcott and Weekes – completed the debacle. Nor did other sports provide more satisfactory results. British players achieved little at tennis; in the London Olympics of 1948 they had to content themselves with four silver medals on the track; Bruce Woodcock, the new hero of the British boxing scene, was exposed as a courageous second-rater once he ventured off the European stage and took on the American heavyweights. Britain could fairly claim to have invented international sport; now it found it increasingly hard to hold its own with even modest distinction.

It would have been surprising if Britain had taken any lead in the world of fashion but the dissatisfaction of its women with the dull austerity of wartime clothing was vividly demonstrated in 1947 when Dior's spring collection introduced what was hailed enthusiastically as the 'New Look'. Cripps viewed with dismay a fashion that involved extravagantly flowing lines and longer skirts, but his objurgations were ignored. The fashion swept Britain in 1948; Princess Margaret, at seventeen, became the first member of the royal family to succumb; with due allowance for age and income the daring eccentricities of today swiftly became the accepted doctrine of tomorrow.

The people's craving for colour and excitement was to be indulged in 1951 by the Festival of Britain. The idea of an exhibition with attendant funfair on the south bank of the Thames had been conceived as long ago as 1945 and nearly abandoned on economic grounds on several occasions in the next few years. It attracted a crop of enemies along the way: from Lord Beaverbrook, who added it to the British Council and

Princess Margaret was the first member of the royal family to succumb to the lures of the 'New Look'. Here, on 16 September 1948, she shakes hands with an apprentice at the Harland and Wolff shipyard in Glasgow, after launching a new oil-tanker.

The pub remained at the centre of British life and the consumption of beer and spirits rose inexorably year after year. This Lambeth pub offers a nicely graduated social mix; charwomen from Whitehall sit at the table, middle-class and white-collar workers stand around.

Mountbatten in the pantheon of those regularly attacked in the *Express*, to Professor Albert Richardson, who predicted disaster and envisaged thousands of visitors being pushed into the river. In spite of such dire pronouncements and a plethora of go-slows and strikes, the festival opened more or less on time. Its most distinctive features were the great, shell-like dome of discovery and the architecturally daring skylon – an apt symbol for the British economy, George VI was somewhat improbably said to have remarked, since it had no visible means of support. More than 8.5 million people visited it, gaped at work specially commissioned from Epstein, Barbara Hepworth, Moore, Sutherland and Lucien Freud; admired the heraldic beasts in plaited straw and the exhibition of artificial limbs; joined Gracie Fields in community singing on the final night. Everyone enjoyed it and by the time it closed only the most inveterate critics had not been silenced.

The British were not without other forms of dissipation. Of the adult male population 81 per cent smoked, 41.6 per cent of the female. Consumption of beer and spirits rose inexorably year after year. More than eleven million people gambled each week on the football pools. There were seventeen greyhound tracks in Greater London alone. More important, the most fundamental questions of sexual morality were thrown open to debate. The year 1948 saw the publication of Kinsey's *Report on the Sexual Behaviour of the Human Male*; its statistical assumptions were suspect and its conclusions questionable, but it still helped in making such issues as homosexuality or the dangers of masturbation open to consideration in non-specialist books and journals. 'Permissiveness' was not yet in vogue; the dramatic change in conventional attitudes towards extra-marital sex was not to happen until the pill had entered the vocabulary of every teenager and the handbag of most girls of seventeen or over; but the old taboos and shibboleths were up for re-examination.

Other forms of morality too were fraying at the edges. The more restrictions there are, the more people will seek to evade them, and if those restrictions have lost the approval of the people, then they will be defied with virtual impunity. As the 1940s drew to their end, the British people began to feel themselves over-governed. It was the age of the spiv; 'it fell off the back of a lorry' became a catch-phrase which covered a multitude of minor illegalities; the 'dirty pound note' was the accepted currency for every dubious transaction. Young delinquents strode the streets looking for trouble, their distinctive uniform long greased-back hair, belted jackets, large loosely-knotted ties. Tax evasion was practised by many thousands who would in other eras have prided themselves upon their honesty. Currency offences increased from 322 in 1946 to 4,583 in 1948. In 1948 indictable offences for the first time passed half a million, almost double the pre-war figure.

'We are a dreary, self-righteous people with a passion for gin, tobacco, gambling and ballet,' wrote J.B. Priestley in 1949. 'We are a nation of sabbath-keepers who do not go to church. We toil to keep ourselves alive, with

The South Bank at the time of the Festival of Britain in 1951. The great shell-shaped dome of discovery dominates the centre of the picture with the precariously balanced skylon to its right. On the near side of the railway bridge is the Festival Hall and the subsequently demolished shot-tower.

Donald Maclean in the British Embassy at Washington a few years before his defection. He is on the right, sitting on the desk; on the left is Nicko Henderson, Second Secretary in the Embassy and himself a future Ambassador in Washington, then Jock Balfour, the Minister, and Denis Allen, the Head of Chancery.

The General Election of 1950; the Labour vote was more or less maintained but the Tory vote rose substantially. Here Aneurin Bevan and his wife emerge from a polling station.

Attlee did not give up without a fight, but he suspected that the election would be lost and that he would never take office again. Gallantly he attends a Labour party revel at the Hammersmith Palais de Dance and chats to the Wallabies, an acrobatic team.

By 1951 Britain was ready for a change. In October, when Attlee went to the country, the Tories secured a small but manageable majority. At the age of seventy-seven Churchill was again prime minister.

three tea-breaks, a five day week, and Wednesday afternoon off for the match.' Physically and mentally exhausted by the rigours of the war, indifferent to extra earnings which would only be taken away in tax, the British labourer was inclined to agree with Tennyson's lotus-eater that surely, surely, slumber was more sweet than toil. Days lost through strikes were not more numerous than at other periods but the burning will to work which marked the German and the Japanese was conspicuously lacking in their British counterpart.

The Labour government, which had lost some of its first fine careless brio in the cruel winter of 1946-7, was palpably running out of steam. Minor accidents of the kind that a thriving administration would shrug off now seemed more burdensome. The Lynskey tribunal revealed no more than that a junior minister, John Belcher, had unwisely accepted somewhat lavish gifts, but his downfall seemed to tarnish the other ministers by association with a world of corruption and sordid intrigue. Another junior minister, Ivor Thomas, resigned his office, denouncing the iron and steel nationalisation bill as 'dogma run mad'. Burgess and Maclean threw the foreign office into disarray when they defected to the Russians in 1951.

Labour's reaction was to prescribe more of the same medicine; no relaxation of state control or the directed economy; more nationalisation – of cement, sugar, certain minerals. Scenting the national mood the threatened industries fought back. Tate and Lyle in particular waged a highly successful campaign in which 'Mr Cube' argued the case against the nationalisation of the sugar industry. The Tories had recovered their morale after their defeat of 1945. Lord Woolton had reorganised the party and built up a young and enthusiastic body of workers. Butler and Iain Macleod had rethought the Conservative philos-

ophy and developed a programme that would work in the post-war and post-Labour world. The Tories spoke of setting the people free, of liberation from bureaucratic dictatorship. George Orwell, whose *1984* was published in 1949, would have been dismayed to see his anti-Communist diatribe thus distorted, but his polemic served as valuable ammunition against the concept of the all-powerful, centripetal state.

The Labour vote held up remarkably well when the government went to the country in February 1950, but the Tory vote rose substantially. After a phenomenally high poll of 89 per cent, Labour won 13.3 million votes and 315 seats, the Conservative 12.5 million and 298 and the Liberals 2.6 million and nine seats. Labour was left with a miniscule overall majority, a disappointing conclusion to what they regarded as the greatest programme of reform that the country had ever known.

It was not their last disappointment. In June 1950 the Korean War broke out and British soldiers became engaged with the forces of fifteen other nations against the Chinese and the North Koreans. The consequences played havoc with the government's plans. National Service was increased to two years, expensive rearmament embarked on, the economic position of the country severely damaged by the rise in the cost of imports. Attlee gained a little credit as an international statesman by his flight to Washington to protest about MacArthur's extravagant bellicosity; but the economic problems caused by the war far outweighed this good.

The government was conspicuously in disarray. Attlee was nearly seventy and a tired man. Cripps and Bevin were sick, with months rather than years of service ahead of them. The young Turks, Bevan and Gaitskell, were at each other's throats. In an effort to curb the pressures set off by the Korean War, Gaitskell introduced a deflationary budget, including *inter alia*,

Britain staged a remarkable economic recovery. By the end of 1947 the pre-war volume of exports had been regained. By 1948, 220,000 motor cars were being sent abroad. Here an Austin is shipped to Singapore from the King George V Dock, London.

charges for false teeth and spectacles procured under the National Health scheme. Bevan resigned, taking with him his henchmen John Freeman and Harold Wilson. Even the remaining ministers seemed to feel that it was time to go.

In fact austerity was easing. Potatoes had come off the ration in 1948, with jam and bread. Milk followed in 1950. The 5s.0d. (25p) limit on restaurant meals had been abandoned. Bananas and oranges, though still not readily available, were no longer rarities. But the pace was not fast enough to satisfy the public. The blame was placed partly on what was felt to be the government's wilful Calvinism, partly on the stifling inefficiency of bureaucracy. The ministry of food alone employed 50,000 civil servants and the annual cost of food subsidies had risen to nearly £500 million a year. Forms had to be completed in tedious detail before any operation could be undertaken. To substitute twenty yards of fence for a hedge at a dangerous corner involved filling in five large forms and providing nine maps, several of them coloured. Examples of such bureaucratic extravagance were easy to find and easier still to ridicule. Prime target for derision was the groundnut scheme, a perfectly rational and constructive plan for growing this estimable plant on 2.5 million acres in Africa, which deserved to succeed but reckoned without drought, baboons, poor soil and the determined lack of enthusiasm of the local peasants.

In October 1951 Attlee tired of leading a government with so narrow a majority and went again to the country. Even with so much going against it, Labour secured a slightly larger share of the popular vote, but they still lost twenty seats to the Tories, who won 321 seats to Labour's 295. With the Liberals holding a mere six seats, that left the Tories with a small but manageable majority. At the age of seventy-seven Winston Churchill was once more prime minister.

The country over which he presided was radically different to that which he had known before the war. Though far from being a full-blooded socialist, still less Marxist state, the composition of Britain's economy had shifted dramatically against private enterprise. Government now intervened in a whole range of situations where previously the citizen had been left to fend for himself. The fact that the Labour government had acted largely in response to the wishes of the British people is shown by the readiness of the Conservatives to accept what had been done. There was to be no rush to denationalise, no dismantling of the welfare state. The monuments set up by Attlee's government were accepted as a permanent part of the social landscape, minor adjustments were in order but wholesale demolition was ruled out. For better or worse the Labour government had laid down the framework of British development in the second half of the twentieth century. For this if for nothing else it deserves remembering as one of the most influential administrations of British history.

KING GEORGE VI was a sorely sick man by the time Churchill once again kissed hands as Britain's prime minister. As early as 1948 tests had revealed that the King was suffering from arteriosclerosis. In 1951 cancer was diagnosed and in September his left lung was removed. No one doubted that he had only a short time to live; equally no one suspected how close the end was, when Princess Elizabeth and the Duke of Edinburgh left at the end of January 1952 for a tour that was to take them to East Africa, Australia and New Zealand.

The Princess and her husband were at Treetops

With the King's increasing ill-health the burden on Princess Elizabeth grew from year to year.
In January 1950 she visited the site of the future Crawley New Town. She is here seen talking
to Mr Silkin, the minister for town and country planning.

Hotel in Kenya on 5 February, enjoying a day or two watching the wild animals before the hard work of the tour began. At midnight the same day the watchman at Sandringham heard the King open his window before going to sleep. He was dead by the next morning. His people had never appreciated him so much as when he was no longer there. They suffered the kind of personal shock which normally only accompanies the death of someone very close. 'Oh, I think it's dreadful,' said a woman working in a department store. 'I'm terribly sorry. I feel as shocked as if it was someone belonging to me.' Such reactions were multiplied a million-fold. George VI, by his unobtrusive courage, decency, kindness, total commitment to his country's needs, had not only won popular confidence but had become a loved part of the family. As so often in a family, only death showed how real that love was.

'*Le roi est mort, vive le roi!*' Elizabeth went up to her tree-top observation post as a princess, she came down as Queen of Great Britain; of Canada, Australia, New Zealand and other countries around the world; Head of the Commonwealth, Defender of the Faith. To some eyes it meant very little; to many others it was all-important. For Queen Elizabeth herself, her honours were accompanied by a sharp sense of loss for her beloved father, by disappointment that she had been deprived of a few more years of relative obscurity with her husband and young children, by doubts about her readiness for her new role. In this she was not alone. 'I really did love him,' said Churchill of King George VI. 'His advice was so good and I could always count on his support in times of difficulty. I hardly know Princess Elizabeth; and she is only a child.' It was not to be long before the prime minister was convinced that 'childish' was no word to describe his new monarch.

There was time for a few days watching game in Kenya. Here she is admiring the view from the primitive bridge that spans the river running through the grounds of Sagana Lodge – the wedding present from Kenya to the royal couple.

The strain of the solemn and lengthy Coronation ceremony behind her, the happy young Queen returns to the Palace.

Chapter Five

The Road to Suez

WHEN HER private secretary asked her by what name she wished to be called on the documents relating to the accession (a reasonable question, since British monarchs – her father among them – not infrequently changed their name on coming to the throne), the new Queen replied 'My own name, of course – what else?' It was the kind of clear and common-sense response which ministers as well as courtiers were to become accustomed to over the next decades. It was also, as will soon be seen, to give rise to much romantic and far from common-sensical extravagance about the new 'Elizabethan Age' which was supposed to be dawning.

Calm, collected, yet strikingly alone, the Queen descended from the royal aircraft at London Airport to be greeted by her prime minister; the leader of the opposition, Clement Attlee; Anthony Eden; the Mountbattens; the Duke of Gloucester. Queen Mary hurried to greet her on her return: 'Her old granny and subject must be the first to kiss Her hand.' The following day, 8 February 1952, the accession council of Queen Elizabeth II took place in St James's Palace. Faced by the cohort of her privy councillors, she appeared, said Vincent Massey, 'a slight figure dressed in deep mourning,' who went through the laborious rituals of the occasion 'with strong but perfectly controlled emotion'. Then it was to Sandringham, to join her mother beside the coffin of the King.

King George VI's body lay in state in Westminster Hall. London was still a grey and battered city, most of its wartime scars unhealed, its streets ill-lit beneath the icy sleet, spring still a distant mirage. Undeterred, nearly 350,000 people queued an average four hours to

Calm, collected, yet strikingly alone, Queen Elizabeth II descends from the royal aircraft at London Airport. The Duke of Edinburgh has lingered a little so that the new monarch is clearly the first to set foot on her country's soil. Attlee and Churchill wait to greet her, with Anthony Eden standing a little behind.

file past the catafalque. The country mourned its dead monarch with genuine sorrow as well as all traditional pomp. The death of the King ushered in a period in which the monarchy was never far from the forefront of people's minds.

Without ever being forgotten, the royal family for most of the time plays a comparatively minor role in national life. It takes mourning or celebration, a birth or a death, a marriage, jubilee or coronation, to catch the largest headlines. This does not mean that it ever ceases to provide excellent copy for the gossip columnist and professional royalty watcher. A feature about the royal family usually adds 25-30,000 to the circulation of any magazine. Even the Duchess of Windsor's memoirs won 300,000 readers for the *Sunday Express*. Nor does it suggest that its popularity is ever less than immense. A series of opinion polls held between 1953 and 1984 has shown that almost 90 per cent of the population consistently support the continuance of the monarchy. The figure has occasionally risen a little just before some royal festival or fallen after the announcement of a royal pay-rise, but broadly it has proved constant. Within the Labour party, where republicanism might reasonably be expected to represent a serious force, an anti-monarchist resolution was rejected by ten

votes to one in 1923 and the issue has not been considered worthy of subsequent debate. The reward of Mr William Hamilton for his many years of sniping at the royal family has been to see his considerable talents ignored and to be excluded from any office.

In early 1952, however, the monarchy was comparatively unobtrusive. For the next two or three years it was to be relentlessly publicised, almost worshipped. It was the accession of a young and attractive woman, and the spectacular glories of her coronation, which fanned the flames. There can be no doubt that the reverence in which the royal family is held stems not only from a belief that it is useful and picturesque, but also from a conviction that it meets some deeper, almost atavistic need. Great Britain – sophisticated, cynical, technologically oriented – feels itself in some way incomplete without this relic of medievalism, indeed of pre-history. The monarchy provides a focal point for tribal loyalties, an element of mystery, a faint flavour of the supernatural. Of all the royal occasions, none more comprehensively unites the disparate elements of the contemporary monarchy – soap opera, show-business razzmatazz, glamour, dignity, mystery, archaic ritual – than a coronation. The coronation of Queen Elizabeth was to set new standards for the

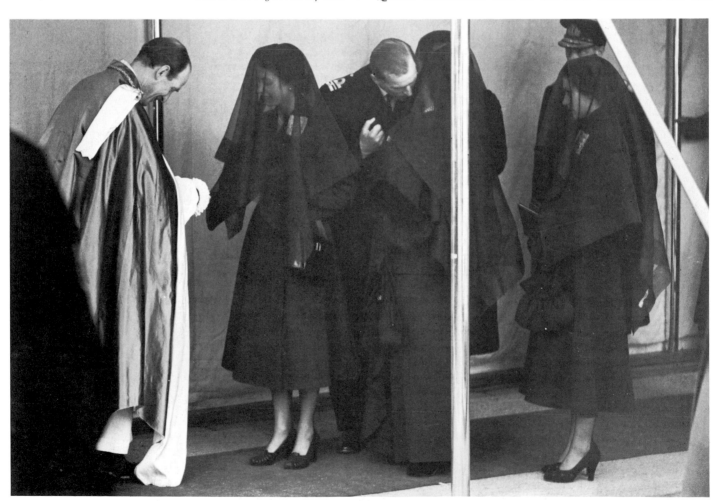

The Queen shakes hands with the Dean of Windsor after her father's funeral service in St George's Chapel. The Duke of Edinburgh embraces the Queen Mother; Princess Margaret and the Duke of Windsor stand to one side.

One of the Queen's earlier engagements, on 10 April 1952, was the traditional distribution of Maundy money at Westminster Abbey.

The Queen at the dinner party for the Commonwealth prime ministers in Buckingham Palace in December 1952. Three years before there would only have been five prime ministers at the dinner – over the next decades the number would grow dramatically.

Commercial exploitation was rife and a gamut of official souvenirs was approved by the Coronation Souvenirs Committee of the Council of Industrial Design. One of these select objects was this Chinese-style paper lantern bearing a portrait of the Queen. It is interesting to speculate what the rejected items can have looked like!

A few days before the Coronation it seemed that Britain was drowning under a monstrous flowering of flags and bunting. Decorations varied from the domestic to the most grandly civic: fifty-year-old Mrs Ellen Sutton (opposite, bottom) ornaments her four-roomed council flat while Fleet Street (above) rejoices in proudly triumphal arches.

A group of peers shuffle around while waiting to take their seats in the Abbey.

splendour of its spectacle and the total involvement of the people.

The occasion was almost marred at the outset. Queen Mary died on 24 March, 1953, just over two months before the date scheduled for the coronation. Some people expected that the ceremony would be postponed or at least curtailed, but the old Queen had performed her last service to the monarchy when she insisted that her death should not be allowed to affect the arrangements. The preparations continued unabated.

To anyone who remembered the coronation of King George VI, the unrolling of events in the months before the ceremony would have come as no surprise. Initially there were many who took or affected little interest in what they dismissed as irrelevant, out-of-date, and very much an affair for Londoners. In February 1953 less than half the population expected to vary its routine to take account of the festivities. By April the figure was 69 per cent. Two weeks before the coronation it was difficult to be in Britain, impossible to be in London, without being constantly assailed by evidence of what was going on. Every street, every village, was rehears-

A forest of periscopes rises above the crowd in Trafalgar Square. Comparing this crowd scene with those of twenty years earlier it is interesting to note how far the hat and cap have lost their sway (though some, of course, may have been removed in sympathy with those behind whose view was being blocked).

ing its plans for its own particular celebration. The focus of national interest was Buckingham Palace and Westminster Abbey, but a multitude of minor carvivals blossomed around the country.

The emphasis on the new 'Elizabethan Age' became even more strident. Links with the antique past were stressed. The last vestige of the holy oil with which the monarch was anointed had been destroyed during the war but Savory and Moore concocted a no doubt authentic substitute. The *Daily Express* created a tableau featuring the ballet dancer, Margot Fonteyn, in a farthingale; the inventor of the jet engine, Frank Whittle, in doublet and hose; and other worthies in appropriately Tudor costume. An arts and crafts exhibition at Sutton town hall typically featured not only a tea cosy emblazoned with the royal arms but a model of Henry VIII's palace of Nonesuch made out of matchboxes. National regeneration was the theme – under its new Queen Britain was to recapture the explosive vigour and zeal that had marked its predecessor some 400 years before.

Few tricks were missed in efforts to exploit the commercial potential of the coronation to the full.

Tickets for seats in the stands changed hands on the black market for £40-£50 while a balcony in a choice site overlooking the route cost as much as £3,500. A deluge of souvenir pots, mugs, plates, medallions and similar bric-à-brac flooded the market. Union Jacks and bunting were produced in gigantic quantities. The popular musicians followed the trend. Particularly favoured was 'In a Golden Coach', with so-called lyric by Noel Gay and sung unctuously by Donald Peers:

> *In a golden coach*
> *There's a heart of gold*
> *That belongs to you and me*
> *And one day in June*
> *When the flowers are in bloom*
> *That day will make history.*

Television was the great novelty of the occasion. A spectacular boom in sales and rentals preceded the event, those who had no set arranged to pass the day with more fortunate neighbours. Nearly half the population saw the procession and ceremony, watching on 2.7 million television sets. That they were able to see the religious service was thanks to the Queen: the

The Bishops pay homage to the crowned Queen.

The proclamation of Elizabeth II as Queen in the City of London.

For months before the Coronation the energies of the nation seemed increasingly to be absorbed by preparations for the occasion. Here workers at Fladbury Mill add to the many thousands of miles of flags and bunting which adorned the streets of Britain.

technicians insisted that the heat and light would be overpowering; the cabinet strongly advised that the cameras should be excluded; the Queen ruled that her people had a right to participate.

Outside, the route was packed. Some two million people secured a view, even if only through home-made periscopes. At least 30,000 camped in the Mall the night before, furnished with radios, thermoses, blankets and very necessary waterproofs. The news that Edmund Hillary and Sherpa Tenzing had become the first men to set foot on the summit of Everest cheered their damp and chilly vigil. The service was broadcast to the crowds outside the Abbey. It should have been an ecumenical occasion – five Roman Catholic bishops were invited to attend, but the offer was politely declined. They could have found nothing to complain of in the admirably well-intentioned prayer:

The Lord give you faithful Parliaments and quiet realms; sure defence against all enemies; fruitful lands and upright Magistrates; leaders of integrity in learning and labour; a devout, learned and useful clergy; honest, peaceable and dutiful citizens.

All over the country the honest, peaceable and dutiful citizenry detached itself from its television sets and settled down to celebrate. At Ripon forty characters dressed in Pickwickian style lunched at the Unicorn Hotel; there was morris dancing at Watton Hall Park in Liverpool and submarines open to the public at Birkenhead. The pageant master at St Albans combed

Street parties were held all around the country, either on Coronation Day itself or within a few days of it. This group of children clearly feel that the real thing has very little more to offer than their own celebration.

England for a chariot fit to carry Boadicea: 'It must be historically correct. If we can't find one we shall have to use a milk-float.' Everywhere there were bonfires, games for the children, dancing for the adults, singing, feasting.

'The Country and Commonwealth last Tuesday,' proclaimed no less an authority than the Archbishop of Canterbury, 'were not far from the Kingdom of Heaven.' The words were extravagant but there were more than enough witnesses to the mood of national exaltation to show that something extraordinary had happened. There were those who argued that the splendours of the coronation damaged the nation by lulling it with romantic daydreams and visions of a greatness that was no longer there. Certainly the politicians were not conspicuously more faithful nor the clergy more useful after the ceremony than before. Yet an immense fillip was given to the country's morale, a sense of community and goodwill generated, something of value must have been left behind.

Only a fortnight after the coronation the country came abruptly down to earth when the story broke in the *People* that Princess Margaret wished to marry her mother's comptroller, Group-Captain Townsend, handsome, gallant, well-liked by all, yet divorced and with his former wife still alive. Townsend was hurriedly shipped abroad and the story rumbled quietly for two years till it erupted again in the autumn of 1955. The establishment ranged itself against the people. Newspaper polls showed a large majority in favour of letting the young couple marry, yet Lord Salisbury dragooned the cabinet into opposition; *The Times* boomed grandiloquently about the duties of royal blood and the ill effects any dereliction would have upon the Commonwealth. In the end Princess Margaret resolved the question by announcing that she had decided against the marriage. With some regret the national press abandoned a story that had filled its pages so satisfactorily for so long.

The Queen would have attached much importance to views expressed by the leaders of the Commonwealth on this or any other issue. Her role as Head of the Commonwealth was not one she took lightly. At the end of 1953 she embarked on what was to be the first of many grand tours of her dominions – to Canada, Jamaica, Fiji, New Zealand, Australia, Ceylon, Malta and Gibraltar. The statistics were awe-inspiring: 43,618 miles travelled, 276 speeches listened to, 102 delivered, 508 renditions of the national anthem, 6,770 curtseys received, 13,213 hands shaken. In Malta, after almost six months, she was reunited with her children, and so at last it was home again to a Britain that seemed notably more cheerful and less dowdy than the country she had left behind her.

SOME WOULD say in spite of, some thanks to the new Conservative administration, Britain in 1953 was at last a conspicuously more prosperous and hopeful country. What was remarkable was how much of the economic and social structure of pre-war Britain had survived the recent revolution. Much had changed. In spite of the continuing austerity, the poor were better fed, better clothed, better cared for medically and better housed than in 1939. Yet more remained. There were 178,000 domestic servants employed in 1951 as opposed to 707,000 in 1931, yet it was still possible for Lord Derby's deranged footman to shoot the butler and the under-butler and leave his employer with enough staff to serve dinner. When the Duke of Westminster died in 1953 his estate was valued at well over £20 million; the following year it was calculated that the richest one per cent of the population owned 43 per cent of the private wealth of the kingdom, the richest 10 per cent almost 80 per cent. The public schools announced their imminent bankruptcy but continued to survive. An egalitarian society was still far away, and neither Conservatives nor Socialists seemed likely to attain it. In September 1952 Christopher Hollis remarked that the two parties were in all essentials the same: they were 'like two old sieves, arguing which of them has the most holes.' Dick Bentley made the same point in the popular radio programme *Take It From Here*. 'Have you seen Jimmy Edwards's new suit?' he asked. 'It's a conservative suit – the same as a socialist cut, only they're more polite about it.'

If the Socialists had failed to socialise Britain, the Conservatives proved equally restrained when it came to unscrambling what *had* been achieved. In principle denationalisation was part of the Tory programme, but when it came to practice, all the government did was to restore road haulage to private ownership and make a slow start on iron and steel. The mines were left under the Coal Board and the public amenities left untouched, the National Health Service was accepted by everyone as an essential part of the country's life.

Churchill, indeed, seemed resolved to present a resolutely non-partisan approach when he selected the members of his government. Field Marshal Alexander as minister of defence, General Ismay as commonwealth secretary, Walter Monckton as minister of labour, were all appointments from outside the party. The 'overlord' system, by which ministers without precise departmental duties were put in loose charge of a group of departments, also introduced, until it perished in 1953, men who though conservative in tendency, were not strictly party politicians. Churchill made another innovation too; in 1953 Florence Horsbrugh became the first woman to serve in a Conservative cabinet.

It was, however, 'to set the people free' that Churchill had been elected, and to this his government addressed themselves with a will. At last the system of rationing was laid to rest. Tea came off the ration in 1952, sweets and sugar in 1953, and the following year the process was completed with butter, cheese, margarine, cooking fats and meat. The ministry of food prophesied the most dire consequences, with crowds storming the food shops to secure their share while

Gordon Richards was a royal jockey but he was sadly not mounted on a royal horse when he rode Pinza to victory in the Derby in Coronation year four lengths ahead of the Queen's Aureole. No one would think this was the case from the cheerfulness with which the Queen and the Duke congratulate him.

The golden State Coach, drawn by eight greys and originally built for King George III, stands outside Westminster Abbey as the Queen emerges. The brilliant colours of the coach and its attendants contrast vividly with the damp and gloomy weather.

At the end of 1953 the Queen embarked on the first and one of the longest of what were to be many tours of the Commonwealth countries. Here she is at the final stage at Brisbane in Australia, leaving a civic reception at the Exhibition Grounds.

The romantic saga of Princess Margaret and Peter Townsend caused much distress to the main protagonists and endless entertainment to the prurient press and public. When the story finally ended in 1955 the newspapers felt that they had been deprived of part of their birthright.

After almost six months of continuous travel, the Queen and the Duke are reunited with their children aboard the Royal Yacht at Tobruk in Libya and from there went on to Malta.

supplies held out. In fact the opposite occurred; stocks proved ample and in several categories, once the glamour of shortage had been removed, consumption actually declined. The ministry of food soon followed its system of controls and was absorbed into another ministry.

With it perished a host of other restrictions. The Tories were apt to claim exclusive credit for a process that had been begun under the previous government, but they did do stalwart work in hacking down the jungle of controls that had grown up during the war. 'In the past three years,' boasted Butler in 1954, 'we have burned our identity cards, torn up our ration books, halved the number of snoopers, decimated the number of forms and said good riddance to nearly two thirds of the remaining wartime regulations.'

Partly cause, partly effect of the new liberalisation was the increasing prosperity of the nation. There was far more money around. If the average wage in 1938 be taken as 100, it had risen to 176 by 1943, 229 by 1949 and 323 in 1954. Yet while wages had more than trebled, prices had little more than doubled. The disastrous impact of the Korean War had begun to wear off by 1952, and the terms of trade turned dramatically to Britain's benefit. Taxes remained high but they were at last being reduced and further reductions could soon be expected. The shops were full, new cars were coming on the market, and there was money with which to buy them.

The comfortable showing of the balance of payments cloaked a disastrous drop in competitivity. The people paid themselves more but did not produce more to justify the increase. Between 1950 and 1954 British exports rose by six per cent, in the same period exports from the countries of the EEC rose by 76 per cent. In a period of world-wide growth, with the terms of trade favourable and competition from such countries as Japan still a remote threat, it could still seem to the short-sighted that all was well. It would not be long before recession, a rise in the price of raw materials, fiercer competition, made the true position painfully clear. Nor did the attitude of the unions suggest that things were liable to change radically for the better. Suspicious of the intentions of the new government, the working man was determined not merely to retain all he had won but to wrest more advantages from his employer. 1953 and 1954 in particular were years of industrial unrest; the railways took the lead in demanding wage increases beyond those which arbitration had awarded, the dockers, miners, electricians, engineers were hard on their heels. Walter Monckton had been appointed to the cabinet to keep the unions sweet, and interpreted his mandate as calling for concession upon concession. The conservative leadership of the union movement made his task easier, but the death of Arthur Deakin in 1955 spelt the end of right-wing dominance. The accession of Frank Cousins in the Transport and General Workers Union pointed to the future.

Another way in which the new government notably did not attempt to reverse the policy of its predecessor

The gap between rich and poor was still vast and in the 1950s conspicuous expenditure became once more possible if not socially acceptable. Here Sir Bernard and Lady Docker inspect their new Daimler. A feature of the special Hooper coachwork was a mirror in the roof – no doubt of use for adjusting tiaras.

In spite of the changes in society there were still 178,000 domestic servants employed in 1951. Here the approved indoor uniform of members of the newly formed National Institute of Houseworkers is shown to the world. The Institute's function was to raise the prestige of domestic labour and attract more workers to the field.

The Coronation of Queen Elizabeth II. The procession on its way back from the Abbey winds its way under Admiralty Arch on the home stretch up the Mall to Buckingham Palace. Some two million people lined the route, many dependent on home-made periscopes for any view of the proceedings. Half the population is believed to have watched on television.

The Queen attends a garden party at Buckingham Palace in 1953. For once the weather seems to have been kind – too often such occasions were marred by rain, to the great detriment of the women's hats and the (frequently hired) tail coats.

Florence Horsbrugh, appointed minister of education in Churchill's new administration and the first woman to serve in a Conservative cabinet.

was over the colonies. Even if it had wanted to, the Tory administration could never have re-established the Indian empire; instead it continued resolutely down the path that led to further grants of independence. The path was not a smooth one – the horrors of the Mau Mau revolt in Kenya and the protracted civil war against the Communists in Malaya were expensive both in lives and money – but by 1954 a multi-racial government had been installed in Kenya and elections the following year in Malaya prepared the way for self-government. With a federation established in Rhodesia in 1953 it seemed not too much to hope that a stable, multi-racial society should soon be capable of running affairs in that part of Africa as well.

In the summer of 1955 Churchill suffered a severe stroke. Most people felt his retirement was already overdue, but the recent death of George VI and the long illness of the heir-apparent, Anthony Eden, encouraged him to remain in office. R.A. Butler loyally held the fort while his seniors convalesced, but Churchill's recovery was far from complete. An infirm old man before, he was now close to senility. In April 1955 he retired, his final flourish a dinner for the Queen at No.10 Downing Street. Monarch and prime minister had grown close to each other in the years since the

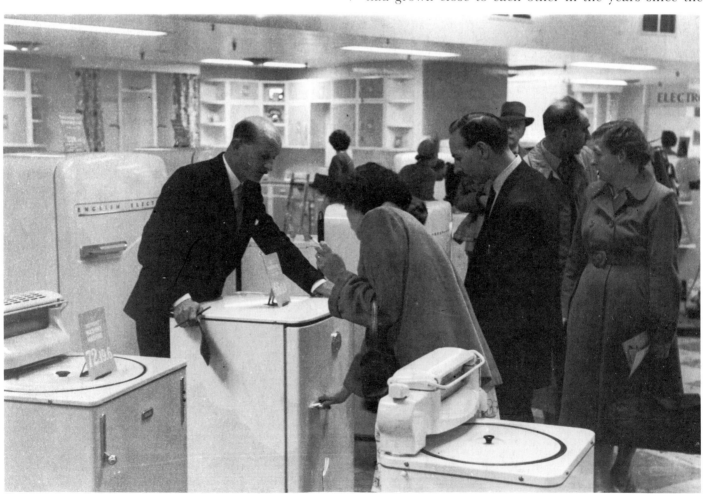

By September 1955 the economic journalists were talking about a new wave of prosperity, with television sets, refrigerators and washing-machines coming within the reach of many workers. This scene in the household department of Selfridges in Oxford Street shows the new range of possibilities.

The shops were once more filled with luxuries. A London hosiery firm tried to boost its sales of high quality silk stockings by organising a competition to find the world's perfect legs. The winner was Barbara Picnett of Australia.

Increasing prosperity did not disarm the suspicions of the average industrial worker who was intent on wresting more advantages from his employer while the going was good. Here, at the end of 1953, engineering workers march through the streets of Birmingham as part of a nationwide twenty-four hour stoppage.

The Queen and the Duke of Edinburgh at Balmoral with Prince Charles and Princess Anne.
The photograph was taken in 1954 when the future Prince of Wales was almost six.

Calder Hall in Cumberland, the world's first full-scale nuclear power station, is opened by the Queen in October 1956. At the time it seemed to open up a great future, both for Britain's energy needs and for the export market.

accession. With which prime minister had she most enjoyed her audiences, she was once asked. 'Winston, of course, because it was always such fun,' she replied. But she knew well that it was more than time for him to go.

In theory her prerogative was to select Churchill's successor, but there was never any doubt that Eden must be the man. He resolved to go quickly to the country. By the time he did so Conservative fortunes were running high. In a budget that turned out to be disastrously inflationary but was none the less popular at the time, Butler had cut taxes dramatically, taking 6d (2½p) off income tax. Macmillan had achieved equally popular results with his housing programme. His target had been 300,000 a year; in 1954 the figure was 347,000, 40 per cent of them from private builders – more than double the proportion under Labour. The Labour party for its part was as usual disunited, split this time over German rearmament. For the first time since the nineteenth century a government in power increased its majority. The Tories won practically half the popular vote, giving them 344 seats to Labour's 277. With 2.7 per cent, the Liberals secured only six seats. The Communists received 33,000 votes – a figure that seemed pitiful enough but was to shrink even further in future years.

A few months later Clement Attlee followed Churchill into retirement. His disappearance heralded a bitter struggle between the right and the left of the Labour party, headed by Gaitskell and Bevan respectively. Gaitskell won, by a sufficiently impressive 157 votes to Bevan's 70. With Churchill and Attlee, Bevin and Cripps all departed, only Eden remained of the senior ministers who had fought and won the war. The country no longer existed in the shadow of conflict: post-war Britain had a new identity.

MOST EVIDENT of the changes, and most notable in its effect on the nation's behaviour, was the triumph of television. The pace, at first, had been slow. The service had reopened in 1946, and the royal wedding in 1947 and Olympic games in 1948 won some attention, but television was still an expensive toy, with only a few hours a day of transmission and no choice of what to view. In early 1947 there were less than 14,000 licence holders; even in 1949 two out of every three Britons had never seen a television set. Then came explosion. Fourteen thousand licences became three quarters of a million by 1951. The coronation provided an immense further stimulus. Licences for sound radio still outnumbered television by five to one in 1953 but in 1954 (the year in which *The Archers* reached their thousandth performance), the proportion fell to three to one, and the following year to two to one.

Most fashions start at the top and filter down, yet television was initially resisted by those who felt themselves to be of the intellectual and social elite. Little by little every bastion fell. Those who feared the effects that the mindless frivolity of much of the broadcasting might have on children were forced to admit that, when

For the first time since the nineteenth century a government in power increased its majority.
This huge crowd collected around the statue of Eros in Piccadilly Circus early in the morning
of 17 May 1955 soon learned that the Tories had won nearly half the popular vote, giving them
344 seats to Labour's 277.

In April 1955 Winston Churchill retired as prime minister. His final flourish was a dinner at 10 Downing Street for the Queen. When asked on one occasion with which prime minister she had most enjoyed her audiences, the Queen replied: 'Winston, of course, because it was always such fun.'

properly used, the educational value was immense; the serious minded who scoffed at quiz shows and soap operas found that the news and documentary programmes could be of the highest standard; the last barriers were to crumble when the serialisation of *The Forsyte Saga* in 1967 transformed British habits, so that to telephone a friend between 8.30 and 9.30 pm on a Saturday evening became a solecism if not grounds for a quarrel.

Those who feared that television would vulgarise the nation were reinforced in their apprehension when Independent Television, with paid advertisements providing the revenue, was introduced in 1954. The appointment of Kenneth Clark to chair the Independent Television Authority lent some respectability to the enterprise, but the mandarins of the BBC still viewed their upstart rival with some contempt. The contempt was not dismissed when, by the end of the first year, seven people were watching ITV for every four loyal to the BBC, but there was none the less soul-searching for that. Was it the function of the BBC to uplift and educate or to entertain; and if the former, what was to be done when the British public perversely chose to be entertained instead? In fact a compromise was reached: the BBC paid rather greater heed to its popular following than really suited it; ITV was kept up to its cultural mark by Kenneth Clark and his

Anthony Eden, Churchill's successor, called a general election shortly after he became prime minister. Here he addresses a meeting outside Uxbridge underground station.

colleagues; and it was generally accepted that the competition had been good for everyone.

One of the first victims of television was the traditional pictorial magazine. Why buy *Picture Post* for news photographs when one could see them more quickly and in motion on the screen? Circulation began to fall sharply, in line with cinema attendance. The daily newspapers, however, appeared unscathed. In 1955, 611 newspapers were sold each day to every thousand Britons as opposed to an equivalent 353 newspapers in the United States. The *Daily Mirror* still enjoyed the largest circulation of any daily paper at 4.725 million, with the *Daily Express* a highly respectable second at just over four million. The *News of the World*, with its potent brew of mutilated corpses, adulterous stockbrokers and the occasional delinquent vicar, put them all to shame with its sale of eight million copies every Sunday.

The dance-halls were soon to suffer like the cinemas from the greater convenience of finding one's entertainment at home, but for the moment they still throve. More than 200 million clients a year sampled their attractions, most of them practising the traditional arts of the foxtrot or the waltz, others the still more traditional country-dancing, and a few the rhythms from South America that enjoyed something of a vogue – the rumba, the samba and, in the right circumstances, the

The age of television dawned. In early 1947 there had been less than 14,000 licence holders but the Coronation proved an immense stimulus and by 1954 the new medium was well on the way to displacing sound radio. The social habits of the British people were about to be dramatically amended.

The cinema was the first form of public entertainment to suffer from the competition of television but the dance-halls too soon began to record dwindling attendances. In January 1954, however, the Wimbledon Palais de Dance was still in vogue. Note the 'poodle' hairstyle which was in fashion at the time.

ebullient conga. Popular songs were also little different from those of earlier years – 'Doggie in the Window' was the outstanding success of the age.

The theatre was more innovative. In 1956 the harsh, protesting shout of the young John Osborne in *Look Back in Anger* blasted a new realism into a London theatre whose conventional values had already been shaken the year before by the bleak uncertainties of Beckett's *Waiting for Godot*. In the eyes of a professional iconoclast like Kenneth Tynan the commercial theatre could never recover from these hammer blows; the commercial theatre was unaware of its demise and continued to thrive with inordinately successful musicals like *The Boy Friend* and *Salad Days*. In 1952 Agatha Christie's *The Mousetrap* began a run that, well over a generation later, seems to be set for eternity.

With *Lucky Jim* Kingsley Amis, though with broader comedy and less embittered spleen, did for literature what Osborne had done for the stage. In *Lord of the Flies* William Golding demonstrated alarming perception of the vagaries of the nature of boy and, perhaps, man. Both these were widely read as well as esteemed, yet it was the cosily social novels of Angela Thirkell, the detective stories of Agatha Christie or the modish fantasies of Ian Fleming that helped to swell library lendings to 360 million books a year by 1956. The spectacular growth of the public library system in the decade after the war, entailing as it eventually did the destruction of almost all the old commercial lending libraries, was one of the two most conspicuous developments in the world of books; the other, the growth of the paperback, also did much to spread the reading habit in the golden age for authors and publishers before television began here too to make its powerful attractions felt.

The new freedoms introduced by the Tories opened up the possibility of travel abroad to many who had never thought of it before. Foreign currency became readily available, the first cheap air flights were introduced in 1952. It was still a long way to the concrete jungles and steak and chips of Torremolinos or the Costa Brava, but the march to the sun had begun. Perhaps because, having tasted foreign cooking, the British decided their national cuisine was lacking, perhaps because the middle classes were now doing it for themselves, perhaps because the housewife had learnt to make the best of the meagre and unpalatable wartime rations, the standards of cooking notably improved. First at home, then in the restaurants, there was greater variety in the dishes served and more thought given to their preparation. The first *Good Food Guide* appeared in 1951 and Elizabeth David's invaluable contributions to British eating came regularly in the early 1950s. But the revolution did not go very deep; the greater part of the population still seemed content with the sort of fare it had always accepted.

Life was getting better in a variety of ways. In December 1952 the last great pea-souper fog descended in the London area. Cars were abandoned, pedestrians groped helplessly around areas which they thought they knew as well as their own sitting-room; in the sitting-rooms themselves acrid yellow fumes seared the throat; at the annual cattle show some of the finest beasts in the British Isles were painfully asphyxiated. At least 4,000 people died. But it was the last fine flourish of the killer fog. New legislation restricted the use of coal on domestic fires, established smokeless zones, raised the chimneys of power-stations. Air became much cleaner and, as the grime of many decades was stripped from London's buildings, a half-forgotten architecture re-emerged – only too often to fall prey to the demolition man and the developer.

Another threat to Britain's breathing was identified in 1953 when a link between smoking and lung cancer was established to the satisfaction of the medical profession if not the tobacco manufacturers. No government enjoyed attacking an industry that yielded huge revenues and provided much employment, but gradually the pressure on the smoker was stepped up – through harsh taxation, restrictions on advertising,

The values and conventions of the traditional West End stage were disrupted in 1956 by the harsh, protesting shout of the young John Osborne in Look Back in Anger, *a landmark in the British theatre.*

The spectacular growth of the public library system, accompanied as it was by the virtual disappearance of the commercial lending libraries, was a phenomenon of the post-war decade. Many books were distributed by mobile libraries, as here at Swanley village, near Dartford in Kent.

health warnings on every packet of cigarettes. With alarming insouciance Britain's youth ignored the advice of its elders, but the elders themselves increasingly took alarm at the risks involved. Meanwhile Britain's wild life was under a different threat. In 1953 and 1954 the nation's roads were made hideous by the corpses of rabbits, eyes popping in an agonising death, victims of the imported disease myxomatosis. For a time it seemed the rabbit population would be exterminated; then a new breed of myxomatosis-resistant rabbit rose from the hecatomb of its ancestors and the race was restored – to the dismay of farmers and gardeners but to the satisfaction of most other people.

Britain was still largely homogenous, but things were beginning to change. In 1949 the coloured population was ony 25,000, predominantly West Indian or Chinese and centred in long-established colonies in Liverpool and Cardiff. The British tended mildly to distrust all foreigners and had little enthusiasm for the periodic waves of immigration from Ireland, but the tradition of the open door for would-be immigrants was a long and honourable one, and would not readily be discarded. Then unemployment in certain Commonwealth countries and restrictions on immigration into the United States led to a dramatic inflow. Three thousand West Indians arrived in 1952 and 1953, then in the first nine months of 1954 alone the figure rose to 8,000. The new immigrants for the most part clustered together and were little seen by the country at large; there was ample scope for them in an expanding economy; the British public was not yet seriously concerned. When at the end of 1953 the *Sunday Times* warned that a serious colour problem could be building up, there was little immediate response. Enoch Powell's day was still to come.

Organised religion continued to decline. There were still nearly two million communicants on Easter Day 1952, but the middle-aged and old were in the majority and the total was falling by some 20,000 a year. A poll in Derby in 1953 showed that nine in every ten families

1954 was the year of Billy Graham. Millions attended his meetings and many thousands found God through his preaching (though most seemed to lose Him again pretty promptly). Here he addressed a massive audience at Wembley.

The 'pea-souper' fog accompanied the commercial lending library into abeyance, and was less generally lamented. Legislation restricting the use of coal and establishing smokeless zones ensured that this scene at Ludgate Circus in London was never repeated.

As the 1950s advanced there was a sudden rush of coloured immigrants, predominantly from the West Indies. Three thousand arrived in 1952 and 1953, then 8,000 in the first nine months of 1954. The determination of some in this group to conceal their faces suggests they were not very sure of their welcome.

Britain pioneered the first jet airliner. The De Havilland Comet is here shown on the tarmac of Rome's Ciampino Airport. Piloted by John Cunningham it had just flown from its home airport, Hatfield near London, in two hours two minutes, breaking all records in so doing.

The campaign against nuclear weapons meanwhile gathered force. In August 1956 a march took place from London to the research station at Aldermaston. It was to become an annual event. This photograph shows the 1958 demonstration; the column, shepherded by the police, is winding its way along a country road in Berkshire.

owned a Bible but that little more than one in ten of the citizens went regularly to church. But there was some revivalist excitement; 1954 was the year of Billy Graham, the American evangelist, whose crusading meetings at Harringay Stadium were attended by 1.3 million people. It seemed too that, for every person who stopped attending church, twenty started sending Christmas cards. By 1956 the annual total had risen to 500 million, an increase of 100 million in five years.

The average Briton in 1956 spent 30 per cent of his income on food, including 3½ lbs of bread a week, and 16 per cent on drink and cigarettes. Twice as many had telephones as before the war, twice as much gas was used. Three million more lived in the cities, while the population of the countryside remained more or less the same. Far fewer worked on the land, while by 1954 there were almost eight tractors at work for every one in 1939. Three million cars were on the roads by 1956, and a million motorcycles. More than a million people travelled each day into central London and another quarter of a million into other parts of Greater London. The British every year became more mobile, more rootless, more dependent on a variety of machines and gadgets for their transport, comfort and entertainment.

Technologically they were still among the leaders of the world. In aeronautics L.P. Twiss in a Fairey Delta was in 1956 the first man to fly at more than 1,000 mph. Britain pioneered the first jet airliner. The Comet, powered by four de Havilland Ghost engines, had originally been developed for military purposes. When it made its first commercial flight in 1952 it seemed that its potential was unlimited. Then came three disastrous crashes within a year. Confidence was shattered, foreign orders withered away, and by the time metal fatigue was diagnosed and conquered Britain had lost its lead. In rocketry, too, Britain was in the forefront. HMS *Girdle Ness*, Britain's first guided missile ship, was commissioned in 1956, and even as late as

Anthony Eden remained undisturbed by the growing opposition to his belligerent policy over Suez. At the Conservative party conference at Llandudno in October 1956 he defended his line and was given a rousing reception. His wife Clarissa supported him staunchly; the Lord Privy Seal Mr R.A. Butler, in the centre of the picture, looks (and was) decidedly more sceptical.

1960 the British had little to learn about ballistic missiles from the two super-powers. Ingenuity and expertise, however, were not enough to keep up in the space race without an immense investment of money and effort which no second rank power could afford. In this field too Britain was to slip back into a minor role.

But it was over nuclear power that the opportunities seemed greatest. In 1956 Britain opened at Calder Hall, in Cumberland, the world's first full-scale nuclear power-station. As with the Comet, a great future seemed secure, both because of the limitless potential for exports and because for Britain in the 1950s, with no known oil resources and a finite supply of coal, it appeared that nuclear power would be the basis for national prosperity. Edwin Plowden, the Chairman of the UK Atomic Energy Authority, insisted that Britain must continue to develop nuclear power 'with energy and faith'. The only other possibility, he said, was 'not to go on as we are. For a nation that has to live by industry in a competitive world, the alternative is to become progressively poorer and less secure.' When he spoke there seemed no reason to doubt that Britain would continue to lead the world.

Britain's civil nuclear programme was then a matter for pride so far as the whole people was concerned; nuclear weapons were becoming a subject of greater controversy. The decision to manufacture a British atom bomb had been taken in 1947, without public debate and with hardly any discussion in cabinet, the cost hidden among the supply estimates. In 1952 the first British atom bomb was exploded. The Russians had set off their first nuclear device three years before and the most common reaction to this latest blast was one of satisfaction that Britain had caught up with the super-powers. Then second thoughts began to be expressed, redoubled when it was realised that the government was now committed to producing a hydrogen bomb as well. Could the use of nuclear weapons

ever be permissible? it was asked. If not, what purpose could there be in Britain developing them? If yes, then should Britain squander resources in an effort to duplicate what the United States had done already? It was the moral case against nuclear arms that proved the most powerful. In August 1956 took place the first march to the research station at Aldermaston. The Aldermaston march was to enter national folklore; a great annual demonstration in which churchmen and politicians, labourers and professional men, women and children, cranks and exhibitionists, marched together, united in nothing except their conviction that nuclear arms were evil and should be banished from the earth. In its first year, however, the march was dismissed by most of the press as well-intentioned but misguided folly that had attracted little support and would undoubtedly soon wither from lack of encouragement.

To the British government, and in particular to Anthony Eden, with his doubts about Europe and conviction that Britain's role should be that of a third, if smaller super-power, the atom bomb was a vital symbol of national prestige and independence. To propose that Britain should renounce it was not merely folly, it was almost treasonable. Eden fancied himself as an international statesman and saw himself acting as intermediary between Russia and the United States. When the Russian leaders, Bulganin and Khrushchev, visited England early in 1956, it seemed that his dream might become reality. It was unfortunate for him that the success of the visit was tarnished when the intelligence services whimsically despatched a naval frogman, Commander Crabbe, to inspect the bottom of the Russian cruiser which had brought the two statesmen to England and which was awaiting them at Portsmouth. Crabbe disappeared – killed or kidnapped by Russian guards or, perhaps more probably, victim of a

The Russian leaders, Bulganin and Khrushchev, visited Britain early in 1956. All was amity as they laid a wreath at the cenotaph in Whitehall, but the success of the visit was marred by the abortive effort of Commander Crabbe, a naval frogman, to spy on the Russian cruiser which had brought the two statesmen to Portsmouth.

heart attack – and a scandal followed, in which the British authorities and Eden as the ultimate authority were made to look spectacularly foolish.

Eden had better cause than this to see himself as a figure of international significance. The long and embittered war between France and its former colonists in Vietnam had come to a bloody climax when a French army was cut off and forced to surrender at Dien Bien Phu. Eden had played a prominent part in the conference at Geneva that followed and could justifiably claim much credit for the settlement by which Vietnam was partitioned between a communist north and a pro-western south. His diplomatic dexterity, however, though it enhanced his country's prestige, did not make it into a super-power. The fact was that Britain's tenuous claim to membership of the big three had survived largely thanks to Churchill and his wartime intimacy with Eisenhower. Now that Churchill was no longer in office the old intimacy had disappeared. The unreality of Britain's claim to greatness was about cruelly to be exposed.

The last British troops left the Suez Canal zone in June 1956. A month later Egypt's radical leader, Gamal Abdel Nasser, nationalised the canal so that its revenues could be dedicated to building the Aswan high dam – a project which had previously been supported by the Americans but had been unceremoniously abandoned by them in dissatisfaction at Egyptian foreign policy. His action was certainly discourteous and probably illegal. Eden's response was to brand him a second Hitler and to dismiss all who sought to negotiate a settlement as latter-day Municheers bent on appeasing a dictator. The British and French connived with the Israelis to create a situation whereby the latter attacked the Egyptians, whereupon an allied force 'intervened' to separate the warring forces and to protect the canal. To many Britons and to most of the rest of the world, this seemed

The Anglo-French military intervention which followed Nasser's nationalisation of the Suez Canal split the nation. Here a crowd, consisting predominantly of university students, parades in Albert Square, Manchester in the vain hope of stopping the operation.

like unwarrantable aggression, immoral out of all proportion to the provocation that had inspired it. The military operation was slow and cumbersome but competently carried out; the political consequences were appalling. The Russians huffed and puffed, the United Nations stormed, President Eisenhower threatened dire economic consequences unless the troops were withdrawn. This last was the clinching factor. The operation was called off with only half the canal zone occupied and the Egyptian forces still fighting. Anthony Eden, by now seriously ill, retreated to Jamaica to convalesce.

Suez split the British nation as no other event had done or was to do in the first sixty years of Elizabeth's life. It was not a split on traditional lines, Conservative against Socialist or establishment against radicals. It was an open secret that the Queen was deeply disturbed by what she felt to be a blow at the fabric of the Commonwealth and her cousin, Lord Mountbatten, the First Sea Lord, several times threatened resignation; yet a majority of the miners, the dockers, the more bellicose sectors of the Labour movement, were vociferously in favour of what they felt to be a proper exercise of Britain's power against the 'reds and wogs'. Hugh Gaitskell, the Labour leader, was initially in cautious support of military intervention and his followers were by no means unanimous when the party moved into opposition, yet many Conservatives had serious doubts and two members of the government resigned. The foreign office, almost to the last man, condemned the operation; in the Armed Services feeling was almost equally strong in favour of it.

Families were divided, old friendships broken. A journalist who admitted that he wrote for the *Economist*, a magazine notoriously unsound in the eyes of the loyalists, found himself shunned in his own club. The *Observer*, which under the editorship of David Astor unequivocally condemned intervention, was banned from homes where it had been a staple of Sunday reading for many years and suffered a sharp fall in circulation. Even today there are many people who date events as being 'before Suez' or 'after Suez'; few indeed who were more than children at the time cannot remember precisely where they were and what they were doing as events unfolded. With tragic precision it marked the end of Britain's role as a world power and cleared the way for the 1960s.

Eden returned from Jamaica unrepentant. 'I am convinced,' he said, 'more convinced than I have been about anything in the whole of my public life, that we were right . . . and that history will prove it so.' He failed to satisfy either his colleagues or the British people. He had to go. Ill health was the official, indeed a valid reason, but if he had been radiantly fit it would have made no difference. On 8 January Eden journeyed to Sandringham to deliver his resignation to his monarch. He left a country in alarming disarray. It remained to be seen whether all the Queen's horses and all the Queen's men would be able to put it together again.

2 November 1956, and soldiers board the troopship Dilwara *at Southampton on their way to the Middle East.*

Hugh Gaitskell, the Labour leader, was initially in cautious support of intervention, but his doubts quickly grew and he ended by leading his party in determined opposition to any military action. Gaitskell died prematurely in 1963, felt by many to have been one of the greatest prime ministers Britain never had.

A tranquil photograph of the young family taken by the children's uncle, Antony Armstrong-Jones, in the gardens of Buckingham Palace.

Chapter Six

The Years of Affluence

1956 to 1964

THOUGH THE phrase may have been taken out of context and used unfairly against him, Macmillan's unwary claim that the British people had 'never had it so good' has stamped ineradicably the eight years of Conservative government between 1956 and 1964. They were, indeed, years of national self-indulgence, lotus-eating perhaps, in which Harold Macmillan, that Circe of the hustings, lulled the British electorate into the conviction that all was for the best in the best of possible worlds. For a time, indeed, it was.

When Eden resigned it seemed most probable that his deputy, Butler, would succeed him. But too many of the Tory leaders believed that Butler's role over Suez had been, if not disloyal, then certainly equivocal. Lord Salisbury was deputed to make soundings before advising the Queen whom she should send for. 'Do you favour Wab or Hawold?' he asked in his patrician lisp, and Harold unequivocally carried the day. To the general public it seemed that he had been selected because his ducal connections and grouse-moor image conformed to the standards of the establishment Tory.

They underestimated the subtlety and skills of one of the most professional politicians to reach Downing Street in the twentieth century.

Macmillan made it his first priority to heal the scars of Suez. There were to be no recriminations, no witch-hunts for guilty men. Unity must be restored within the party, bridges rebuilt with the Commonweath and the United States. He retained Selwyn Lloyd, Eden's foreign secretary, as evidence that he did not intend to do penance for British foreign policy; included Julian Amery in his government, who had rebelled because he felt Eden had called off the operation too rapidly; yet also brought back Edward Boyle, who had resigned in protest at military intervention. Then he turned his attention to the outside world.

In this task he had no ally more efficacious than Queen Elizabeth. In 1957 she undertook five state visits, to Portugal, France, Denmark and – far the most important from the point of view of repairing the damage done by Suez – to the United States and to Canada. Of these the visit to France was the most

The Queen visited Canada in 1957, an important step in repairing the damage done to Britain's reputation by the Suez affair. She is opening the Canadian Parliament, the first reigning monarch ever to do so.

It was the age of 'Supermac'. Here the new prime minister, impeccably dressed for the occasion, is watching the 1957 Derby at Epsom. It was won by Lester Piggott on Crepello, in the second of his nine victories in the race.

Selwyn Lloyd, Eden's foreign secretary and at first retained in that position by Macmillan, later became chancellor of the exchequer and is here shown leaving the treasury on the way to present his first budget. He is carrying the famous red dispatch box.

spectacular in its stage-management; the vision of the Queen and President de Gaulle processing down the Seine in a brilliantly lit *bâteau mouche* while a jungle of fireworks blazed above them is one that lived in the minds of the Parisians for many years. The visit seemed to offer hope – alas fleeting – that the *entente cordiale*, strained by the unhappy ending to the joint venture in the Middle East, might blossom to the benefit of both countries and of a united Europe.

The Queen never flagged in her readiness to serve as an instrument of British foreign policy by visiting whatever countries her ministers told her would repay the attention. By preference, however, she concentrated on the Commonweath. This could pose problems. She was due to visit Ghana in 1961 but her advisers were reluctant to let her go because of the unrest caused by the increasingly dictatorial rule of President Nkrumah. Shortly before the visit a statue of Nkrumah was blown up in Accra. She was unperturbed. A Russian visit to Ghana was also in the air; how deplorable it would be, she commented, if the Queen showed herself afraid to visit a Commonwealth country in which Khrushchev was subsequently fêted. She was equally indifferent to murder threats from French separatists in Quebec when she visited Canada three years later. It was her duty to go; personal safety and comfort were of secondary importance.

Nevertheless she was not immune to criticism. In 1957 Lord Altrincham published in the *National and English Review* an editorial in which he accused the royal entourage of being 'stuffy and tweedy', said that the Queen's voice was 'a pain in the neck' and that it

The royal family indulged in some cautious modernisation. In 1957 the antique and snobbish ceremony of the presentation of debutantes came to an end. This is Miss Ullein Reviesky, the last deb.

The Queen made her first descent to a coal mine at Kirkaldy, Scotland, in July 1958.

Baby Prince Andrew is the centre of attention at Balmoral in September 1960. The Queen's corgi basks in its privileged position.

In September 1957 Prince Charles began to attend a boarding school, Cheam, near Newbury in Berkshire. He is here entering the school. His father and the headmaster, Peter Beck, appear decidedly cheerful – but then they haven't just left home for the first time.

conveyed the impression that she was 'a priggish schoolgirl'. Malcolm Muggeridge, who had written an article in the *New Statesman* the year before under the title 'The Royal Soap Opera', now joined in the fray. The explosion of indignation that greeted these attacks was proof, if proof were needed, of the love in which the British people held their monarch. It was also absurdly disproportionate to the offence. Lord Altrincham was challenged to a duel, insulted in public, physically attacked by an elderly Empire Loyalist and bombarded with angry letters, the more vicious ones anonymous. Malcolm Muggeridge had his contract with the BBC suspended. Some of the Queen's sager advisers saw danger in a situation where mild and constructive criticism gave rise to such a stupendous pother.

The royal family was as aware as anyone that criticism from those who were well-disposed deserved careful consideration. Prince Philip, in particular, was resolved to bring efficiency and modern business methods to court circles. The royal children were to be educated with a minimum of fuss and formality and Prince Charles was despatched to the preparatory school of Cheam which, while admittedly an expensive

Another important royal visit in 1957 was that to Paris. In the glass-encased saloon of a bâteau mouche the Queen and the Duke of Edinburgh process down the Seine. A spectacular firework display was part of the evening's programme.

private institution catering for the upper and upper-middle classes, provided something a great deal nearer to a democratic upbringing than had been enjoyed by any other future British monarch. The antique and snobbish ceremony of the presentation of debutantes was ended in 1957. The bombed ruins of the chapel at Buckingham Palace were converted into an art gallery and opened to the public, exhibiting selections from the awe-inspiring royal collection. In 1957 the Queen's Christmas broadcast for the first time was seen live on television.

In 1960 Princess Margaret made her personal contribution to the democratization of the royal family. Her fiancé, Antony Armstrong-Jones, had been educated at Eton and Cambridge and was the stepson of an earl, but he was still the first commoner to be received into the inner circle of the royal family. Endless jokes were made on the theme of 'Keeping up with the Joneses', but the British people were genuinely pleased that Princess Margaret had found happiness after her earlier troubles and that she had stepped outside the charmed circle of foreign royals and the upper aristocracy. 'She's doing the right thing,' said a tobacconist

The engagement of Princess Margaret to Antony Armstrong-Jones in 1960 delighted everyone who wished her well after the former troubles. Here she visits the Vaudeville Theatre with her fiancé and talks to Julian Slade and Dorothy Reynolds, co-authors of Follow the Girl.

October 1959, and the Tories break all records by increasing their majority in three general elections in succession. Here a crowd in Trafalgar Square watches the results on a giant electric scoreboard. The Tory lead rose to 102.

who spoke for Britain. 'He's one of us. His family have paid income tax.' Armstrong-Jones – Earl of Snowdon as he was shortly to become – was also refreshingly remote from the stuffy courtiers whom Lord Altrincham had excoriated. A photographer with a background in the world of fashion and theatrical design was hardly conventional material for a royal brother-in-law. At least 300 million people in thirteen countries watched the wedding on television and the crowds that lined the route were hardly less vociferous than they had been for Elizabeth's wedding.

Armstrong-Jones's family had to endure the fierce blaze of publicity. There was nothing new in this, save in its intensity. As techniques of news-reporting became more powerful and more sophisticated, so the public appetite grew for any snippet of information connected with the royal family. In the first eighty-eight days Prince Charles spent at Cheam, there were sixty-eight stories about him carried by the newpapers. When, as a fourteen-year-old at his next school, Gordonstoun, he ordered a glass of cherry brandy in a local pub, the story earned notoriety beyond that to be expected by the mass-murderer or the adulterous film star. The burden of publicity was to become almost intolerable when he began to have girl-friends and look for a wife, but that, in 1957, was mercifully remote.

THE EARLY days of Macmillan's government saw a fierce assult on the Armed Services. Winston Churchill's son-in-law, Duncan Sandys, one of the toughest and most pragmatic of contemporary politicians, was appointed minister of defence with a mandate not only to cut out dead wood and save money, but also to transform the Navy, Army and Airforce from the rump of wartime forces to a modern fighting force capable of meeting the needs of the 1960s and onwards. National Service was to be abolished in 1960 – the new Services would have no room for such costly amateurism; the days of the fighter and the bomber were numbered, ballistic missiles were the weapon of the future. Inevitably some thriving babies went out with the bathwater, mistakes were made, false economies introduced, but the operation as a whole was overdue.

The savings were not sufficient to satisfy the chancellor of the exchequer, Peter Thorneycroft. Early in 1958 Thorneycroft and the other treasury ministers resigned in protest at the failure of the rest of the cabinet to support them in curbing the estimates of the various spending departments. The government was experiencing 'little local difficulties' said Macmillan airily – a comment which did much to fortify the reputation for unflappability that was his stock in trade. Heathcote Amory took Thorneycroft's place and the following

*Harold Macmillan played a vigorous part in the 1959 electoral campaign. Here he is in the
High Street of Dartford speaking in favour of a promising young Tory candidate,
Mr Peter Walker.*

*Peter Thorneycroft was Macmillan's first chancellor of the
exchequer. He is here seen at a party conference at Brighton,
appealing for a national crusade against inflation. Early in 1958,
dissatisfied at the support his colleagues in the cabinet were giving
him in curbing official spending, he and his treasury team
resigned. Macmillan commented airily that the government was
experiencing 'little local difficulties'.*

*In 1961 Anthony Wedgwood Benn was deprived of his
parliamentary seat on the death of his father, Lord Stansgate. He
refused to accept the situation, stood for parliament and was
returned again and is here shown with his wife and son waving
his Certificate of Election after again being denied the right to
take his seat. He won his point a few months later when
hereditary peers were allowed to renounce their titles and stand for
the House of Commons.*

The Queen and Queen Elizabeth, the Queen Mother, ride in the Irish State Coach to the wedding of Princess Margaret and Mr Antony Armstrong-Jones. There were endless jokes about 'Keeping up with the Joneses' but the British people as a whole were delighted.

The crowd flows up the Mall towards Buckingham Palace after Princess Margaret's wedding. They were to acclaim the newly married couple with almost as much zest as they had cheered her elder sister and Prince Philip thirteen years before.

Nigeria became independent in 1960. There was jubilation outside Nigeria House in London and a crowd gathered, including many Nigerians in national dress.

year introduced a generously tax-cutting budget. There are no rights or wrongs in economics, but the evidence suggests that the respective chancellors were responding too late to events rather than dictating their course. Thorneycroft failed to reinflate when expansion was urgently called for, but by the time Amory did his work the brake was needed more than the accelerator. Steady progress was the aim of every chancellor; erratic Stop-Go the usual result of his activities.

Amory's budget was good enough for the electorate, however. The general election of 1959 was unique in that the Tories increased their lead for the third time in a row; from twenty in 1951 to sixty-two in 1955 and 102 in 1959. A Liberal revival under their new leader, Jo Grimond, which had seemed hopeful a few months before, ended in disappointment with the number of Liberal voters doubled but their seats unchanged. The result was a remarkable tribute to the political dexterity of Macmillan and a sad commentary on the divisions that racked the Labour party.

Macmillan made several changes that affected the House of Lords. First in 1958 life-peers were invented, an innovation that some feared might presage the end of the hereditary peerage but has so far done little towards this end. Then in 1961 hereditary peers were allowed to renounce their titles and take their chance with the commoners. Lords Stansgate and Hailsham, henceforth Anthony Wedgwood Benn and Quintin Hogg, hastened to avail themselves of the chance and by so doing proclaimed themselves candidates for the leadership of their respective parties. The Earl of Home, now secretary of state for foreign affairs, took no such step, nor did anyone think that he would do so.

Scottish nationalism became a force to be reckoned with. Some Scots objected to the designation of the Queen as Elizabeth II, arguing that she was the first Queen Elizabeth of Scotland. Extremists blew up the odd pillar box to make their point.

But it is perhaps most of all with decolonisation, in particular in Africa, that Macmillan's name is associated. Cyprus, where luckless British soldiers had long found themselves caught in the cross-fire between Greek and Turk, was settled in 1959. There was a last moment of hideous drama when the plane of the Turkish prime minister crashed at Gatwick as he arrived to sign the treaty, but he survived and the ceremony took place at his bedside in the London Clinic. Ghana and Malaya became independent in 1957, Nigeria in 1960, Sierra Leone and Tanganyika in 1961. The West Indies followed swiftly, with Jamaica and Trinidad in 1962. East Africa presented problems, with large white-settler populations, but Uganda also graduated to independence in 1962 and Kenya in 1963. The most worrying outstanding problem was the Rhodesias. The Government was convinced that the best solution was a federation of the two Rhodesias and Nyasaland, but that this could not be imposed on a reluctant population. Nyasaland and Northern Rhodesia were deeply suspicious of the white minority rulers of Southern Rhodesia and opted for secession. By 1963 a resentful Southern Rhodesia was left as the solitary colony in what had once been British Africa. The response of the predominantly white electorate was to harden its line, and in April 1964 Ian Smith became prime minister, dedicated to lead Southern Rhodesia to independence without allowing the black majority to secure control. The stage was set for confrontation.

The South Africans watched with dismay as the tide of independence swept down their continent. In 1960 it was announced that there would be a referendum to decide whether the country should become a republic.

South Africa became increasingly isolated as more of the continent became independent. In April 1960 there were clashes outside South Africa House. Admirable sang froid *is shown by all.*

The clamour to 'Ban the Bomb' became ever more vociferous – no need to ask what *bomb. In March 1961 the slogan, in yellow letters four feet high, was daubed across Stonehenge. Archaeologists were not amused, claiming irreparable damage could easily have been done.*

While the debate was on Harold Macmillan made a celebrated journey through Africa, ending up in South Africa. There was a 'wind of change' blowing throughout the continent he told his hosts; they would ignore it at their peril. They resolved to ignore it nevertheless. South Africa became a republic and so was required to apply for readmission to the Commonwealth. For other countries this had been a formality; in the case of South Africa opposition from the new Commonwealth countries would be fierce. At Sharpeville, ten weeks after Macmillan's visit, sixty-seven Africans were shot down. By the time of the Commonwealth conference in March 1961, the prospects for South African readmission were remote. The prime minister, Verwoerd, decided to accept the inevitable with dignity and withdrew South Africa's application. Here too stark confrontation was to be the way of the future.

It seemed fleetingly as if things might be different in Northern Ireland. In 1956 a new wave of violence had begun, based largely on the Republic. For almost six years the campaign continued; then abruptly it was suspended in February 1962 to give way to a few years of peace. Scotland seemed to be going the other way,

though with little real violence yet apparent. Scottish nationalism, always grumbling quietly in the background, erupted into militancy by the start of Elizabeth's reign. The Stone of Scone, on which British monarchs had been crowned for centuries, was taken away from Westminster Abbey and removed to Dunfermline, whence Edward I had stolen it in 1296. It was recaptured with no harm done. Hardly more serious was the row over pillarboxes. The Scots argued that these should not bear the insignia E II R since in Scotland the Queen was only E I R. Militants blew up the odd box to make their point. A compromise was reached when it was agreed that the higher of the two designations should always be adopted – so that the next King James would be James VII. Since the next King was not going to be King James but King Charles – III of Scotland as well as England – the Scots had not gained very much. So far the campaign for Scottish devolution concentrated on trivia of this kind; it was not to be long before more substantial issues came into question.

The Communists posed as trivial a political threat as ever, but industrially they proved capable of working themselves into positions where they could do much

The Queen with Lord Harlech and Mrs Kennedy at the unveiling of a memorial to President Kennedy at Runnymede. Three years earlier the Queen, Jackie Kennedy and Eleanor Roosevelt had been voted 'the most admired women in the world' in a poll in the United States.

harm to the nation. By skilled chicanery and the apathy of most of the members they had gained control of the Electrical Trades Union. The worm turned, when the Communists rigged the election so as to secure the general secretaryship for a party member. With Frank Chapple heading the counter-attack, the Communists were assailed in the courts and routed at the polls; the union returned to democracy.

The communist threat from without provided the government's justification for its determination to remain a nuclear power. A truly independent deterrent, however, became ever less feasible. The government pinned its faith in the American air-borne missile, Skybolt, and in recognition of its importance accepted in 1958 that American nuclear weapons should be based in the British Isles. Unfortunately the Skybolt programme proved a costly failure and was abandoned. Briefly Britain's nuclear armoury seemed without a future. Then at Nassau in 1962 President Kennedy offered Britain the submarine-launched missile, Polaris, on condition that the nuclear striking force, though under the command of Whitehall, should be earmarked for NATO uses. Macmillan accepted the terms with alacrity. With four nuclear submarines to provide the launching platforms, Britain could remain a nuclear power for a quarter of a century at least.

The critics of Britain's nuclear role grew more vociferous. The Aldermaston marches at Easter continued, though with flagging zeal, and in 1960 came the first mass demonstration in Trafalgar Square organised by the Committee for Nuclear Disarmament. Between 60,000 and 100,000 people attended – the first the figure suggested by the police, the second by the organisers. In September 1961 a still larger demonstration lasted until midnight, at which point the police swooped and made many arrests, including such celebrities as Canon Collins, the 'Red Dean' of Canterbury (Hewlett Johnson), John Osborne and Vanessa Redgrave. The government appeared undisturbed by this opposition.

They were more affected by the hostile attitude of the French. Macmillan's Nassau agreement with Kennedy had followed hard on a meeting with De Gaulle and was interpreted by the French leader as, at the worst, rank treachery, at the best, proof that Britain's loyalties were with the United States rather than Europe. At another time this might not have mattered much; in 1962 it represented a crippling blow to British foreign policy.

The Queen and the Duke of Edinburgh on the balcony of Buckingham Palace after the ceremony of Trooping the Colour in 1964. The Queen holds the infant Prince Edward in her arms and exhibits him proudly to the huge crowd outside.

Nassau, December 1962. President John Kennedy greets Harold Macmillan before the fateful conference that was to secure Britain the Polaris missile, but incidentally cost her the chance to enter the Common Market when De Gaulle applied his veto early in the following year.

The gramophone and the photographs of Liberace identify the girls in this picture as being worshippers at the shrine of this cult-figure. Sales of gramophone records continued to rise dramatically.

The hula-hoop became a transitory craze, though not habitually among bowler-hatted gentlemen.

Schools became larger, lighter and more imaginatively planned. This is the brand-new Garratt
Green comprehensive school in Wandsworth, built at a cost of £735,000 and opened in 1958.
The photograph shows the Assembly Hall, where an informal group is at work.

By 1960 Macmillan had become convinced that on grounds both economic and political Britain must join the EEC. He saw Britain as being at the centre of three interlocking circles – Europe, the Commonwealth and the Anglo-American alliance – but he had come to believe that the second two could not suffice unless Britain enjoyed the strength it would gain from Europe. Britain, said the American secretary of state, Dean Acheson, had 'lost an Empire and failed to find a role.' Macmillan accepted the truth in this and found the solution in full membership of the European community. He applied to join in 1961 and throughout 1962 British ministers, led by Edward Heath, laboured diligently to negotiate satisfactory terms. The Commonweath was won over to grudging acquiescence, all major difficulties were eliminated, and then at the beginning of 1963 De Gaulle imposed his veto. Great Britain, he said, was not, perhaps never would be, a loyal European. To let in the British would be to admit a Trojan horse financed by American capital and stuffed with American ideas.

As is not unusual, the indignation that the British felt at their rejection was far stronger than their desire to join. The British people in 1963 had no very strong views about Europe. Labour had moved predominantly against entry, though a wing of the party under Roy Jenkins was passionately European. The Tories were for Europe, though a largely right-wing fringe was equally passionately opposed to the idea. The Communists were against entry, the Liberals for it. Nobody asked the people what *they* felt. Probably if they had been consulted they would have said that they were quite happy as they were. They would have had some justification for this point of view.

THE BRITISH lower and middle classes at the start of the 1960s were more prosperous than they had ever been. There were fewer houses without electric light, running water, indoor lavatories. Refrigerators, vacuum cleaners, electric kettles were not now luxuries but part of the equipment of the average home. Hire-purchase – no longer something to be ashamed of – brought such delights within the reach of millions. Television and the telephone were taken for granted in all but the poorest or most self-consciously old-fashioned homes. Cars were not yet considered a basic necessity but their use was spreading ever more widely. The young had money to burn; on gramophone records, magazines and, for the slightly older, drink and cigarettes.

The schools were larger, lighter, better equipped, more imaginatively planned. Whether it followed that the education they provided was therefore superior was a matter of opinion. The socialist dream of vast educational establishments which could offer appropriate styles of schooling to children of every age, social background and level of intelligence was taking a long time to work out. Many Tories were prepared to offer a cautious welcome to a system which presented a way of escape from the harsh rigidity of the eleven plus examination, but size offered its own problems too, and there

New universities opened almost every year. One of the most ambitious architecturally was Sussex University, designed by Basil Spence. Falmer House, its social centre and refectory, won the British Architects' Bronze Medal for outstanding merit.

The first fifty-five miles of motorway were opened in 1959. As the photograph shows, a central barrier was not then considered essential.

Richard Beeching in June 1961 on the point of taking over as the first Chairman of the new British Railways Board. He had moved to his new job from ICI. The 'Beeching axe' was to fall savagely and close a myriad branch lines. The picture behind him depicts one of the new Scottish Region electric trains which had recently come into discredit after a series of technical setbacks.

were soon horror stories circulating about drugs, delinquency, and a breakdown of standards in the comprehensive schools of the cities. Most of the stories were no doubt exaggerated but there was enough truth in them to give the doubters cause for genuine alarm. The Conservative government gave local authorities no encouragement to extend the comprehensive system, but equally did nothing to check them.

It was to the universities and polytechnics that the Tory government particularly addressed itself. In the late 1950s Britain was said to have proportionately fewer students than any European country except Turkey. The Robbins report of 1963 recommended vast and rapid expansion. Eight new universities were initiated, including those of Sussex, York, Keele and East Anglia, and the existing establishments – Oxbridge or red-brick – were greatly extended. London University was to grow from 16,000 in 1961 to 46,000 in 1981. Rapid growth sometimes involved a fall in standards and what some felt to be undue emphasis on new and fashionable subjects such as sociology, but the end result was that many received higher education who deserved the chance but would formerly have been denied it.

The people's expectations of holidays also rose impressively. By 1964 four million Britons were taking their annual holidays abroad. Motor caravans began to appear in large numbers on British roads, as sure a harbinger of summer as the swallow or the daffodil. More than 180,000 were in use by 1959, though half of

Rock-and-roll swept the country in 1958. Bill Haley and his Comets, more than anyone else responsible for the success of this noisy and energetic diversion, are here rehearsing at the Dominion Theatre in Tottenham Court Road. Aficionados will wish to know that Johnnie Grande is playing the accordion, Al Rex and Ruddy Pompilli are prostrate while playing the bass and saxophone respectively, Franny Beecher is on the electric guitar, Billy Williamson on the steel guitar while Mr Haley himself cavorts in the centre.

these served as substitute houses. The roads themselves made the most substantial advance since before the war. The first fifty-five miles of motorway were opened in 1959, from Luton to Dunchurch – 'a quarter of a century late by international standards' as *The Times* loftily remarked, but better late than never. The motorways were desperately needed; for every one family that had owned a car in 1950 there were two in 1960, and the pace was accelerating. But the motorist was not allowed to have it all his own way; the first radar speed traps were used by the police in 1957, while parking meters and traffic wardens became a feature of the London scene the following year. Meanwhile that redoubtable eccentric, Dr Barbara Moore, kept the flag of the pedestrian flying by stumping across the English countryside, proclaiming the merits of walking as a way to health.

Those who favoured rail as a means of transport found themselves progressively more disadvantaged. Richard Beeching, the chairman of the transport commission, was given a mandate to make the railways pay, or at least lose substantially less money. He set about it by seeking to close half the stations and a third of the route mileage, which together contributed only two per cent of the total revenue. The Beeching axe fell ferociously and closed a myriad branch lines that had become an essential support of rural life. The bus and

In the late 1950s, the 'teddy-boy' – flamboyant, innovative, vulgar to some – was a conspicuous feature of the urban scene. Here, at St Luke's Church, Skerton in Lancashire, a teddy-boy is married. He and his best man wear powder-blue suits edged with black velvet. The colour of the bride's dress, however, is not recorded.

the private motorcar helped to fill the gap but many suffered great inconvenience. For the railway enthusiast it was some consolation that an Anglo-French study group reported in favour of a channel tunnel designed for trains rather than motor vehicles, but this did little to console the innumerable country dwellers who found themselves cut off from their traditional method of travel and supply.

New and more ambitious means of travel were meanwhile evolving. In 1960 an Anglo-French agreement was negotiated for the manufacture of the world's first supersonic airliner, soon christened Concorde. By 1964 the estimated cost had already almost doubled, the British share rising from £80 million to £140 million. A purely British invention, the Hovercraft, came off the secret list in 1959 and had its first test run in June of that year.

Such novelties were appropriate to an age which the press was soon to call the 'swinging sixties' though it really began three years earlier. Flamboyant, innovative, slightly vulgar, the period did indeed have rather more of an authentic flavour than most eras graced with a similar label. The dances of the day were characteristically frenetic. Rock-and-roll swept the country in 1958 – if there is one noise characteristic of the end of the 1950s it is Bill Haley and his Comets with their 'Rock around the Clock'. In 1961 the twist arrived from Paris, inflicting severe strains on the muscles and joints of many who fancied that they could keep up with the teenagers and found too late that they could not. The first discothèque, the Saddle Room, was opened in Park Lane. Then, in 1963, came the full flowering of that extraordinary talent from Liverpool that was to sweep the world. The Beatles achieved fame and popularity beyond that of any other group of musicians before or since, a renown based on hard work, charm and a genuinely original creativity that happened to coincide with a shift in popular taste. Their song 'I Want to Hold Your Hand' became top of the pops in 1964 and they dominated the charts for season upon season. The hysterical adulation lavished on them by the young alarmed both the elderly and the police, whose task it was to keep control at their concerts, but the persona they projected of clean and amiable, if mop-headed young men was in fact more beneficial than harmful.

It was a period in which to be young was automatically to possess certain virtues and the establishment – a name for the traditional ruling elite which came into vogue at this time – was assumed to deserve contempt and mockery. *Beyond the Fringe* set a theatrical fashion for satire, which was extended to television with the lively and iconoclastic *That Was The Week That Was*. John Freeman pioneered a new form of television interviewing – abrasive, penetrating, and with little respect for the values of the older generation – and the same elements flavoured the BBC's slick, irreverent, magazine-type programme *Tonight*.

In 1962 a group of these clever young men launched an enterprise that was to prosper beyond even their

In 1963 a group of young musicians from Liverpool broke through into the full flowering of a talent that was to sweep the world. They had great ability, charm and capacity for hard work, but more than any of these they had the good luck to coincide with a shift in popular taste which they both initiated and profited by.

Over-enthusiastic fans at a showing of the rock-and-roll film Rock Around the Clock *cause havoc in a cinema in Burnley, Lancashire, and incur the wrath of the manager. £150 worth of damage was done – vandal techniques have evidently improved since then.*

The twist arrived from Paris in 1961 – 'the wackiest, gayest dance since the Charleston' wrote a contemporary apologist. This photograph was taken at the Satire Club, run by Lord Ulick Browne.

Frenetic dances were part of the age dubbed the 'swinging sixties' by the Press. It was a period in which to be young was automatically to possess certain virtues, and the establishment was assumed to deserve contempt.

Satire became fashionable, notably in television's lively and iconoclastic That Was The Week That Was. *David Frost is squatting on the studio floor, in front of a group that contains Lance Percival, Roy Kinnear, Millicent Martin and, behind Millicent, William Rushton.*

The Beatles were more popular, more famous and made more money than any other group of musicians in recorded (or recording) history. One euphoric critic of some repute compared their creative skills to that of Beethoven.

expectations. *Private Eye* was set up to report the news that no one else dared mention and to jeer at the shibboleths that everybody else held sacred. Its appearance was cheap, its content often still more so, yet it unearthed much scandal that would not otherwise have been exposed, and made people laugh. Within a year its circulation was over 30,000 and it was soon as widely read as the *Economist*, *Spectator* and *New Statesman* put together. The more conventional press meanwhile fought hard to retain its readers; in 1962 the *Sunday Times* introduced the first colour supplement and 'investigative reporting' took on a new *réclame* as journalists turned every stone for something that they could fearlessly expose.

Television completed its conquest of the nation. By 1964 there were 12.6 million licence holders, 30 per cent of all families owned a set. More watched ITV than the BBC and the introduction of BBC2 in 1964, avowedly to cater for minority interests, did nothing to redress the balance. In 1960 Granada showed the first episode of an unpretentious serial set in a provincial city; *Coronation Street* was quickly to become and to remain the most popular programme in the British Isles. The advertisers relished this new medium and paid highly for a chance to exploit it. A 'licence to print money' was how Roy Thomson somewhat unwarily described the television franchise, and huge fortunes were made by those who succeeded in this new industry.

The cinema lost what television gained. Over 800 cinemas closed between 1954 and 1959, and though the pace slackened after that, the fall in attendances continued inexorably, by 20 per cent in 1959 and another 20 per cent in 1960. Good films were still made, notably *The Loneliness of the Long Distance Runner* and *Saturday Night and Sunday Morning*, and relatively low-budget and undemanding productions like the 'Carry On . . .' series did well, but the commercial successes tended to be spectacular creations which benefited from the larger screen – *Lawrence of Arabia* or the James Bond films, which started in 1962 with *Dr No*. Spectaculars were a risky and expensive business, however. *Antony and Cleopatra*, with Richard Burton and Elizabeth Taylor, proved a costly failure, celebrated mainly for launching the stormy romance that rivalled *Coronation Street* in its popularity and, almost, longevity.

The traditional theatre, too, was under attack. The Gilbert and Sullivan copyrights ran out in 1961 and half a million devotees petitioned parliament that they might be extended so as to protect the sacred texts from

Coronation Street was first shown in 1960 and to the surprise of everyone soon established itself as the most popular television programme in the British Isles. This it has remained, though few indeed of the original cast remain, here seen sheltering in a mission hall after a gas main has fractured.

desecration. They failed, and desecration duly followed, many felt to the considerable advantage of the operas. The following year the Crazy Gang appeared for the last time together. On the credit side the English Stage Company of the Royal Court and Theatre Workshop at Stratford-by-Bow produced original and often exciting work. The Royal Court made Beckett and Ionesco familiar if not always popular, while Shelagh Delaney's *A Taste of Honey* and Brendan Behan's *The Hostage* both made their way from Theatre Workshop to the West End. In 1959 the Mermaid became the first theatre to open in the City of London for 300 years, and four years later the National Theatre Company, directed by Laurence Olivier, opened at the Old Vic until such times as it could move to its permanent home on the South Bank.

Britain was being pulled down and built up again at hectic speed. What was to become an intolerably protracted saga began in 1959 when a plan was presented for the redevelopment of Piccadilly Circus, to be dominated by a monster tower 165 feet high, with a large, blank wall for illuminated advertisements. The project met with angry opposition and was the first of many similar designs to find its way to the wastepaper basket. But other tall buildings began to proliferate: New

Ian Fleming's hero, James Bond, was translated to the screen with spectacular success. Here Sean Connery portrays him in the first of what was to be a vastly profitable series, Dr No, *with Ursula Andress as his nubile girlfriend.*

Antony and Cleopatra, *made in Rome and starring Richard Burton and Elizabeth Taylor, proved a disastrous failure but it launched a protracted romance between the leading players that earned them notoriety never dreamt of by the characters they portrayed.*

Tower blocks began to sprout in most of the larger cities. Their clean-cut lines and the wide open spaces that surrounded them seemed to offer an attractive alternative to the decayed houses that are seen in this view of Sheffield. The snags soon revealed themselves.

The stately home industry began to thrive in the 1950s. Though not the first to open to the public, the Duke of Devonshire's palace of Chatsworth led the way. Some of the 264,000 visitors that went there in 1955 are here seen strolling in front of the East façade.

The rebuilt Coventry Cathedral, designed by Basil Spence, was consecrated in May 1962. This photograph shows the East wall, dominated by Graham Sutherland's great tapestry.

Zealand House in the Haymarket and the Vickers building in Millbank in 1961, the Hilton hotel in Park Lane in 1963, and loftiest of all, the Post Office Tower in 1964. These were all in London, but residential tower blocks began to sprout in many of the larger cities. To the planners they seemed to offer cheap and attractive housing units surrounded by open spaces in which cars could park and children play; the snags only revealed themselves when the towers were built and in use. The pace of building on the outskirts of the larger towns and cities meant that vast fortunes were made by developers, speculators and lucky landowners.

But it was not always a case of demolition and redevelopment. In 1958 it became clear that No.10 Downing Street and the adjoining houses were on the point of collapse. A report was commissioned, which made an overwhelming case for razing the buildings to the ground and starting again and then went on to conclude that what was needed was extensive and extremely costly refurbishment. Conservation began to be spoken of, not yet imbued with a potency that made it menacing to the developers but still an irritant in their grand, modernist designs. It was encouraged by the growth of a new industry, the opening of stately homes to the public. The Duke of Devonshire's palace of Chatsworth led the way, with 264,000 visitors in 1955. Blenheim and Woburn were not far behind, and the Duke of Bedford changed the rules of the game when he added a fun fair and a zoo to his majestic home. The results were dramatic: Woburn had almost half a million visitors in 1958. All over the British Isles aristocratic householders wondered whether they too should not be exploiting this new fashion. Meanwhile the National Trust continued on its somewhat more dignified way; Waddesdon and Hardwick Hall were two of the greater houses added to their collection.

Organised religion fared no better than it had in the previous decades. A poll in 1958 showed that 79 per cent of the adult population believed it was possible to be a good Christian without ever going to church; only 41 per cent accepted the existence of a personal God, while almost three-quarters 'regarded the Christian religion as a good thing provided it did not interfere with their private lives.' The church itself showed signs of wear and tear; by 1962 the average age of the clergy was fifty-three and there was a shortfall of 7,000 priests. The rebuilt Coventry Cathedral was consecrated the same year, however, and in one sense at least seemed very much alive, being visited by two million sightseers in the first twelve months.

The British public was as much obsessed with sport as ever, and had still less athletic triumphs to celebrate. It was in 1953 that English football lost its proudest record when the national team was for the first time beaten on its own soil – by Hungary at Wembley. The result plunged every football follower into mourning, and the grief took on a sharper edge five years later when England's most successful and favourite team, Manchester United, was destroyed in an air crash near Munich. The captain and six other players were killed

A vertiginous view of the Post Office Tower, then in the final stages of completion and opened to the public in 1964. The revolving restaurant, with its astonishing view of London, was to be damaged by an IRA bomb, but the structure of the tower was unaffected.

In 1953 an English football team for the first time lost on English soil, beaten by Hungary at Wembley.
Here the English goalkeeper, Merrick, is bypassed to give the Hungarians their fourth goal.

British football suffered a far sadder blow five years later in 1958 when England's favourite
and most successful team, Manchester United, was aboard an aircraft that crashed near
Munich airport. The captain and six other players died in the disaster.

in the disaster. Cricket offered moments of glory, as in 1956 when England defeated Australia by four matches to one and Laker took an astonishing nineteen wickets for ninety runs in the fourth Test; but the overall picture was not one of spectacular success – a more typical year being 1964 in which nine out of ten Test matches were drawn and the tenth – also against Australia – lost. Wimbledon produced a brief satisfaction when, in 1961, two English girls – Angela Mortimer and Christine Truman – met in the final. It was the first time for forty-seven years that the foreign challenge had been so comprehensively beaten off and it was not to be repeated – nor did Britain's male players ever seem likely to achieve a comparable distinction.

The frozen-food revolution was in full swing. By 1960 360 million packets of frozen fruit and vegetables were being sold, as opposed to a mere 100,000 six years before. The result was that the consumer enjoyed far greater variety throughout the year – and if some of the goodness was lost in the process it would probably have been boiled out anyway by traditional British cooking methods. For not much else had changed in the average British kitchen. Powdered coffee had begun to make

inroads into the ranks of tea drinkers but half the adult population still started the day with a cup of tea and 85 per cent drank it with their breakfast. A cooked breakfast was regularly eaten by half the men and a third of the women. A third of the population ate roast beef on Sundays. By far the most usual time for the evening meal was between six and six-thirty; two-thirds of the population still called it tea or high tea.

Despite such evidence of continuity, it sometimes seemed to the more conservative members of society that everything was being changed, often to no good purpose or positively to the disadvantage of the nation. 'With it' entered the language; if one was with it one was aware of the evolution of society and actively participating; if religious one read the New English Bible and not the fusty old seventeenth-century version; if theatrical one was *au fait* with Beckett; if operatic one had seen, or at least knew about, Britten's *Midsummer Night's Dream* and Tippett's *King Priam*. One rejoiced when the farthing was abolished in 1960 and felt no nostalgic twinge when the handsome, white five pound note went the same way the following year. If one was with it one felt it wholly proper that the tram should be withdrawn from Sheffield, the last city to

1956 was a good year for English cricket when England defeated Australia to take the Ashes. This is the team for the first test at Trent Bridge. Standing: Parks, Richardson, Cowdrey, Moss, Appleyard, Graveney and Lock; Seated: Watson, Bailey, May, Laker and Evans.

*In 1961, for the first time for forty-seven years, two English girls contested the final of the
Ladies Singles at Wimbledon. Angela Mortimer, the winner, is here shown in play against Christine Truman. The
British men players achieved no such success, nor did the girls repeat their achievement.*

The Queen shows that she is not immune from the preoccupations of any other harassed mother, trying to control her rampaging son, Prince Edward, at the Windsor Horse Show. Princess Margaret's daughter, Lady Sarah Armstrong-Jones, is the other combatant.

employ those inflexible juggernauts; one saw nothing odd about the removal of the BBC's evening news from its hallowed slot at nine pm to an equally arbitrary and apparently no more convenient ten.

But to be truly with it one had to be liberal in one's own eyes, laxly permissive in the opinion of the censorious. In 1957 the Wolfenden report was published, which recommended that homosexual acts between consenting adults in private should no longer be a criminal offence. Two years later Penguin Books were allowed to publish an unexpurgated edition of *Lady Chatterley's Lover* and made a rich killing out of the sale of 1.5 million copies within a few months to a curious and usually disappointed public. Dr Fisher, the Archbishop of Canterbury, rebuked the bishop who had given witness at the preliminary prosecution under the Obscene Publications Act, but himself visited the Pope in December, 1960, a piece of liberalism which some felt still more heinous. Equally controversial had been the publication of Nabokov's blackly erotic farce *Lolita* in 1959, a book which many believed to be both more skilfully written and more shocking than Lawrence's laborious exercise in sexual honesty.

Gambling was a feature of the age. There was gambling organised by the government, made possible by the introduction of premium bonds. ERNIE made the first draw in June 1957, the maximum prize was £1,000. Then there was bingo, a new gambling craze based on the old-fashioned housey-housey which at least provided a use for some of the redundant cinemas. But such novelties were as nothing compared with the time-honoured ways of losing money, above all on horse racing, the dogs and the pools. Something approaching £1,000 million changed hands as a result of betting and gambling in 1961, twice what it had been even a few years before.

No wonder, said the moralist, that such excesses were accompanied by a sharp increase in violence. The misbehaviour of football crowds was a relatively well-established phenomenon, but for them to destroy the trains that took them to their matches was something new. In 1961 nine out of ten carriages were wrecked in a train returning from Llanelli. It had been a 'moving den of hooliganism' said the magistrate bitterly. Juvenile delinquents were responsible. It was all the fault of their unwonted security and prosperity, he declared.

One of the last trams to run in England is here seen in action with Sheffield Town Hall in the background.

D.H. Lawrence's turgid and singularly an aphrodisiac novel Lady Chatterley's Lover *was first published in its unexpurgated version on 10 November 1960 after a protracted and entertaining trial. Here office workers queue to buy it in their lunch hour.*

Gambling seemed more popular every year. Bingo took over at many of the now unwanted cinemas. Here 900 take part in a bingo session at the former Trocadero cinema at the Elephant and Castle in South London.

Dr Geoffrey Fisher, the Archbishop of Canterbury, chose a dinner at the Mansion House held in connection with a YMCA appeal to repine at the delinquency of modern youth and the failure of parents to bring up their children under proper control.

'Mods and rockers' – a target for the Archbishop's criticisms – indulged in tumultuous battles at several of Britain's coastal resorts in the summer of 1964. A youth is dragged from the beach at Brighton, appearing notably unconcerned by his predicament.

The great train robbery in 1963 attracted vast popular attention and earned unexpected dividends for the owners of Leatherslade farm, where the robbers hid out. At 2/6d (12.5p) a time entrance money, the farm did a merry trade.

Coloured immigration began to reap a crop of violence. In 1958 a mob of 5,000 negro-baiting rioters stormed through London's Notting Hill armed with stones, home-made bombs and knives. The rioting went on into the early morning and many arrests were made.

Hostility to the coloured immigrant was by no means the only or even the most common reaction. The other side of the coin is shown at Waterloo station, where a group of London students gather to welcome the new arrivals.

The Queen inspects her corps of Beefeaters, or Bodyguard of Yeoman of the Guard, in the garden of Buckingham Palace.

The explanation would have been more convincing if similar antics by West Indian youths a decade or so later were not attributed to their insecurity and poverty. In 1964 it was the turn of the mods and rockers, gangs of loutish youths who dressed in an *outré* form of tribal uniform and fought their wars at the seaside resorts of Britain, to the dismay of the more respectable citizenry.

The ending of National Service in 1964 would make things still worse, predicted the pessimists. Others saw a correlation between the growth in juvenile delinquency and the decline in the number of dogs – only 2.5 million in 1957 against four million at the turn of the century. The cat population, observed the canine champions balefully, had remained constant or risen. Certainly youth, with money in its pockets and time on its hands, was likely to make mischief and accounted for much of the petty theft and pointless vandalism that afflicted the country. How many of the three-quarter of a million indictable offences committed in the United Kingdom in 1961 could be attributed to teenagers is more debatable. It is unlikely that they could claim credit for the theft of Goya's portrait of the Duke of Wellington from the National Gallery, or for the great train robbery of two years later. In this spectacular crime the Glasgow-London mail train was ambushed and £2.5 million stolen. By the end of the year eighteen people had been charged; the skilled organisation and daring of the enterprise won much admiration and, but for the violence used on the guard, the criminals would have found themselves public heroes.

There were many eager to link the rise in the crime rate with growth in coloured immigration. In the mid 1950s, when jobs were scarce, immigration had slowed up, but when the British economy boomed, so did the numbers of those coming from abroad to share in the new prosperity. Fear of controls on entry increased the rush and so made controls more necessary. When the Immigration Act of 1962 removed the automatic right of entry of Commonwealth citizens, coloured immigration was running at 136,000 a year and there were already 172,000 West Indians, 80,000 Indians and 25,000 Pakistanis in the country. It was only 0.7 per cent of the population, but ten years earlier it had been 0.2 per cent. The sudden flow made assimilation difficult and led to sporadic violence. 'Nigger-bashing' became a favourite sport of the Teddy boys – progenitors of the mods and rockers – and there were outbreaks of racial violence in Nottingham and Notting Hill where many of the newcomers had ensconced themselves. But it was not only violence the immigrants had to endure. A property racketeer, Peter Rachman, lent his name to the language and 'Rachmanism' became a byword for the exploitation of coloured city-dwellers, crowded into slum tenements and made to pay high rents or indulge in crime and prostitution.

The property racketeer Peter Rachman had the dubious honour of adding a new word to the British language. One aspect of 'Rachmanism' is here shown when coloured residents are evicted from their home – most probably one small and squalid room – in London's Maida Vale.

Increasing unemployment was one of the factors that led to popular disenchantment with Macmillan's government. A group of youths march down Oxford Street in protest against the lack of jobs. They seem to have sensibly decided to have some fun at the same time.

COLOURED immigration was only one of Macmillan's worries in the early 1960s. It was becoming progressively more difficult to conceal the fact that economically Britain was lagging far behind its rivals. By 1957 the 26 per cent of the world market in manufactured goods that Britain had secured had dropped to 20 per cent; every year now saw a further decline, to the benefit particularly of Germany and Japan. In aeronautics and in the provision of nuclear power Britain's lead had been eroded. Unemployment was mounting. An announcement of the government's plan to abolish retail price maintenance forfeited the sympathy of many of the Tories' traditional supporters. The white-collar workers were irritated by the pay-pause which had cut down their lead over the less well qualified. In March 1962 a Conservative majority of nearly 15,000 at Orpington was turned into a Liberal majority of 7,800. It was one of the most shattering defeats in a by-election that a post-war government had experienced. A ferocious purge in the autumn of 1962, in which Macmillan dismissed seven out of his twenty-one senior ministers including the lord chancellor, the chancellor of the exchequer and the minister of defence, failed to reverse the tide. The only question seemed to be whether the Liberals could turn Orpington into a national crusade that would leave them as the chief party of opposition.

Early in 1963 Hugh Gaitskell died. After an embit-tered battle Harold Wilson defeated the right-wing George Brown as the new leader of the Labour party. He was a lesser man than his predecessor but a far more formidable politician. It was now sure that any misfortune that overtook Macmillan's government would be exploited to the full.

Misfortunes came thick and fast. In the summer of 1963 the British public was entertained by one of the most spectacular scandals in high life ever to reach the papers. The action centred around Lord Astor's splendid home, Cliveden, perched high above the Thames. The *dramatis personae* included the secretary of state for war, John Profumo; Stephen Ward, an osteopath with a profitable sideline as society pimp; Captain Ivanov, the Russian naval attaché; Christine Keeler and Mandy Rice-Davies, two girls of slender reputation, the first of great beauty, the second a fount of raucous and refreshing wit. Macmillan had been assured by Profumo that he had not had an affair with Miss Keeler. The prime minister had believed him, and had been made to look a fool for his pains. In retrospect it seems that he deserved sympathy and some respect rather than rebukes for his credulity, but at the time the stench of scandal seemed to permeate the whole administration and Macmillan left the impression that he had been naive and did not know what was going on. The country as well as the party was losing confidence in his leadership – the first being damaging to a Tory leader,

In spite of the growing affluence of most of the country there was still much poverty to be found. This scene in a slum tenement in Oldham, Lancashire, could have been repeated in many places (though one suspects the child's face was dirtied specially for the occasion).

The government experienced a crushing setback at Orpington in March 1962 when a Tory majority of 15,000 was turned into a Liberal majority of 7,800. A triumphant Eric Lubbock proclaims his victory.

The government was dogged by scandals, none more sensational than the 'Profumo affair' which for months claimed the headlines in the summer of 1963. Here are the two women at the heart of the affair; the ebullient and irreverent Mandy Rice-Davies and the lustrously beautiful Christine Keeler.

the second disastrous. When in June 1963 Philby was identified as the 'third man' who had warned Burgess and Maclean of their impending arrest and it was discovered that he was now snugly in Russia, Macmillan's reputation suffered a further blow. It was he who had formally exonerated Philby in 1955. There had been another sensational spy trial only two years before, after which George Blake had been sentenced to forty-two years' imprisonment. It seemed security under the Conservatives had ceased to exist.

A politician as deft as Macmillan might well have retrieved a situation which was parlous but not impossible. Shortly before the Tory party conference in October 1963, however, he retreated to hospital for a prostate operation. Tired and ill, he decided to take the chance to resign gracefully. The succession was wide open and for the first time in many years it seemed that the royal prerogative to appoint a prime minister might be more than the appending of a rubber stamp to a decision that had been made elsewhere. The obvious candidates were R.A.Butler, by far the most senior of the contenders and the hero of most of the parliamentary party; Lord Hailsham, the popular favourite who was said also to be preferred by Macmillan, and Reginald Maudling, who had little support and soon

At much the same time Harold Philby was identified as the 'third' man who had given Burgess and Maclean a chance to flee the country. The revelation was particularly damaging to Harold Macmillan, who had formally exonerated Philby some years before.

When Macmillan retired as prime minister in October 1963, the decision to appoint Alec Douglas-Home, formerly the Earl of Home, as his successor caused great surprise and some resentment. Home quickly called a general election, which he lost. Here he addresses an election audience in his constituency.

retired from the fight. Butler was distrusted by the party hierarchy, who found him devious and unpredictable; Hailsham was viewed with some reserve by his cabinet colleagues, who doubted his judgment and thought he had made a fool of himself on television. Macmillan produced, as from a hat, the man whom probably he had envisaged as his successor from the start: the Earl of Home. When the Queen visited her prime minister in hospital she was advised to invite Lord Home to try to form a government.

The decision, reached in private conclave, to put forward an outsider from the House of Lords, caused some dismay in the Conservative party. Iain Macleod and Enoch Powell resigned from the government; others grumbled, but Hailsham and Butler were not the men to revolt against their monarch's nomination. Alec Douglas-Home, as he was now to become on renouncing his title, emerged as prime minister. His courage, generosity and decency were unbounded, but he could never escape the image of the grouse-shooting aristocrat who worked out his economic problems with the help of a box of matches and whose cadaverous features on television conveyed a misleading impression of irresolution and even fatuity. He was the 14th Earl of Home, and though he might retort that his rival

was presumably the 14th Mr Wilson, the latter's combination of home-spun wisdom with ostentatious mastery of the new techniques and technologies, gave him a vast advantage with the electorate.

Douglas-Home's brief reign was dominated by the forthcoming election. It was marked by the last appearance in the House of Commons of Winston Churchill on 27 July 1964. An all-party motion was passed expressing the House's 'unbounded admiration and gratitude for his services to Parliament, to the nation and to the world'. It was almost the only moment of goodwill in an embittered session. The government were more successful at winning back popular support than at first seemed likely, but they could not overcome the conviction of the British people that after thirteen years of Conservative rule it was time for a change. When the election came in October the Tory vote was down by nearly 1.8 million; the Labour vote virtually unchanged, the Liberals, by dint of fighting 150 more seats than at the previous election, gained some 1.5 million votes. The result in seats was, as usual, less satisfying to the unlucky third party; Labour won 317 seats, the Tories 303 and the Liberals a miserable nine. It was close but Labour had clearly gained the day and Mr Wilson was prime minister.

Alec Douglas-Home speaking again in his brief reign, this time in Kent, but the picture is dominated by the poster supporting his adversary Harold Wilson. The British electorate was convinced that after thirteen years of Conservative rule it was time for a change. Labour won 317 seats against the Tories' 303 and a miserable nine for the Liberals. Mr Wilson became prime minister.

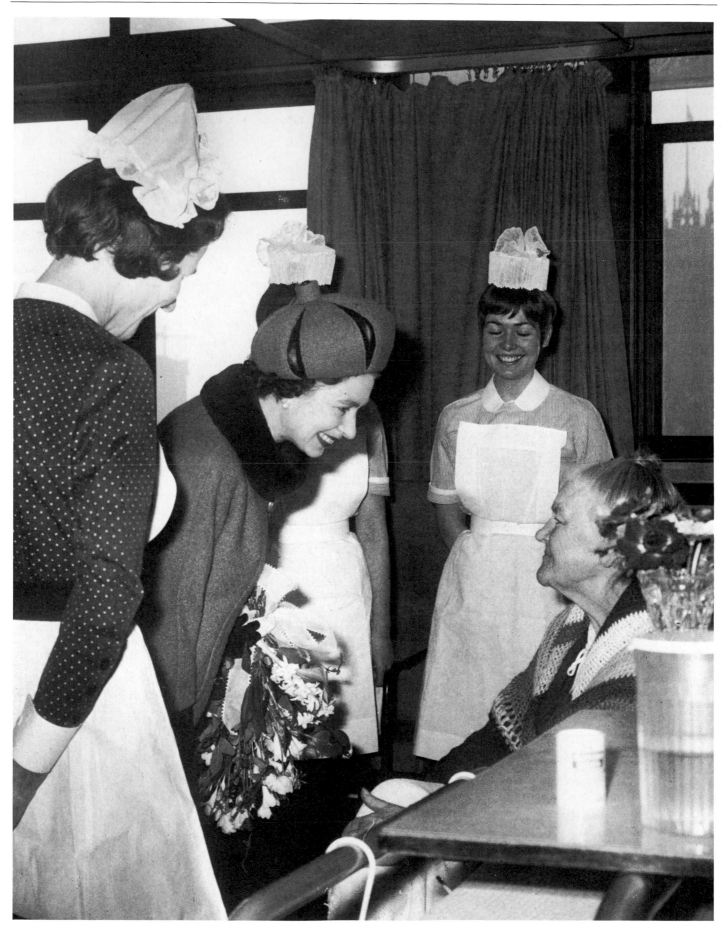

*On 28 February 1968 the Queen opened the £60,000 Dimbleby Laboratory at St Thomas'
Hospital in south-east London. During her tour of the wards, she paused to talk with 83-year-
old Mrs Mary Hearn.*

Chapter Seven

The Years of Uncertainty

1964 to 1976

ON THE FIRST of January 1973 Britain formally became a member of the European Community. It was one of the most momentous events of British history. Viewed through the telescope of history the years immediately before it will seem a period of preparation for the climactic moment, the years after a period of adjustment. Harold Wilson would hardly have thought as much in 1964. Since Macmillan had favoured entry, the Labour leader had felt bound to be sceptical about the project's merits. He had no intention of risking a second rebuff. His views were soon to change, but when he came to power plans for British entry into the Common Market were in the pending tray, perhaps even the wastepaper basket.

Wilson had won the election as the antithesis of everything that Douglas-Home was supposed to stand for: he was professional, incisive, an authority on economics, at ease with the modern world. The new technology was his particular delight. He saw it as his destiny to drag Britain into the 1970s. He set up the Fulton committee to reform the civil service, which he believed to be ossified and dominated by amateurs. The committee duly recommended drastic reforms, but by the time it reported the prime minister had other things on his mind and little was achieved. He set up a brand new ministry of economic affairs under George Brown to manage the country's return to prosperity, but it had little idea what to do or how to do it, and it too came to nothing. However, something was saved for progress; in 1965 he awarded the Beatles MBEs in the Birthday honours' list; a gesture that was felt by his supporters to be bold, classless and admirably modern.

The 1970s saw the development of new technology. The Anglo-French supersonic airliner, Concorde, was developed by the British Aircraft Corporation at Fulton in Bristol. Here the British prototype makes her maiden flight.

In the 1965 Birthday honours' list the Beatles were awarded MBEs. Wilson's admirers considered this an imaginative and admirably modern gesture; others did not and some holders of the honour returned it to the Palace.

When the Beatles paraded at Buckingham Palace to receive their decorations a hysterical mob of fans besieged the gates and the police had the greatest difficulty in holding them at bay and keeping the entrance open.

Harold Wilson, Britain's new prime minister, leaves his home at Southway, Hampstead on 19 October, 1964 for his first working day in his new job. Behind him Mrs Wilson closes the door.

George Brown, Labour deputy leader, was to prove one of the most talented yet tempestuous members of the new administration. Here he is opening the National Dairy Festival in June 1964.

Winston Churchill died in January 1965. The state funeral in St Paul's Cathedral was attended among others by General de Gaulle. He stands, in the centre of the picture, beside the Grand Duke Jean of Luxembourg. In front stand Prince Michael of Kent, Princess Marina and the Duke of Kent.

Douglas-Home, meanwhile, retired gracefully from the leadership of the Conservative party, having first set up a new system for election by ballot which would avoid involving the Queen in the embarrassment of having to fish around for advice on whom to nominate. The party was resolved to look for a new man, and one who was not in the traditional image of a Tory grandee. They found him in Edward Heath, solidly middle-class, lacking in patrician graces, formidably accomplished and yet clumsy, almost uncouth. A few months after he took over the party his predecessor, Winston Churchill, died. 'The greatest heart in England ceased to beat,' proclaimed Harold Macmillan grandiloquently, He adopted Churchill's own words for an epitaph: 'In war, resolution; in defeat, defiance; in victory, magnanimity; in peace, goodwill.' Sir Winston lay in state in Westminster Hall from 27 January 1965 till his state funeral three days later. A multitude came to pay their last respects; the queue in bitterly cold weather, stretched over the Thames and far down the south bank. More than twenty-five million people, half the population, watched the funeral on television.

With his tiny majority, Wilson found himself hard-pressed to keep both right and left wings in order. He introduced a bill to renationalise steel, largely to placate the left, and found himself confronted with the revolt of Woodrow Wyatt and Desmond Donnelly on his right. In the event it was 1967, after his position had been strengthened by a further election, before the thirteen largest steel companies were taken back into public ownership.

But it was Rhodesia which proved the most vexatious problem. Ian Smith refused to accept the five principles which the British insisted must be the basis for a grant of independence, and on 11 November 1965 the Rhodesians went it alone, making a unilateral declaration of independence. Economic sanctions, including an oil embargo, were applied and at Lagos the following year Wilson claimed that the rebellion would be ended 'in a matter of weeks rather than months'. He reckoned without Rhodesian ingenuity and efficacious help from the South Africans. Spasmodic negotiations aboard a British warship at Gibraltar failed to break the deadlock and in 1970 Rhodesia declared itself a republic. Diplomatic representation was withdrawn by every country except

The Reverend Ian Paisley became the most powerful Protestant voice in Northern Ireland. He is addressing a meeting in the Shankill Road area of Belfast, a stronghold of his followers.

South Africa and Portugal and the world settled down while economic pressure from without and black resistance from within gradually eroded the capacity of the illegal government to run the country.

At the same Lagos conference as Wilson had made his unwise boast about Rhodesia, it was unanimously agreed to set up a Commonwealth secretariat in London. Queen Mary's old home, Marlborough House, was offered as a headquarters. But the strengthening of Commonwealth ties could not conceal the fact that Britain's role as a world power was almost over. In 1967 the government decided to halve its establishments east of Suez and to withdraw completely within a few years. All that remained of the Empire were a few scattered and often embarrassing relics. In 1968 there were great ructions over reports that the government planned to hand over the Falkland Islands to Argentina and a pledge was extracted that sovereignty would never be surrendered without the consent of the inhabitants. The following year a farcical 'invasion' of the West Indies island of Anguilla involved 250 troops and thirty-five policemen, who contrived to restore order and establish stable government.

Bernadette Devlin, the nearest the Northern Irish Catholics could get to Joan of Arc, was elected to the House of Commons when only twenty-two and is here shown arriving in April 1969 to make her maiden speech – a characteristically intemperate but impressive debut.

Violence mounted in Ireland as extremists took control on both sides. Here, in 1969, a building is set alight by a Londonderry mob. Firemen were stoned by the crowd.

That the people felt the Labour government had on the whole done a good job with inadequate means was shown in 1966 when a general election increased the nominal majority of one to a highly respectable ninety-seven. The only cause for government regret was that the turnout was the lowest since the war, a fact which reflected more on the inability of the Tories to attract voters than the potency of Labour policies in deterring them.

Wilson's second tour in office was dominated by economic troubles exacerbated by his reluctance to devalue the pound. By the time devaluation was forced upon him at the end of 1967, crippling external debts had been accumulated and industrial expansion at home held back by deflationary measures. The value of the pound was then cut by 14 per cent to $2.40 – the hitherto unimaginable spectre of a $2 pound seemed a real if still remote possibility. 'This does not mean that the pound in your pocket . . . has been devalued,' said Wilson hopefully – another of those glibly optimistic prophecies to which the prime minister was prone, and which usually rebounded against him.

The government's other main initiative proved equally ill-fated. Alarmed by the industrial anarchy which the trade unions were permitting to exist, Barbara Castle introduced a white paper called 'In Place of

On 11 February 1974 Prime Minister Heath got his General Election campaign under way by introducing the Conservative party manifesto Firm Action for a Fair Britain.

Strife' which envisaged measures to curb unofficial strikes, such as an obligatory conciliation period and a compulsory ballot before a strike could be called. Appalled by this attempt to curb the British shop-steward's democratic right to destroy his country, the unions rallied in opposition, with the home secretary, James Callaghan, supporting them within the cabinet. Wilson and Mrs Castle abandoned their project in favour of a voluntary agreement – a measure of which the voluntary nature was more evident than the agreement.

Ireland provided nothing to cheer the general gloom. By 1970 extremists were taking control on both sides. The dubiously reverend Ian Paisley was by now the most powerful Protestant voice in the North while the IRA had split into two factions: one socialist, working through political means; the other, the provisionals, dedicated to violence. As the killings grew more frequent and the Northern Irish government weaker, more troops were moved in. It made no difference whether a Tory or a Labour government was in power in Westminster; in Ireland things grew inexorably worse. On 30 January 1972 – Bloody Sunday – thirteen people were killed during an illegal march on Londonderry. The British Embassy in Dublin was burnt down in retaliation while in the House of Commons Bernadette Devlin – the nearest thing the Northern Ireland Catholics could come to a home-grown version of Joan of Arc – pulled Reginald Maudling's hair and called him a 'bloody hypocrite'. In desperation the Northern Irish government was suspended and direct rule from Westminster imposed. A brief truce followed but soon the violence resumed, with Britain as an additional target. There were car bombs outside the Old Bailey and Scotland Yard, bombs in Westminster Hall and the Tower, bombs in Birmingham that killed twenty-one, and wounded 170. When the British ambassador was murdered in Dublin in 1976, it was the culmination to a campaign of terrorist atrocity that had achieved nothing save to cause untold human misery.

In spite of all setbacks, Wilson went to the country in June 1970 with some confidence. Temporarily at least devaluation seemed to have worked; a record budgetary surplus had been recorded. But the country had not forgiven the government's tergiversation over devaluation, nor its failure to impose order on the unions. Aided by some bad trade figures which discouraged Labour voters at the last moment, the Tories swept back with a majority of thirty-seven. The Liberals fared worst, losing only 10 per cent of their popular vote yet ending up with half the seats they had held before. Edward Heath was the new prime minister.

THE QUEEN saw Harold Wilson depart with genuine regret. On his first appearance as prime minister at Buckingham Palace he had refused to wear a long coat but compromised on striped pants and a short black jacket. The Queen was unperturbed by this solecism and the two got on famously. One of the advantages of a

*The Prince of Wales as an undergraduate at Trinity College, Cambridge. The royal family felt it
necessary to explain why a new, scientifically oriented provincial university had not been chosen
instead of this establishment institution.*

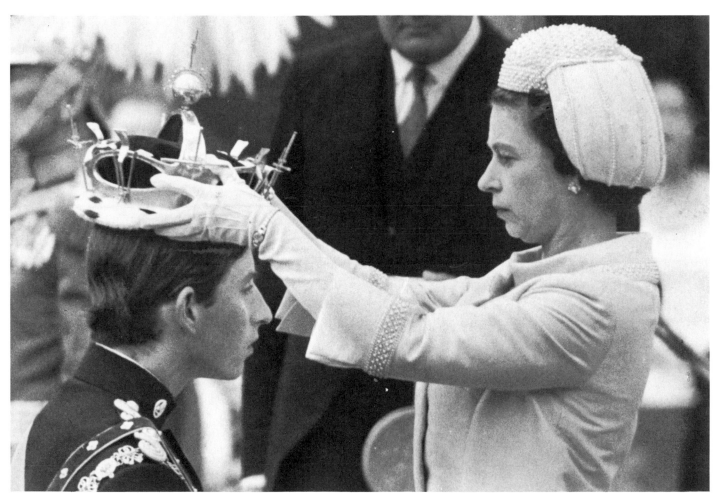

*The investiture of the Prince of Wales in Caernarvon Castle. Previously the Prince had spent a
term at Aberystwyth University, learning Welsh. The Welsh nationalists were not appeased and
the ceremony took place against a backcloth of spasmodic and usually ill-executed violence.*

hereditary monarch as opposed to an elected president as formal head of state is that the first can be genuinely above party. The Queen judged her ministers by what they were and what they wanted to do rather than by any party label. She enjoyed Wilson's company and thought him unlikely to do anything silly – that he was a Socialist rather than a Conservative was immaterial.

The important thing about the monarchy, said Prince Philip in Canada, was that 'if at any stage the people feel that it has no further part to play, then for goodness sake let's end the thing on amicable terms without having a row about it'. Wilson, for one, had no doubt the monarchy still had a part to play, but the Queen did not need him to tell her that the nature of the role required much thought and careful definition and that such rethinking was certainly no less urgent under a Labour than under a Tory government. The royal family had to continue to modernise itself, though as little as possible at the cost of dignity and pageantry. It was a difficult line to follow.

Prince Charles's future was one preoccupation. Harold Wilson was one of the group of sages who conferred upon the possibilities – the Archbishop of Canterbury and Lord Mountbatten being among the others. When the decision was announced to send him to Trinity College, Cambridge, the Duke of Edinburgh

felt it necessary to explain why a new, scientifically-oriented provincial university had not been chosen. Proximity to Sandringham and family connections were given as the slightly unconvincing reasons. The Prince did however spend a term at Aberystwyth learning Welsh before he was invested as Prince of Wales in Caernarvon Castle in 1969. The ceremony, picturesquely stage-managed in television-traditional style, took place against a backcloth of Welsh nationalist violence. On the morning of the investiture two terrorists blew themselves up while fixing a bomb to a bridge.

From every point of view it seemed to the Queen that state occasions of this kind were the better for being rarities. Too many circuses sate the palate and involve too much expenditure. It was decided that the celebrations of the Queen's silver wedding and the wedding of Princess Anne to Captain Mark Phillips in November 1973 should be family affairs, to be relatively low key. The royal family did not wish to seek greater notoriety than was anyway thrust upon it. However, nothing could stop Princess Anne hitting the headlines the next year when a madman tried to kidnap her from her car in the Mall and fired six shots, wounding her bodyguard and others. 'If the man had succeeded in abducting Anne, she'd have given him the hell of a time while in captivity,' remarked her father proudly.

Husband and wife exchange glances at the end of a thanksgiving service at Westminster Abbey – one of the many public engagements undertaken to celebrate their silver wedding anniversary on 20 November 1972.

On 14 November 1973 Princess Anne married Captain Mark Phillips in Westminster Abbey.
The wedding was treated as a fairly low-key family affair but was still celebrated with
considerable grandeur. Lady Sarah Armstrong-Jones is the bridesmaid taking charge of the
bouquet and Prince Edward is the page nearest to the camera.

So far as was compatible with security – or even further in the opinion of some of her advisers – the Queen was determined to get as close to as many of her subjects as was possible. 'I need to be seen to be believed in,' she once observed. The first royal walk-about took place in New Zealand in 1970; then she did the same in Coventry the following month and the concept soon became accepted as a commonplace. But it was on television that the royal family were seen most widely and most intimately by their subjects. It began in 1966 with a series on 'The Royal Palaces of Britain', presented by Kenneth Clark. The films were a success, and were followed three years later by *The Royal Family*. For seventy-five days on 172 locations the everyday life of the Queen and her close relations was followed by the cameras. Forty-three hours of film were cut to 110 minutes. The result was, not surprisingly, favourable to the royal family – 'a large-scale commercial', said William Hamilton, arch-critic of the monarchy. It was also enormously popular. More than 68 per cent of the population watched the film and found to their surprise that the Queen and her family were human, relaxed, industrious and often remarkably funny. Their view of the Queen was changed radically by what they saw. Polls showed that only 27 per cent of the population had thought her outspoken before they saw the film; afterwards the figure rose to 42 per cent; 49 per cent had thought her powerful before, 64 per cent after; 69 per cent had believed her in touch with what was going on; the film increased the figure to 81 per cent.

William Hamilton had discovered that by far the largest number who wrote to applaud his criticism of the monarchy based their views on its expensiveness or the personal extravagance of its members. Every time larger sums had to be voted to meet the rising costs an outcry arose and the number of republicans grew perceptibly if slightly. In 1969 the Duke of Edinburgh was interviewed on American television and stated bluntly that the royal family would 'go into the red' the following year. The civil list had not been increased since the accession. On a following programme he remarked – only half in joke – that they might well have to move into smaller quarters. To avert so unwelcome an economy Heath in 1971 set up a select committee, as a result of whose recommendations the civil list was raised to just under £1 million. Ten years later it was more than four times as great, but by then inflation had been accepted by all concerned as an inevitable feature of British life.

On 5 June 1968 the Queen attended the centenary banquet of the Trades Union Congress at the Guildhall. She is seated between George Woodcock, the general secretary of the TUC (who seems in a minority in eschewing a dinner jacket) and Lord Wright.

On 7 September 1973 Mr Victor Feather (centre, smiling) retired as general secretary of the TUC. Joining in a rendition of 'Auld Lang Syne' are president Joseph Crawford (left) and the new general secretary Mr Len Murray.

In 1970, while on a visit to New Zealand, the Queen first mingled informally with the crowds. The idea of the royal 'walkabout' soon became a commonplace and in November 1972, after a luncheon in the Guildhall to celebrate their silver wedding, she and the Duke of Edinburgh strolled among the crowd in the City of London.

British industry was in trouble in the early 1970s. British Steel was a particular cause for concern, as much as any part of it the great works at Ebbw Vale in Wales which is here shown with horses grazing placidly on the hillside above it.

INFLATION WAS to be one of Heath's bugbears during what was to be his unhappy period in office, and was to grow still worse after his departure. The British people had become used to a moderate annual inflation, averaging about 3 per cent per annum. This began to rise in the mid 1960s, fuelled mainly by the increased demand for raw materials which forced up prices. The countries which grew rich as a result, particularly the oil producers, fomented the process as the 1970s wore on, by spending much of their vast new revenues in the industrial west and turning an inflationary fire into a raging furnace. The worker saw his standard of living eroded by the rising cost of living and demanded wage increases that would more than compensate for his loss. Heath's administration tried to shelter behind courts of inquiry which awarded massive pay increases to dockers, dustmen, post-office workers. The Ford Motor Company, always to the fore in raising wages, offered its workers 33 per cent spread over two years. A panic-stricken attempt to impose a limit on wage and price increases did little to check the trend. An Arab-Israeli war in 1973 forced up the price of fuel and limited its supply. Both factors helped to cripple the industrial recovery which was long overdue. The age of cheap food and raw materials was over. In 1970 retail prices had risen by 6.4 per cent; by 1974 the figure reached 15.9 per cent; in 1975 it hit a terrifying 25 per cent.

Hyper-inflation, the spectre of a society in which savings could be wiped out overnight and currencies rendered meaningless, seemed a real possibility.

Heath had come to power dedicated to the revival of British industry, posing as a hard-faced businessman who believed in backing success and letting the lame ducks perish. But in the climate of the early 1970s much of British industry seemed, if not lame, then at least faltering. The crash of Rolls-Royce symbolised the problem at its starkest. As late as 1960 half the world's aircraft had been powered by Rolls-Royce engines; the firm was the brightest jewel in Britain's industrial crown. Now, helped on its way by a disastrously mis-negotiated contract for the production of engines for the American Tristar, it tottered towards bankruptcy. The government concluded that this lame duck at least must be saved and, in effect, nationalised the greater part of it. Other eminent casualties followed, and Heath's successors found themselves called upon to rescue Harland and Wolff, Ferranti, British Leyland and Burmah Oil. The public sector was rapidly aggrandised, often to the government's dismay. As with the growth of the British Empire in the eighteenth and nineteenth centuries, it seemed as if the nationalisation of British industry was going to happen piecemeal and more or less by accident.

The economic climate made it both more urgent and

In the early 1970s much of British industry seemed to be faltering: the crash of Rolls-Royce symbolised the problem at its starkest. Here workers are shown in 1969 assembling the latest model at the Crewe factory.

The Queen at the opening of the Victoria line, a long awaited extension to London's underground system. She would probably have contrived to remain almost equally unruffled if she had been doing the journey at rush-hour.

The Queen, Prince Charles and the youthful Prince Edward on the ramparts at Windsor. Prince Edward surveys the cannon with all the satisfaction of a small boy who has just discovered a particularly enjoyable toy.

The Queen takes the salute at the gates of Buckingham Palace as part of the annual ceremony of Trooping the Colour. Unlike so many royal occasions, which are dogged by rainy weather, the Trooping usually seems to fall on a warm and sunny day.

A protracted coal strike in 1972 led to almost total victory for the miners, thanks partly to the success of miners' pickets in turning away lorries from the power stations, like this one at Ferrybridge. It was largely the memory of this defeat that led to the government standing firm when the miners struck again at the end of 1973.

Victims of economic malaise and the inexorable decay of the Welsh mining industry, these unemployed miners at a Wrexham employment exchange in May 1970 provide an uncomfortable echo of the Britain of the early 1930s.

more difficult for Heath to push through the reform in industrial relations which he believed essential. Many of the features of his Industrial Relations Act were similar to those which Mrs Castle, with Wilson's backing, had tried to pass under Labour auspices, but any illusion Heath might have cherished that this would ensure him a degree of bipartisan support was quickly dispelled. The unions believed that the new act would make it more difficult for them to look after their members; they resolved to defy it to the limits of the law, and if necessary beyond, and in this attitude they were supported by the parliamentary opposition and, it sometimes seemed, condoned by the law itself. When the leaders of the dockers were on the point of ending up in jail, the court of appeal quickly found a way to quash the verdict; when five dockers were actually imprisoned for contempt of court, a strange beast called the official solicitor, hitherto unheard of or else believed extinct, was summoned from desuetude to secure their liberation.

Early in 1972 a prolonged and bitter strike had ended in almost total victory for the miners, who had held out for and secured even better terms than an anyway generous committee of enquiry had awarded them. It was perhaps the recollection of this defeat which led the government to stand firm when the miners at the end of 1973 rejected a pay offer that went to the limits of the statutory curbs. It was hardly a propitious moment to seek a battle. The oil shortage

In the winter of 1973 hospitals were hit by the industrial action of ancillary workers. At St James's Hospital in Balham, affected more than any other London hospital, a nurse adds another bag of rubbish to the already overflowing pile.

The miners' strike in 1973 led to a ban on overtime by the railwaymen and the imposition of a three-day week. Here a buyers' clerk at Liberty's department store in Regent Street works by gaslight on a day when the electricity was cut off.

Unemployment and bad labour relations were at the heart of the 1974 election campaign. This march of members of the Amalgamated Engineering Union (the AEU) was one of many which manifested working-class opposition to Heath's government. Heath went to the country on a platform of democratic government against the unions; under his leadership the Conservatives won more votes than Labour but five seats less.

For several weeks squatters occupied what had once been the palace of the Rothschild family in Piccadilly and which was standing empty awaiting demolition or a new use. One graffito not shown in this picture was the bodeful: 'We are the writing on your wall.'

that had followed the latest war in the Middle East had led to the imposition of a 50 mph limit on all roads and restrictions on the heating of buildings. The power stations were short of fuel. When the railwaymen banned overtime in support of the miners it was announced that a three-day week would be imposed on industry from the beginning of the New Year. The government and the TUC failed to find a solution and an all-out coal strike was announced for 9 February. Heath thereupon called a general election; the miners were trying to bring down an elected government, he proclaimed, and the rule of democracy must be restored.

He almost won. If he had not been unlucky with the trade figures and had not had to grapple with attacks from Enoch Powell, on the Common Market, and Campbell Adamson, director-general of the Confederation of British Industries, who somewhat surprisingly chose this moment to denounce the Industrial Relations Act, he would have been prime minister for a second tour. If he had handled the medium of television with half the dexterity of his rival, Harold Wilson, he still might have won. As it was the Conservatives won more votes than Labour but five seats less. Under its new leader, Jeremy Thorpe, the Liberal party had increased its vote to six million, more than half that of the two main parties, yet still had only fourteen seats. Heath tried to do a deal with them which would have secured the continuation of a Conservative government, but the Liberals were only prepared to sell their support in exchange for a commitment to proportional representation, which would give them a fairer share of seats in the House of Commons. This Heath would not accept – nor would Wilson, but at that point it seemed more suitable to the Liberals to support the left rather than the right. Though he survived only by the tolerance of the minority groups, Wilson was in power again.

But Heath left one monument behind him. It had not taken the Labour government long after its return to power in 1964 to conclude, first that membership of the Common Market did offer a chance of prosperity and security for Britain, and second that it was hard to see where to look elsewhere for a similar opportunity. This belated conversion was ill-rewarded, however. Wilson and George Brown toured the Continent on a mission of reconciliation, but they signally failed to win support in Paris. Before Great Britain would be acceptable to the community, ruled De Gaulle, a radical transformation of its economic and political affiliations with the rest of the world would first be necessary. When Britain put in its formal application to join, the French vetoed it.

Even De Gaulle, however, was not immortal, and with his resignation in 1969, resistance to British membership of the Common Market crumbled. Heath first established that the new French president, Georges Pompidou, was amenable to the idea of British entry, and then launched negotiations to sort out the terms. These were lengthy, tough and sometimes rancorous, but little by little even the most intractable

The Labour party found it impossible to maintain a united front on the issue of Britain's entry into Europe. Roy Jenkins for one believed it too important an issue to allow questions of party advantage to sway his judgement. Here, at the party conference at Brighton, he seems to be symbolically disassociating himself from the anti-marketeer James Callaghan.

On 28 October 1971, at the end of a marathon debate in the House of Commons, the
government had a majority of 112 in favour of its proposal that Britain should enter the
European Economic Community. Not all were gratified, as is shown by this demonstration in
Downing Street by a group of anti-marketeers.

Under its new leader, Jeremy Thorpe, here with his wife Marion
during the 1974 campaign, the Liberal party increased its popular
vote to six million and won fourteen seats. This made it possible
for Harold Wilson to form a new Labour administration.

In January 1972 Britain acceded to the Common Market and on
1 January 1973 became a member. The die was cast.

The decimalisation of the currency was anticipated with some dismay by the more conservative or elderly sections of society but in the event it passed off without too much disturbance. The children took to it like ducks to water and were soon observing the difficulties experienced by their elders with amused contempt.

A defiant slogan proclaims the boundary of the staunchly Catholic section of Londonderry. Someone with a black sense of humour has amended 'free' to 'carefree' – a piece of wit that is made to seem even sicker by the presence of the armed and apprehensive troops.

The Queen, with a cluster of small boats far beneath her, formally opens Scammonden Water near Huddersfield.

problems were solved and compromises arrived at by which Britain's peculiar responsibilities to the Commonwealth were recognised and accepted either as permanent or only gradually to be phased out. Britain acceded to the community in January 1972 and formally became a member a year later. So far as the average citizen was concerned, the effects at first were imperceptible, but it was the start of a process which was to affect almost every aspect of national life as the conventions and habits hallowed by the centuries were modified to reach harmony with similar practices on the Continent.

Since the Conservatives had negotiated the terms of entry, Labour was in honour bound to look askance at them. Wilson pledged that when he returned to power he would first renegotiate the more unacceptable items and then submit the result to a referendum. This was enough to drive Roy Jenkins and other European-minded members of the party into revolt and, in the case of Jenkins, to his resignation as deputy leader. The concessions which the new Labour government in the event won from the other members of the community were of trifling importance but gave Wilson enough to justify him in recommending to the electorate that they should support remaining in the Common Market in the referendum that was fixed for June 1975. It was the first time that the British people had ever been invited to express their views in such a way. Roy Jenkins and the Socialist marketeers worked actively with fellow enthusiasts in the Conservative party. The Labour left and Enoch Powell and his fellow-thinkers among the Tories were quite as vociferous on the other side. The result was an overwhelming victory for Europe. Every region of the British Isles except the Shetland and Western Isles, hardly major centres of population, voted to remain in the Common Market; overall there was a two to one majority in favour of acceptance: 17.4 million for, 8.5 million against. The result was so emphatic that it was hard to believe the issue was not settled for ever; and particularly memorable for reflecting almost exactly the division of votes in the House of Commons.

'The new links with Europe will not replace those with the Commonwealth,' said the Queen in her Christmas message for 1972. 'They cannot alter our historical and personal attachments with kinsmen and friends overseas. Old friends will not be lost. Britain will take her Commonwealth links into Europe with her.' It was a pious hope and not one which the history of the last fifteen years suggests has been fulfilled. The Commonwealth has survived but its ties have inevitably been weakened. Probably this would have happened anyway, but Britain's membership of the European Community has been a factor in speeding up the process. This was not by express intent. When the British voted 'yes' in the referendum they conveyed no wish to loosen the bonds of the Commonwealth but accepted that, in the last quarter of the twentieth century, Britain could no longer afford not to be part of Europe. That was a momentous decision enough.

ANYONE WHO imagined that the British would mark their membership of Europe by rapidly adapting their way of life to conform to their Continental cousins reckoned without the intensely conservative nature of these new Europeans. Enormous though the surface changes might appear, the structure of society was still surprisingly similar to what it had been thirty or even fifty years before. The richest one per cent of the population still owned a quarter of the nation's private wealth – substantially less than a decade before and vastly less than the 66 per cent of 1926, yet a long way from an egalitarian society. Ninety-six per cent of the stocks and shares belonged to five per cent of the population. Tens of thousands of families lived below the official poverty line, though a surprisingly large number of these owed their plight not to the inadequacy of their income but to their failure to claim the benefits that the state was bound to pay them.

There was continuity too in where people lived. Over three-quarters of the people born in Britain still lived

Coloured immigration was now becoming one of the most controversial of current issues. It caused problems in many unexpected areas, as for instance when legislation was introduced making it compulsory for motor-cyclists to wear crash-helmets and the Sikhs complained that this was incompatible with the rules of their religion which prescribed the wearing of a turban.

within a mile of their place of birth. The census of 1971 showed that the population had grown by 2.6 million in the last decade, an increase of 5.5 per cent, and that more than half this growth had been concentrated in London and the south-east, but the movement of population away from the north and the abandonment of the countryside were slowing down. The work force continued to shift from outmoded industries to the new sources of wealth but on the whole this was achieved without major migration. An exception was the mining industry, whose manpower was reduced from half to a quarter of a million between 1960 and 1970, with little industrial unrest but to the grave detriment of the mining areas.

Coloured immigration provided the most evident departure from the past. There were still few black or coloured faces to be seen in country villages or provincial towns, but in certain cities and areas of Greater London something close to ghettoes had been established. In 1968 an influx of Asians from Kenya began,

In April 1968 Enoch Powell took up the issue of immigration in an emotive speech in the House of Commons in which he spoke of the river Tiber 'foaming with blood'. Here, in September of the same year, he raises the question again at the party conference.

Powell's opposition to immigration won some support among the workers, as was shown when dockers and other unionists marched to Westminster a few days after his Commons speech.

The investiture of the Prince of Wales at Caernarvon Castle in 1969. The occasion was picturesquely stage-managed in television-traditional style by his uncle by marriage, the Earl of Snowdon.

For seventy-five days on 172 locations the everyday life of the Queen and her close relations was followed by the cameras for the preparation of the film The Royal Family. *Here the photographers record the Queen chatting with the Poet Laureate, Cecil Day Lewis, and Robert Graves, when the latter was presented with the Queen's Gold Medal for Poetry in 1968.*

The Notting Hill carnival, supposed to encourage 'peace and love', on several occasions ended in violence but there was much goodwill as well. Here a policeman lends his helmet to one of the celebrators.

In 1972 the first party of Ugandan Asians, banished from their homes by President Amin, was airlifted into Britain. This forlorn little group of refugees is waiting for a train at Bishop's Stortford station, Hertfordshire.

7,000 in the first three months alone. Attempts had already been made to legislate against racial discrimination and the Race Relations Act of 1968 sharply penalised any attempt to treat the new arrivals as inferior citizens when it came to housing, jobs or the supply of goods and services. At the same time the automatic right of entry was removed from those whose parents or grandparents had not been born in the United Kingdom. A voucher system limited immigration to 1,500 a year with their dependents – say 7,000 in all.

This did not satisfy Enoch Powell. In a celebrated speech in Birmingham on 20 April 1968 he spoke of Britons being 'made strangers in their own country' and declared balefully: 'Like the Roman I seem to see the River Tiber foaming with blood.' Such emotive phrases led to his dismissal from the shadow cabinet, but also won him much popular support. He received more than 100,000 letters, nearly all applauding him, and the dock-workers marched to Westminster to support his point of view. It was clear that many of the inhabitants doubted the wisdom of creating in Britain the racial tensions that were so evident in the United States. The mass flight of Asians from Uganda in 1974 increased their doubts, and economic depression accentuated the problems experienced both by the immigrants and their hosts. Unemployed, inadequately educated, and with the feeling that society was against them, many black youths turned to violence. 'Mugging' entered the vocabulary to connote robbery with violence in the streets, often directed against the elderly. It was by no means a crime confined to the immigrants, but the public often felt it was. The carnival at Notting Hill in 1976 started in fiesta and ended in ugly clashes between police and black youths.

Race was one of those issues on which almost everybody was ready to express an opinion, often intemperate. The death penalty was another. The execution of Ruth Ellis for shooting her unfaithful lover, and of Evans, for a murder which was almost certainly committed by Reginald Christie, had stirred doubts among all but the most convinced supporters of hanging. In 1957 the death penalty was restricted to poisoners or murderers of policemen and in 1965 even this was suspended for a five-year trial period. In deciding to do this, parliament was almost certainly in advance of popular feeling; even if it had not been, the particularly macabre and sadistic 'Moors Murders' and the murder of three policemen in a London street would have stirred up demands for the restoration of hanging. Undisturbed, parliament in 1970 turned suspension into permanent abolition. The sensational murder by Lord Lucan of his children's nanny in 1974, followed by his disappearance, filled the newspapers for months but had little effect on public sentiment towards the death penalty.

Another issue that stirred strong passions among the British was education. The drive towards comprehensivisation continued – vigorously while a Labour government was in power, more cautiously when the Tories

One of the most gruesome of modern murder trials was that of Myra Hindley (top, left) and her lover Ian Brady (top, right). The 'Moors Murders' involved the cold-blooded killing of children in the most macabre and sadistic circumstances.

(Above) Another celebrated murder case involved the Earl of Lucan, his wife and their nanny. Lord Lucan was accused of killing the nanny, presumably in mistake for his wife. He disappeared and has never been brought to justice, though 'sightings' of the peer have from time to time been reported. Here he is with his wife on their wedding day in November 1963.

took over, but always onwards. By 1970, 31 per cent of those receiving secondary education were at comprehensive schools. The middle classes, for the most part, deplored the damage done to the grammar schools by the process. Their particular disapproval, however, was reserved for what they felt to be the long-haired and degenerate students. The late 1960s saw an outburst of unrest in the universities and polytechnics; the students demanding better facilities, larger grants, more of a say in the organisation of their syllabuses and daily life. The London School of Economics was temporarily closed because of the disturbances; at Essex University a group of visiting MPs was forced to suspend its meeting under threat of violence.

No such troubles plagued the Open University – the University of the Air, as Wilson originally called it. Set up in 1969 in the new city of Milton Keynes, it sought by correspondence course and broadcasting to enable

The waif-like Twiggy captured the affection, first of Britain, then of the United States. Her angular gracefulness and lack of what might be called a figure was peculiarly well suited to the fashions of the day.

In January 1972 Britain acceded to the Common Market. The opposition was vociferous and indefatigable,
as this demonstrator makes clear. It was not till the referendum of June 1975 that it
was finally demonstrated that two-thirds of the population were in favour of Britain's entry.

Long-haired schoolboys and turbulent undergraduates seemed particularly rife at this period and roused the wrath of all the more conservative members of society (a group which contained many Labour supporters). A group of long-haired boys (above) is pictured outside the gates of Whitchurch High School in Cardiff after they had been sent home by the headmaster for refusing to take even a few inches off their locks. The turbulent undergraduates (top) not surprisingly are at that former heartland of radical youth, the London School of Economics.

those who had missed university to acquire degrees nonetheless. By 1971 it had 20,000 students, by 1975, 50,000. Nearly a third of these were teachers improving their qualifications, but many of the other students were drawn from the working classes. In an age of massive unemployment the service did much to maintain morale and offer a ray of hope to those who saw no future in their former occupation.

Television proved an invaluable if costly supplement to the support which sound radio gave the Open University, but the educative value of the medium was shown most vividly in the great series that were shown in the late 1960s and early 1970s: Kenneth Clark's *Civilisation*, Bronowski's *The Ascent of Man*, *The World at War*. The first of these in particular was enhanced by the introduction of colour television in 1967. This appeared just in time for Wimbledon – with the courts looking very green and the balls very white – and was at first considered an expensive luxury. Only 35,000 sets had been sold by the end of the year. Even after five years there were still fifteen million monochrome licences to 1.6 million colour, but by then few doubted that black and white television was on the way out.

Popular though programmes like *Civilisation* or even *The Forsyte Saga* might be, the highest ratings were time and again achieved by such fare as *It's a Knock Out*, the *Morecambe and Wise Show* and the *Miss World* competition. *Dad's Army* began in 1970 and *Coronation Street* continued its remorseless progress. The irreverent surrealism of *Monty Python's Flying Circus* infuriated some

and delighted more. But sound radio was not supplanted by its more flamboyant cousin; twenty-five million still listened every day for an average hour a head.

The relentless drop in cinema attendances began to level out, as the cinema adapted itself to the needs of the age. The old cathedral-like halls were broken up into nests of smaller cinemas or converted in part into restaurants, bingo halls or bowling alleys. Resolved to concentrate on lavish productions which television could not match, the cinema moguls produced a series of disaster movies: *The Towering Inferno*, *The Poseidon Adventure*, *Earthquake*, and above all the bloodthirsty exploits of an indian-rubber shark in *Jaws*. Many films lost money, but when a jackpot was hit it could still be on a spectacular scale: *Murder on the Orient Express* grossed more than any British film had done before, while *The Godfather* made $250 million – twice the takings of British cinemas in a whole year. Another expedient denied to television also did well – pornographic movies filled the halls of Soho, while softer porn – such as Marlon Brando in *Last Tango in Paris*, took £500,000 in British cinemas.

A blow for liberty, said some – for pornography, said others – was struck when the Lord Chamberlain's power to censor plays was abolished in 1968. He had been made to look slightly ridiculous three years before when he banned certain homosexual scenes in John Osborne's *A Patriot for Me*. Osborne refused to modify the material and the Royal Court Theatre turned itself

The Open University – 'The University of the Air' as Harold Wilson originally called it – was set up in 1969. It made as much use as it could afford of television. Here Professor Maxim Bruckheimer, Dean of the Mathematics Faculty, is recording a programme for future transmission.

The Queen on the lawn at Balmoral, surrounded by a covey of doting labradors with a slightly supercilious corgi in the background.

The exhibition of the treasures found in the tomb of the Egyptian monarch Tutankhamun, on loan from Cairo, proved a phenomenal success when it came to the British Museum in 1972, attracting 1.6 million visitors. Here the Queen inspects Tutankhamun's death-mask when she opened the exhibition.

Celebrated though such television programmes as Kenneth Clark's Civilisation *might justly be, the highest ratings went time and again to programmes like the* Morecambe and Wise Show.

Monty Python's Flying Circus, *with its vulgarity, wit and irreverent surrealism bemused and irritated some but delighted more. John Cleese's celebrated 'silly walks' were one of the more peculiar features of a bizarre programme.*

into a club and put on the play unexpurgated. Kenneth Tynan celebrated the victory of freedom with the highly profitable *Oh! Calcutta*, a gallimaufry of lubricious sex and dirty language. In more edifying vein Andrew Lloyd Webber and Tim Rice evangelised profitably in a series of epic musicals: *Godspell, Jesus Christ, Superstar* and *Joseph and the Amazing Technicolor Dreamcoat*.

Art throve, at least if a nation's artistic health is to be measured by the attendance at museums and galleries. The British Museum had three million visitors in 1975; the National Gallery more than two million; on 2 January 1976 attendance at the Victoria and Albert Museum was so great that the doors had to close at 3.30 pm. The Hayward Gallery on London's South Bank opened in 1965. The Tutankhamun exhibition at the British Museum in 1972 was a phenomenal success, attracting apparently endless queues and 1.6 million visitors. For those more concerned with the contemporary scene, the poster style 'popart' gave way to the abstractions and three-dimensional trickery of 'opart'. The Tate Gallery manfully strove to keep abreast of such vicissitudes. But it was the price of art that most engaged public attention. In 1970 Lord Radnor's portrait of Juan de Pareja by Velasquez was sold for a record £2.3 million and disappeared to the United States in spite of the National Gallery's struggle to acquire it. A spate of great paintings followed it on to the market, including Van Dyck's 'Study of Negro Hands', Domenichino's 'Adoration of the Shepherds' and Titian's great 'Death of Actaeon'. The Titian was sold to the Getty Museum but rescued for London at a cost of £1.76 million.

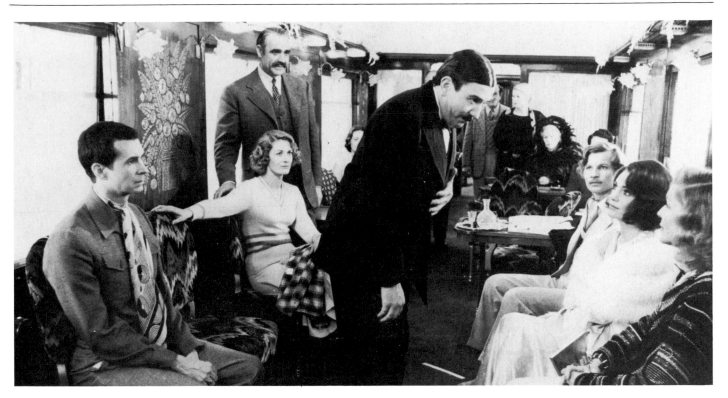

*Greatest money-spinner of the generation for the British cinema was the film of Agatha
Christie's* Murder on the Orient Express. *Almost everyone involved seemed to be a major star
and the film was made on the lavishest of scales, but the gamble paid off.*

*Andrew Lloyd Webber and Tim Rice achieved a curious and commercially most successful mix
with a series of epic musicals cum religious dramas.* Godspell, Jesus Christ, Superstar *and
(above)* Joseph and the Amazing Technicolor Dreamcoat *were all box-office triumphs.*

It was in 1967 that the giant tanker, the Torrey Canyon, *ran aground off Land's End and broke in half.*

'London Bridge is broken down', said the nursery rhyme, and the work of breaking began in 1968, when it was sold for $2.4 million, to be reconstructed over the Colorado river. It is alleged that the purchaser thought he was getting Tower Bridge.

'Fanfare for Europe'. The Queen arrives with her prime minister, Edward Heath, who more than any other single man had been responsible for making it come about that Britain joined the Common Market and reversed many centuries of insular policies.

Francis Chichester, sixty-five years old and thus qualified for an old age pension, returns in triumph to Plymouth in March 1967 having sailed single-handed around the world in his boat Gipsy Moth IV. *The 28,500 mile journey took 107 days to Australia and 119 for the second lap.*

Tony Jacklin revived some of the glories of the past when in 1970 he became the first British golfer to win the US Open Championship.

Michael Angelow (no relation as Private Eye *would say) also made sporting history of a kind when he 'streaked' across the cricket ground at Lords during a test match against Australia. Alan Knott is the British batsman surveying the scene.*

In 1966 England relived old glories when it defeated West Germany on 30 July to take the World Cup. The Queen presents England's captain, Bobby Moore, with the coveted trophy.

Red Rum by far surpassed the achievements of any other steeplechaser when it won the Grand National in 1973 and 1974, came second in the two succeeding years and won again in 1977. Here it is jumping Becher's Brook on the second time round in the 1974 race. Brian Fletcher is the jockey.

Alderman Joseph Cairns with the Queen in Belfast in July 1966 when she opened the Queen Elizabeth Bridge. Such a relaxed visit would be unimaginable today, for 'the troubles' escalated and British troops were sent to Northern Ireland in August 1969.

The royal yacht Britannia *sails past one of the vast new oil rigs which were beginning to sprout in the North Sea, that of Burmah Oil's* Ocean Kokuei. *In November 1976 the Queen pressed the button which started the flow of oil to the mainland.*

The Velasquez was not the only treasure lost to the country. In 1968 London Bridge was bought for $2.4 million, to be reconstructed over the Colorado River; it is claimed that the purchaser – an oil company – thought it was getting Tower Bridge for its money. The *Queen Mary* went to Long Beach, California, to serve as a floating museum, the *Queen Elizabeth* departed to a still more inglorious end, gutted by fire in Hong Kong.

Britain's national pride was battered too. In 1966 England had won the World Cup, by 4-2 against West Germany after extra time. For three weeks the BBC devoted nearly every evening to the tournament, seven million viewers watched every night. In 1967 and 1968 British teams won the European Cup. But it was the end of an era. In 1970 England was defeated by West Germany when the two teams met again in Mexico. For the 1974 World Cup England failed even to qualify for the final stages; Scotland got there but was soon eliminated. Worse still, for those who consoled themselves with the thought that the British at least could teach the world to lose gracefully, national supporters became a byword for drunkenness, obscenity and hooliganism. When Glasgow Rangers won the European Cup at Barcelona in May 1972 their supporters wreaked such havoc that the club was banned for two years. 'The English disease', the journal of the International Football Association described this mindless barbarism – a rebuke that seemed a little harsh in view of the fact that the Scots were quite as bad.

There were sporting heroes too. Francis Chichester sailed single-handed around the world and came home triumphant to Plymouth. Donald Campbell followed his father Sir Malcolm in establishing world speed records on both land and water before dying in an accident on Coniston Water while trying to improve the latter. Tony Jacklin in 1970 became the first British golfer to win the US Open, though international golf was on the whole dominated by the American giants: Nicklaus, the now veteran Arnold Palmer and the up-and-coming Tom Watson in particular. Michael Angelow, a twenty-four-year-old ship's cook, made cricket history when he streaked naked across the sacred turf at Lords during a test match against Australia. Noblest of all was a horse. The great-hearted Red Rum won the Grand National in 1973 and 1974, came second in the two succeeding years and won again in 1977, a record far surpassing that of any other steeplechaser.

Newspapers changed hands frequently. Here Rupert Murdoch, on the near side of the aisle, and Robert Maxwell, next to him on the far side, await the result of the voting at the News of the World *shareholders' meeting. Murdoch won control and later acquired the* Sun *and* The Times. *Maxwell had to content himself eventually with* The Mirror Group.

The national newspapers seemed to be following Lord Radnor's Velasquez and London Bridge into foreign ownership. In 1966 *The Times* began to print news on its front page and was sold to the Canadian, Roy Thomson. Two years later the Australian, Rupert Murdoch acquired the *News of the World*. Then he bought the ailing *Sun* from the Mirror group, turned it into a tabloid replete with sex and scandals and doubled the sales in eighteen months. By the mid 1970s the *Sun* had the largest circulation in the British Isles. Clothes were still more cosmopolitan, the ethnic vogue was on and the fashion-conscious woman appeared improbably disguised in Afghan sheepskin coat or Peruvian peasant outfit. Before that, however, the mini-skirt had come and gone and trousers for women had moved from the utilitarian to the ultra-formal. Such styles were not invariably well suited to those who affected them but showed off to advantage the cynosure of the times, the waif-like Twiggy, whose gawky gracefulness and non-existent figure conquered first Britain and then the United States. For men hats almost disappeared; braces, sock-suspenders, tie-pins, cufflinks, all the traditional appurtenances of the properly dressed became rarities or vanished altogether.

Regional loyalties were much in evidence, fomented by the local radio stations which were introduced in 1970. By mid 1976 there were nineteen of them, earning more than £12 million a year in advertising revenue. Local patriotism was affronted when an act of 1972 abolished Cumberland and Westmorland; merged Rutland with Leicestershire; butchered Yorkshire; invented strange new areas called Cleveland, Avon or Humberside; and fiddled with county boundaries with scant respect for tradition. The country cricketers very properly decided to ignore such absurd goings-on; in Ringwood, threatened by a Dorset take-over, the citizens marched to the market-place with banners, insisting that their town should remain in Hampshire where it belonged. They won.

Local patriotism was one of the more potent forces in the long-drawn out battle over London's third airport. The need for such an airport had been accepted since 1954 but it was not till thirteen years later that Stansted in Essex was selected as the site. Local fury was so great that the Conservative government lost its nerve and set up a commission which recommended Cublington in Oxfordshire as an alternative. Local fury there proved to be greater still. The government lost its

The mini-skirt was a fashion which flourished briefly, to the delight of tall, slim girls and lecherous old men. It commanded the loyalties of this group of girls who, in 1966, claim to be members of the 'British Society for the Preservation of the Mini-skirt' and parade outside Christian Dior's fashion house.

nerve again and opted for a desolate stretch of marshland on the Essex coast where only a few geese would be likely to complain. The cost of this was so appalling that the incoming Labour government in its turn lost its nerve. Was it to be Stansted after all? Then the happy thought occurred to some civil servant: perhaps no third airport was needed after all. The matter was referred for further consideration – preferably lengthy. The final – so far – decision was announced in June 1985, and Stansted was chosen.

That other drawn-out story, the future of Piccadilly Circus, made equally little progress. A new – third – scheme was commissioned in 1966 which provided for half as much traffic again as its predecessor and was denounced for what its creator had imagined to be its

salient virtue. In 1971 a fourth scheme raised pedestrians on to decks twenty feet above the traffic; this was thought altogether too daring and was smothered almost at birth. Covent Garden market was, however, at last moved across the Thames, leaving plenty of scope for recriminations about the development of the original site. Casson's new elephant house and Lord Snowdon's aviary were generally felt to adorn the London zoo, and Liverpool's Roman Catholic cathedral opened in 1967, a mere seven years after the plans had been finally approved.

For the long-term future of society one of the most significant developments was the increasing availability of the contraceptive pill. In 1974 a free birth control service was introduced with the pill and other

The fruit and vegetable men were at last driven from Covent Garden, to take refuge in a new, efficient, hygienic and thoroughly depressing barracks south of the river. The Queen dutifully inspects it but one suspects that she feels a nostalgic regret for the past.

preventive devices to be had 'on the health'. Penicillin, meanwhile, removed the worst effects of venereal disease, thus, as Lord Moran put it, making 'lust safe for democracy'. Legal abortion in 1967 became more readily accessible. The principal deterrents against pre-marital sex having disappeared, only the moral sanction remained. This proved ineffective. Cohabitation before marriage became tolerated except in the strictest circles and a couple going virgin to the wedding were unusual if not yet unheard of. The new techniques, however, failed to reduce illegitimacy, cases of which were nearly three times as frequent by 1983 as they had been twenty years before.

Some believed that science was serving humanity ill by offering such bewildering opportunities, but most people welcomed the freedom of choice which was now available. There could be no such justification for thalidomide, a drug which was responsible for sending some 300 babies into the world with limbs truncated and other deformities. Nor did the ever more ambitious efforts of the surgeon meet with everyone's approval. The first heart transplant in Britain took place in 1968. The patient lived six weeks. Even though results improved with time it was still asked whether the effort, skill and money could not have been better employed.

On the whole Britain grew healthier. It was safe once more to bathe in the Thames, Tyne and Severn, and fish that had not been seen in those rivers for many years now ventured back there. There were 15.4 million vehicles on the roads by 1975 and pollution from

A new elephant house at the London Zoo was designed by Hugh Casson and was generally approved of by the architectural establishment. The views of the elephants were not solicited.

The new Roman Catholic cathedral of Liverpool was opened on 14 May 1967, thirty-four years after the foundation stone was laid. The architect, Frederick Gibberd, was a Congregationalist. The local inhabitants christened it 'The Wigwam' or 'The Space Capsule'.

The drug thalidomide, prescribed for mothers, was responsible for sending some 300 babies into the world truncated or deformed. Marvels of rehabilitation were done and many children were to lead full and satisfying lives.

In May 1968 the triumphant team of the first ever heart transplant operation carried out in Britain are pictured in London – Mr Keith Ross (left) and Mr Donald Ross join Mr S. Khoja (white coat), *the surgical registrar.*

The breathalyser was introduced in 1967, to help police apprehend the drunken driver. Various brands were put on the market to enable the driver to test himself before setting off. Here one marketed by the theatre ticket firm Keith Prowse is being tried out.

Disaster, costing no human life, but catastrophic for birds and amenities generally, followed the running aground of the Torrey Canyon off Land's End. More than 100,000 tons of crude oil oozed on to the beaches of Devon and Cornwall. The housewives of Marazon are fighting the menace with detergents.

Another disaster struck in 1966 at Aberfan in Glamorgan when a heap of coal-mining waste slipped down the hill after heavy rain and crushed part of the village, including the school. 144 dead, mostly children, were taken from the mountain of rubble.

Ronan Point put a question-mark against the future of the tower-block (already much criticised on social grounds) when a corner of the 23-storey block of flats crumbled in ruins in May 1968.

car exhausts undid some of the good achieved by the clean air acts of previous decades, but breathing was still a safer business. A blow was struck for the pedestrian and sober driver in 1967 when it became an offence to be in charge of a car with more than a specific amount of alcohol in the blood. The breathalyzer was introduced to catch the guilty driver. Evening parties became less merry but the chances of surviving on the road were measurably increased.

In 1966 a pit heap slipped down the side of Aberfan valley in Glamorgan, crushing houses and a school and leaving 144 dead, mostly children. A year later the *Torrey Canyon* ran aground off Land's End and shed 100,000 tons of crude oil on Devon and Cornwall's beaches. In 1968 a corner of a twenty-three-storey block of flats, Ronan Point, crumbled in ruins, to the great alarm of many living in similar tower blocks. And then in 1976 came the great drought. The twelve months ending in April 1976 had anyway been the driest since records began in 1727 and from mid June to the end of August there was unbroken sunshine, with the temperatures in the 80°s or even 90°s. Reservoirs were empty; the Thames was virtually dry in its upper reaches; Britain became sere and brown. On 26 August Denis Howell was appointed minister of drought. His moral authority triumphed: the rains began three days later and continued until October.

HAROLD WILSON'S second ministry was to end shortly before the drought began. It was marked by increasingly bitter battles between left and right for the control of the Labour party. The left seemed to be winning. Michael Foot, then considered alarmingly radical in his views, came top of the constituency elections for the national executive and a programme of sweeping nationalisation was adopted. The dread of a slip into anarchy and then communism increasingly possessed certain of the more conservative and authoritarian elements. Proposals for a para-military force that would help the government in case of emergency were put forward by such worthies as General Sir Walter Walker and Colonel David Stirling, but got nowhere.

Even if the frailty of Wilson's parliamentary position had not ruled out any dramatically socialistic adventures, the economic state of the country would have

The great drought of 1976 transformed the British landscape and turned green to brown. This is Penhow reservoir in Monmouthshire, the scene made more striking by the addition of a group of camels from the safari park at Lord Bath's Wiltshire home of Longleat.

checked them. In 1974 the deficit on visible trade was a disastrous £5,264 million; what was still more awkward for the doctrinaire economists of the left was that invisible exports – notably profits made by the City of London – were £877 million in surplus. Heath had already imposed value added tax in 1973 with exemptions for food, books, children's clothing and a few such favoured categories; the Labour chancellor, Callaghan's, main innovation was to cut back on business entertaining. Wining and dining could in future only be set against tax if overseas buyers were entertained. Foreign businessmen in Britain found themselves suddenly popular, while the smarter restaurants prophesied doom.

Inevitably Wilson's first initiative was to repeal the Industrial Relations Act. Instead he formulated the concept of a social contract. The government would guarantee at least the maintenance of real incomes at their present level and a healthy measure of social reform; in return the unions would impose wage restraint. Unfortunately the social contract was as little contractual as the voluntary agreement had been agreed. As soon as it became clear that wage restraint would impose sacrifices on the working man, industrial chaos ensued. For the moment, however, it seemed a possible way forward. When Wilson called an election in October 1974 he won fourteen seats from the Conservatives and gained something close enough to an overall majority to make his task in the Commons immeasurably easier.

This same election brought to a crescendo the new nationalist spirit that had for some time been growing

Welsh nationalists practise their marksmanship in November 1965. Their object, they told the photographer, was 'to drive the English oppressors out of Wales'. The parliamentary wing of the movement, Plaid Cymru, won its first seat in 1966.

The belief that England was growing rich on 'Scotland's oil' meanwhile fanned the flames of nationalism north of the border. British Petroleum's Forties field was established in 1972, though it was to be another four years before oil would flow to the mainland.

in Wales and in Scotland. The Welsh nationalists had begun to demonstrate and throw bombs in the early 1960s, agitating in particular for greater use of the Welsh language, but Plaid Cymru did not win a parliamentary seat until 1966. The Scottish Nationalist Party (SNP) started even later, the redoubtable Winifred Ewing not taking its first seat, at Hamilton, till 1967. But once well alight, and fuelled by the belief that England was growing rich on Scotland's oil, the nationalist fire burnt furiously. To appease this new force the Labour government in 1968 set up a commission under Lord Kilbrandon to consider what changes if any were necessary to the constitutional and economic relationships between the three countries. It took four years to recommend a measure of devolution, with national assemblies enjoying considerable powers over internal policy sitting in Edinburgh and Cardiff. The proposals stopped far short of independence, but it was hoped would provide enough to satisfy all but the most ferocious nationalists.

The Tories showed little enthusiasm for the project but in 1974's second election Plaid Cymru had captured three seats with 11.5 per cent of the Welsh vote

Harold Wilson's list of resignation honours included Lord Kagan who created a scandal when he was sent to jail for fraud.

Harold Wilson retired as prime minister early in 1976, five days after his sixtieth birthday. Here, at the 1975 party conference, he joins in the ritual singing of 'Auld Lang Syne', linking hands with Barbara Castle and Ian Mikardo.

The new prime minister was James Callaghan, who defeated Michael Foot decisively, though only on the third round of voting. He was four years older than his predecessor.

The Liberal party too selected a new leader after Jeremy Thorpe was involved in a sensational scandal. Here, in 1973, the full body of Liberal MPs is at breakfast. Thorpe is in front of the waiter with David Austick on his right hand and then successively Jo Grimond, Cyril Smith, John Pardoe, Emlyn Hooson, Graham Tope, Russell Johnston, Clement Freud and the future leader, David Steel.

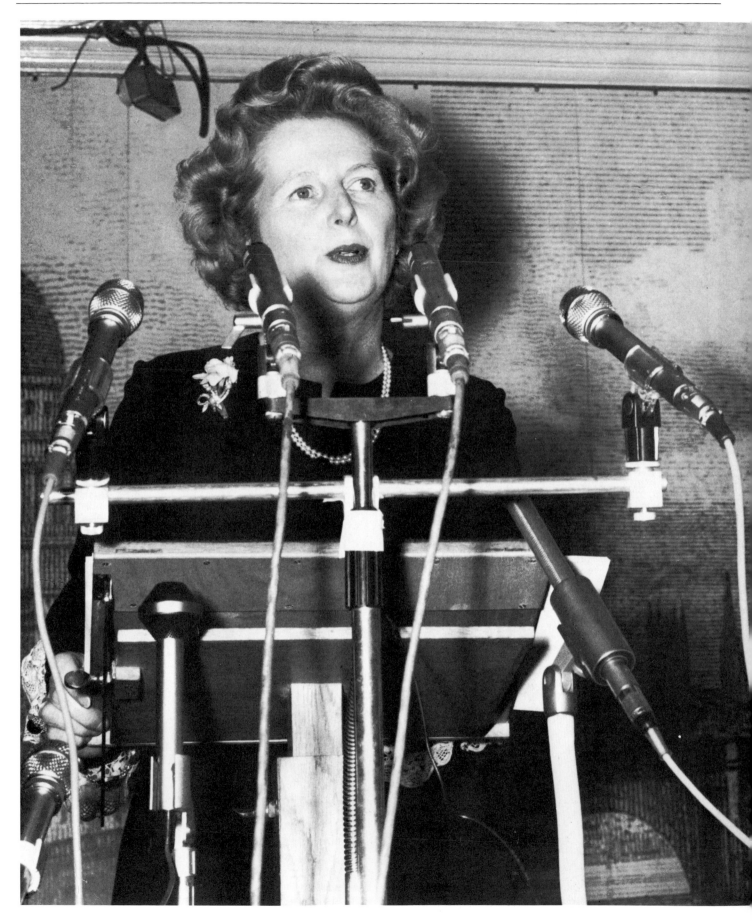

Finally in 1975 Mrs Thatcher became leader of the Conservative party. She is here speaking at the launch of a campaign to keep Britain in Europe. Beside her her predecessor listens intently. Edward Heath had introduced her speech, a courtesy which was not often to be repeated in the ensuing years.

and the SNP eleven with 30.44 per cent of the Scottish. The SNP was close to being the largest party in Scotland. The government settled down to the painful duty of preparing legislation that would be acceptable to the parliament in Westminster and yet satisfy the ambitions of the Welsh and Scottish. There was no shortage of Jeremiahs to prophesy that the end of the road must be the disintegration of the United Kingdom.

'Scotland's oil' was indeed more than just an emotive cry. Natural gas from the North Sea had been coming ashore from the end of the 1960s, and by 1973 13 per cent of national fuel consumption was supplied from this source, but the discovery that there was also oil in exploitable quantities did not come till later. Then the new strikes came thick and fast, particularly in 1972 when BP's Forties field and Brent were both established. In November 1976 the Queen pressed the button which started the flow of oil to the mainland. Predictions about the future varied wildly but it seemed certain that Britain would be self-sufficient in oil within a few years and would reap great advantage for its balance of payments until the end of the century or beyond it.

Wilson retired in March 1976. The announcement was unexpected and gave rise to dark rumours about the reasons behind it, but the Queen for one had known of her prime minister's intention for six months at least. The only flavour of scandal arose from the list of honours which an outgoing prime minister traditionally prepared. Wilson's selection was widely felt to reflect credit neither on him nor on the House of Lords; one of the new peers, Lord Kagan, actually ended up in jail for fraud. Wilson, retiring because at sixty he felt he needed a rest, made way for a successor of sixty-four. Michael Foot put up a stiff fight, but Callaghan beat him decisively on the third round of voting and duly became prime minister.

The other two parties also adopted new leaders. Jeremy Thorpe was involved in a sensational scandal, accused of homosexuality and incitement to murder and chased from office. Going from the ridiculous to the sublime, the Liberals replaced him by the transparently pious and honourable son of a Scottish minister, David Steel. Heath's departure was less dramatic if still acrimonious. The Tory panjandrums at first refused to oppose Heath for re-election as leader and it was left to Hugh Fraser and Margaret Thatcher, who had joined the government in 1961 and later won a reputation at the ministry of education, to take up the challenge. To the consternation of some, Mrs Thatcher led Heath on the first ballot by 130 votes to 119. Heath withdrew in pique; William Whitelaw joined the fray, but nothing could check the momentum gained by his adversary. In February 1975 Mrs Thatcher became leader of the opposition.

The Prince of Wales and Lady Diana Spencer pose for photographs shortly after the announcement that they were to marry. The engagement met with unanimous approval. Lady Diana was patently young, beautiful, well-born, British and Protestant and there was every reason to believe that she was high-spirited and benevolent as well.

Chapter Eight

Steps Towards the Future

1976 to 1985

JIM CALLAGHAN played towards his predecessor, Harold Wilson, a role very similar to that played by Home towards Macmillan; he took over a losing hand and conspicuously failed to conjure success out of disaster. His government limped along for three uncomfortable years, sustained in office by the 'Lib-Lab Pact', the support of the Liberal party offered in the hope that as a *quid pro quo* elections to the European parliament and the new assemblies of Wales and Scotland would be held on a basis of proportional representation. The *quid pro quo* came to nothing and in the long run the pact proved damaging to both the participants.

Callaghan's only hope was to prove that the social contract worked and that his close association with the trade unions bore fruit in stability and industrial peace. He failed signally. The year 1975 had been marked by a squall of massive pay demands and inflationary settlements. The mine workers rejected voluntary restraint: 'The social contract has been breached . . .'

said the militant president of the Yorkshire miners, Arthur Scargill. Curbs on prices and wages imposed by the government checked inflation but at the cost of eroding the traditional differentials between skilled and unskilled workers. In 1977 there were demands for wage increases of 63 per cent for the railwaymen and 90 per cent for the miners, and more than a million days lost to strikes in March alone. The same year saw one of the most ferocious industrial disputes of postwar Britain at the factory of a film processor in north London, called Grunwick. A fifth of the Grunwick work force walked out in protest at management's refusal to negotiate with their union. The men were dismissed; the company refused to reinstate them; and mass picketing began. Day after day there was violence, with members of the government and other left-wing celebrities prominent among the strikers. It was not till July 1978, after 591 days, that the strike was called off and Grunwick left battered but in possession of the field.

1977 saw one of the most embittered and protracted industrial disputes in British history. Police outside the Grunwick film plant in North London battle to keep back the angry pickets as a bus full of workers arrives at the factory.

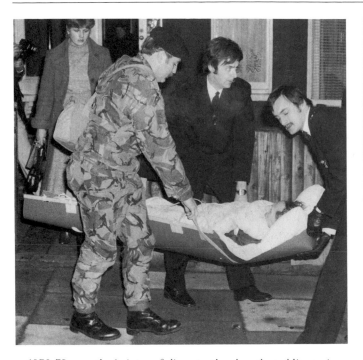

1978-79 was the 'winter of discontent', when the public services were chaotically disrupted by strikes and go-slows and industrial production fell to the level of the three-day week. Here a makeshift ambulance team composed of soldiers and policemen carry a man with a broken femur from a house in Streatham.

Liberal support meant that the death throes of the government were indecently protracted. The House of Lords fiercely mangled any bill which displeased it. In spite of restraints, wage increases averaged over 14 per cent. A suggested guideline of 5 per cent for wage settlements put forward in July 1978 was rejected by the TUC. The Liberals grew ever cooler as their electoral fortunes seemed to wane. Callaghan put a good face on it. Everyone expected an autumn election but he jauntily sang 'There was I, waiting at the church' to the TUC Congress and added: 'I have promised nobody that I shall be at the altar in October.'

His extra eight months did him little good. The 'winter of discontent', 1978-79, was a bleak season in which industrial production fell to the level of the three-day week. It was marked by chaotic disruption in the public services. A strike by school janitors combined with a shortage of fuel oil to close the state schools. If one drove on the snow-bound roads one probably skidded because nobody had gritted them; the ambulancemen were on strike so nobody rescued one after the crash; if one got to the hospital one found it picketed by discontented ancillary workers; and one's corpse was eventually stored in a factory because nobody was at work to bury it. This last detail, above all, sapped the failing credit of the government.

A strike by dustmen led to unsightly and unhygienic mountains of refuse building up in many of Britain's towns and cities. This street in Soho has been rendered almost impassable.

The death of devolution did nothing to restore the situation. The first Scotland and Wales bill met with fierce opposition in the House of Commons. On 4 May 1977 the Queen, in acknowledging loyal addresses from the two Houses of Parliament, declared: 'I can never forget that I was crowned Queen of the United Kingdom of Great Britain and Northern Ireland.' Rightly or wrongly, this was hailed as a not particularly veiled attack on any move towards separatism. An amended and weakened bill was introduced and became law, but with the proviso that 40 per cent of the voters in Scotland and Wales must first support the proposals in a referendum. Already the signs were that support for the SNP was waning; when the votes were taken only 32.85 per cent of Scottish voters were in favour of devolution, only 11.9 per cent of Welsh. Nationalism softly and silently vanished away; at the general election in May 1979 the SNP lost nine out of its eleven seats.

The election was a contest between two styles: the bland, avuncular Callaghan assuring the electorate that all was under control in the best of possible worlds, and the more abrasive and didactic Thatcher preaching radical solutions and old-fashioned capitalistic virtues. Blandness can work admirably when all is going well, but wins little support in times of trouble. The

At the general election of May 1979 the Conservatives triumphed under Mrs Thatcher, who is here seen leaving the polling booth in Chelsea Town Hall accompanied by her husband Denis. Twelve hours later Britain knew that it had its first woman prime minister.

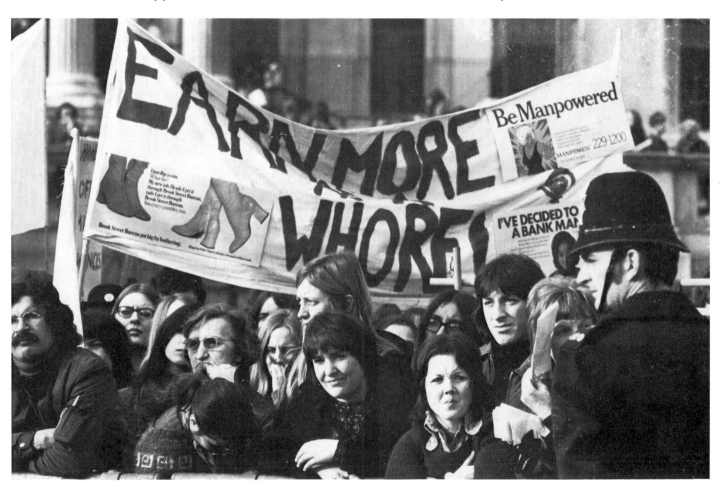

A female monarch and prime minister were not enough to satisfy the feminists. 'Woman's Lib' was one of the crusades of the age, often in pursuit of the most justifiable aims, sometimes dotty. This demonstration in Trafalgar Square appears to incline towards the second of these categories.

Jayne Torvill and Christopher Dean – 'Torvill and Dean' as they were invariably known – became national heroes with the beauty and sensational success of their dance routines on ice. Here they are at the scene of one of their greatest triumphs, the 1984 European Ice Dance Championships in Budapest.

On the occasion of the Queen's Silver Jubilee in 1977 addresses were presented to the Queen by the two Houses of Parliament. Here the lord chancellor is reading the address from the House of Lords.

As feminism grew more clamant, sexual frontiers became blurred. The androgynous Boy George became a hero/heroine of the pop scene and though he took things rather far a tendency towards uni-sex became clearly marked.

Men wore long hair and ear-rings; women were as likely to crop their hair and wear trousers. This outfit was advertised as 'fun wear for the summer', but the fun could have been shared by either sex.

property-owning middle classes, into whose ranks an army of former working-class voters had now moved, wanted to see the unions brought under control, wanted to buy their council house, wanted to keep more of their own money. They gave the Tories a majority of forty-three with 13.7 million votes against 11.5 million for Labour. Mrs Thatcher became Britain's first woman prime minister.

A SITUATION in which both the monarch and the prime minister were women suggested to some of the naiver men that the role of the traditionally under-privileged second sex was not such a very benighted one after all. This argument cut no ice with the feminists, whose vociferousness was so conspicuous a feature of the last decade of Elizabeth II's sixty years. The women had some powerful ammunition to support their case. There were 25.83 million of them, as opposed to 23.9 million men, yet there were only twenty-three woman MPs, no women judges, admirals or generals, precious few directors of large companies, only a smattering of stockbrokers, bankers, senior accountants. In most men's clubs they were allowed only inferior status, if admitted at all. A persistent campaign to achieve equal pay for equal work achieved much success but still left discrepancies in many fields. The Church of England in solemn conclave decided that there was no reason against appointing women priests; approved their ordination in principle; but decided that the time was not yet ripe. There was indeed much of what *Private Eye* delighted to pillory as 'loony feminist nonsense', too much significance was attached to trivial points of vocabulary such as the use of 'chairperson' for 'chairman' or 'humankind' for 'mankind', but the women still had a lot to complain about. Meanwhile the proportion of marriages ending in divorce rose inexorably, most notably among the manual workers and the unemployed. In 1981 the marriage of an unskilled manual worker was four times as likely to break up as that of a professional man.

Sexual frontiers became blurred. Sex changes became, if not frequent, then at least conceivable; James Morris, by becoming Jan Morris and writing intelligently and sympathetically about the process, gained much understanding for those who exist on the frontiers of gender. The androgynous Boy George became a hero/heroine of the pop scene. Trouser suits for women, unisex hair-cuts, ear-rings for men, all became commonplace. The frontiers of motherhood became blurred as well. Test-tube babies, with all the terrifying possibilities for genetic engineering that the technique implied, began to be a subject for experiment and the moral issues of surrogate motherhood, where the fertilised eggs of a particular couple would be allowed to grow within the womb of another woman, caused much debate and confusion.

Women were seen at their most militant at Greenham Common, where they pitched camp outside an American base from which convoys containing potentially nuclear-warheaded Cruise missiles periodically emerged. The women made it their business to interrupt this exercise so far as lay within their powers, and in so doing ran frequently into confrontation with the police. The unfortunate police, indeed, seemed to be in confrontation with almost everybody: Iranian students, picketers at Grunwick, members of the national front, striking coal-miners. One of the most bizarre and bloody incidents came in St James's Square when a Libyan diplomat opened fire from his Embassy and shot dead a policewoman who was trying to control a demonstration against Colonel Gadaffi's regime.

The most spectacular and alarming test for the police came in 1981 when Britain's inner cities erupted in violence. It started in Brixton in April, a riot triggered off by a trivial incident when police tried to question a black man who had been stabbed and a hundred or so black youths jumped to the conclusion that he was being victimised and came to his rescue. Violence spread; some white youths joined in; police, shops, even ambulances were attacked. In July it was the turn of Toxteth in Liverpool; there was looting and arson; a

The frontiers of motherhood became blurred as well. The girl in this picture wanted a baby without marriage and achieved her object by insemination at a Harley Street clinic. Test-tube babies began to be a subject for experiment.

Women were at their most militant outside the American air base at Greenham Common in Berkshire, protesting against the presence of the new, mobile cruise missiles. In December 1982 they sought to encircle the entire camp in a 'chain of protest'.

The Queen visits what must be the best known highway in the British Isles – Coronation Street. While in Manchester she went to see filming in progress on the set of this interminably long-lasting serial.

Brideshead Revisited *was one of the most triumphant successes of British television, both in critical renown and dollar earnings. In the picture Lord Marchmain and his mistress Cara, played by Laurence Olivier and Stephane Audran, are seated, while behind them stand Charles Ryder (Jeremy Irons), Cordelia (Phoebe Nicholls) and Julia (Diana Quick).*

hospital ransacked; Upper Parliament Street a ruin. Next day Moss Side, Manchester, was in flames; then it was Brixton again, Southall, Reading, Hull, Preston. Unemployment was worst among coloured youths aged between sixteen and twenty, and it was this group that provided the core of the disaffected rioters. Lord Scarman, set up to report on the problem, referred to 'concealed discrimination' and urged positive discrimination in favour of the racial minorities so as to redress the balance. The government for its part took alarm at the state of the impoverished and half-deserted inner cities and accepted the need to spend money to put things right.

Crime throve in such an environment, indeed throughout Britain. Just over half a million indictable crimes in 1952 had multiplied five fold by the 1980s. Crimes of violence increased with particular speed. Cases of homicide rose by a mere 50 per cent, though these included cases of peculiar ferocity, notably that of Peter Sutcliffe, the 'Yorkshire Ripper', who in May 1981 was jailed for life on thirteen counts of murder. Crime paid – £26 million was taken in a bullion raid on Heathrow Airport. Sometimes it provided entertainment: the case of a 'madam' in Streatham who ran a

brothel catering for the more wayward tastes of the professional classes caused general delight. Sometimes it stirred moral issues: Dr Leonard Arthur, a respected paediatrician, 'allowed' a baby with Down's syndrome to die and was charged with attempted murder. To the general relief he was acquitted. Less fortunate were the directors of EXIT, the voluntary euthanasia society, whose publication of a pamphlet advising on ways of committing suicide was deemed to constitute a criminal offence. A new, if minor crime was invented in 1983 when the wearing of seat belts in a car became compulsory.

To the more traditional it seemed as if the same degeneration in moral standards was to be seen in the world of first-class cricket. The decay, they held, had started in 1966 when the first one day limited-over matches began to be held on Sundays. Then in 1977 the Australian tycoon Kerry Packer came on to the scene and recruited virtually the entire Australian and West Indian teams and a crop of players from other countries for a series of 'super tests', played under floodlights and with what the cricketing establishment felt to be the most unseemly razzmatazz. The operation was called off after two years, but many of the practices

In St James's Square in April 1980 a Libyan diplomat opened fire from his Embassy's windows at a crowd of demonstrators in the road outside. A policewoman who was trying to control the traffic fell dead. St James's Square was sealed off and the siege of the Embassy only lifted when the occupants filed out and were immediately deported to their homeland.

There were some demands for the restoration of the death penalty, particularly in the case of Peter Sutcliffe, the so-called 'Yorkshire Ripper'. Here a crowd outside the courtroom at Dewsbury makes its views unequivocally clear.

In 1981 came fierce violence in Britain's inner cities, often racial in origin but reflecting too the pressures of poverty and unemployment. Here violence in the Brixton area was followed by an orgy of looting and arson. The singularly dead-looking figure on the pavement is fortunately just a shop-dummy.

After many delays, changes of site and near cancellations the National Theatre at last opened on the South Bank in 1976. A striking example of the 'brutalist' school of architecture, it is hard to believe that this building has the same purpose as the Theatre Royal in the Haymarket, or, for that matter, the new Opera House in Sydney.

After ten years under construction the Thames Barrier opened (or, to be more precise, for the first time closed) in 1984. London at last was free from the danger of flooding, though inhabitants of Chiswick were disconcerted to find that their cellars still flooded at certain times of the year.

Bob Champion won the country's esteem when he conquered cancer to win the world's most gruelling race, the Aintree Grand National, in 1981. Here he stands with his mount Aldiniti.

Sebastian Coe (above) and Steve Ovett (top, left) brought glory to British middle-distance running. Both runners are here seen at Crystal Palace, Coe breasting the tape in August 1977 and Ovett winning the 1,500 metres at the same meeting two years later.

Bjorn Borg, the Swedish champion, won at Wimbledon for five successive years. His court manners were invariably impeccable. The same, alas, could not be said about his graceless though superlatively gifted successor John McEnroe. Borg is here seen congratulating McEnroe after the 1981 Wimbledon final, which the American won 4-6, 7-6, 7-6, 6-4 to end the Swede's long reign.

The demands of politics and sport increasingly conflicted. There was some indignation when the young South African runner Zola Budd was made a British citizen with indecent haste just before the Olympic games. Here she is winning the 1,500 metres at Crystal Palace, despite some barracking during the race.

1981 was the year of Ian Botham. Here he is shown hitting a six in the fifth test at Old Trafford. In 123 minutes Botham scored 118 runs, including six sixes and thirteen fours. At times it seemed that he was winning the series single-handed.

The Queen on Britannia *during the Silver Jubilee Review of the Fleet.*

The Queen, a member of the Women's Institute herself, watches as Robin Ives demonstrates a cucumber slicer at a WI exhibition.

The Conservative party conference of June 1984 addressed itself to the question of the European parliamentary election. Michael Heseltine is seated on the left, with next to him Geoffrey Howe, Margaret Thatcher, the prime minister, and the chairman of the party, John Gummer.

it had introduced proved more long lasting. Politics, too, increasingly exercised an influence on sport: in 1982, for instance, when a group of England's senior cricketers was banned from international matches for playing in South Africa; and in 1984 when waif-like but singularly fleet South African Zola Budd was made a British citizen with indecent haste just before the Olympics, but could only achieve the doubtful distinction of colliding with the American champion and putting her out of the race.

But it was not all so controversial. Bob Champion won the country's esteem when he conquered cancer to win the Grand National on Aldiniti, a horse which, incidentally, had itself triumphed over a broken leg. Coe and Ovett brought glory to British middle distance running; Coe setting world records for the 800 metres, 1500 metres and mile in a single year. Borg won at Wimbledon for five successive years with dignity and superlative skill, though it seemed more in keeping with the times when he was supplanted by McEnroe, whose skill was quite as great but whose dignity was sadly lacking. Jogging was imported from America and became a minor craze; its elder brother, marathon-running, also became curiously popular. Up to 20,000 people at a time, blind men, infants, grandfathers, risked blisters and coronaries as they trotted around

London, Manchester and other venues, racing for glory, charitable causes or just the hell of it. Still more passionate though less lasting popularity was won by the skateboard, a gadget lending itself to displays of spectacular virtuosity, which like canasta, the yo-yo or the hula hoop blazed into prominence and then vanished almost entirely.

Cricket, too, had its moments of less meretricious glory. In 1979 England won the series in Australia by five matches to one, while 1981 was the year of Botham. Deprived of the captaincy, he celebrated in the fourth test by taking five wickets for one run in twenty-eight balls when the Australians needed only thirty-seven to win and in the fifth, when England followed on, by scoring 149 from 148 balls and opening the way for victory. The glory was fleeting though; in 1984 England lost five times in a row to the West Indians. Some honour was regained in India, but no one could claim that it was a golden age for English cricket.

The British were better fed, being able to afford more from a wider selection. The average man had to work only seven minutes to afford a white loaf, against nine ten years before; four minutes for a pint of milk against five in 1971. Deep-freezing emptied a cornucopia of exotic foods into Britain's shops; a greengrocer in a

Take-away meals boomed in popularity. This stall is selling hamburgers and cheeseburgers, but it might as well have been Indian curries, Chinese bean-shoots, Kentucky fried chickens, or the traditional fish and chips.

small provincial town would sport avocados and lychees, mangoes and cumquats; the humblest super-market displayed a range of pâtés and savouries that Fortnum and Mason could not have approached before the war. Ninety per cent of houses had a refrigerator and many a deep-freeze, to be stocked by the pre-cooked foods supplied by a plethora of manufacturers; while Chinese and Indian take-aways, hamburgers and Colonel Sanders' fried chickens supplemented if they did not replace the traditional fish and chips. Britain became a nation of wine-drinkers, consumption treb-ling within ten years, mainly at the expense of beer.

Health foods abounded; even the smallest town seemed to boast its emporium where ruggedly grainy bread and free-range eggs jostled with strange pastes and honey drawn from cyclamen or esparto grass. The food faddist formed part of an ever more strident ecological lobby whose ample apron accommodated a plethora of homeopathic doctors, anti-vivisectionists, advocates of alternative forms of energy such as wind-mills or the tides, protesters against industrial pollu-tion, nuclear waste, blood sports or the use of furs for clothing. Like most lobbies they talked much sense and a certain amount of cranky rubbish.

Health continued to improve. Life expectancy grew, disease was progressively controlled if not conquered,

the cure for cancer proving elusive though methods of treatment became steadily more efficacious. Pollution from factories sank to its lowest post-war level, while emission of lead from cars and lorries dropped substan-tially in spite of the doubling of the number of vehicles over twenty years. Road accidents dropped too, by 17 per cent over the same period. Cigarette smoking was practised by only 38 per cent of men and 33 per cent of women as opposed to 52 per cent and 41 per cent a decade before, though the young conspicuously failed to profit by the example set by their elders. A new terror was introduced by AIDS – Acquired Immune Defi-ciency Syndrome – a killer believed to have been introduced by but not confined to homosexuals.

Sixty per cent of the British now bought their own homes and within those homes there was greater com-fort. Nine out of ten households had their own televi-sion, refrigerator and vacuum cleaner. Three-quarters had a telephone. Some form of central heating was the norm in any house built within the last twenty years. It was as well that such comforts were available – 40 per cent of the population still took no regular holiday away from home and in spite of the abundance of cheap charter flights, 38 per cent had never left the country.

Religion did not become notably more popular though nine out of ten of those asked said that they

Indignation was vociferously expressed over a wide range of social and moral issues. The disposal of nuclear waste was deemed to fall into both these categories. A policeman removes a Greenpeace banner as he picks his way gingerly past a heap of allegedly radioactive mud from Windscale which protesters have dumped outside the Department of the Environment.

The Queen Mother was eighty in 1980 and a thanksgiving service was held for her in St Paul's Cathedral. In his address the Archbishop of Canterbury, Dr Robert Runcie, praised Queen Elizabeth's courage, integrity and enthusiasm. He is here seen welcoming her to the Cathedral.

would deplore the ending of religious education. Six out of ten gave their religion as Church of England, yet of these only 6 per cent had attended church within a week of being asked and less than a quarter within three months – a period that included Christmas. Ecumenism caused much debate, if not a religious revival. The Archbishop of Canterbury visited the Sistine Chapel and the Pope Canterbury – there was much celebratory embracing. Prince Charles's wedding included prayers by the Roman Catholic Archbishop and the Moderator of the Church of Scotland and a lesson was read by the Methodist Speaker of the House of Commons. Ian Paisley thought it was all a papist plot and did not attend – his absence was accepted with equanimity. The new Bishop of Durham caused much debate when he cast doubt upon the literal truth of the resurrection and other cherished Christian tenets. To the theologian it seemed that he had gone no further than Bishops Barnes and Robinson many years before him, but the Almighty evidently felt otherwise since York Minster was struck by lightning and a transept gutted.

The BBC seemed to believe it had inherited the traditional authority and dignity of the Church of

In 1982 Pope John Paul II visited Canterbury, a striking illustration of the new mood of ecumenism in the Christian world. With Dr Runcie, Archbishop of Canterbury, he is approaching the deanery for a meeting with the Prince of Wales.

*In July 1984 one of the greatest architectural treasures of the British Isles was put in peril
when the south transept of York Minster was struck by lightning and set on fire. Damage was
severe but 140 firemen, fighting the flames for more than three hours, managed to save the rest
of the building, including the central tower.*

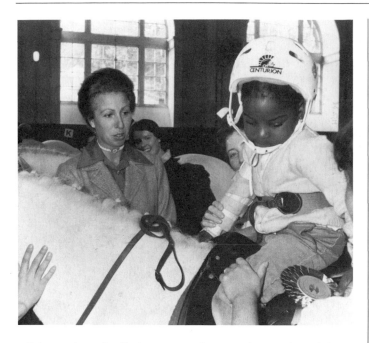

Princess Anne finally began to receive a good press through her work for charity, in particular The Save the Children Fund, on behalf of which she has undertaken several gruelling tours. (Above) The Princess watches six-year-old Tinu Adio-Pereira at a Riding for the Disabled get-together in September 1983.

England. Standards were not to be lowered. Announcers, it decreed, should base their pronunciation on that of 'a person born and brought up in one of the home counties' and 'educated at one of the established southern universities'. Its image was bolstered in 1978 by its ambitious project to screen all thirty-seven of Shakespeare's plays. Not all enterprises were so meritorious however; in 1981 when independent television was winning laurels (and dollars) for its production of *Brideshead Revisited* the BBC could only counter with a cliché-ridden and banal series on the Borgias. The power of television continued immense; more people watched Wagner's *Ring* on television over ten weeks than had attended the festival at Bayreuth since 1876. The average Briton over five watched for twenty hours a week. Television's empire expanded with independent television's Channel 4 and breakfast television from both BBC and ITV. ITV's early morning programme was at first an expensive disaster, but both channels eventually settled down to approximate parity. Early in 1985 the House of Lords went on to the screen. Orthodox television was not omnipotent, however; the provision of films on video noticeably reduced regular viewing.

It struck another blow at the cinema too, where

Early in 1985 the House of Lords was televised. After an initial flurry of public interest the experiment caused little stir, but at least the danger most often advanced by those opposed to televising parliaments – that exhibitionists would hog the cameras – has not so far come true.

attendances dropped alarmingly close to one million a week. It had been thirty times more at its peak. Cinemas continued to close, though sales of films to television helped to boost revenue. The British cinema enjoyed something of a renaissance with multi-Oscar winners like *Chariots of Fire* and *Gandhi*, or cheap and idiosyncratic minor masterpieces like *Gregory's Girl*. The theatre, too, was active. The National Theatre in 1976 at last opened in its vast fortified keep on the South Bank; a theatre for the Royal Shakespeare Company was among the delights of the 'Centre for Arts and Conferences' at the Barbican; and new, less formal, theatre groups sprang up all over the country. Musicals seemed particularly in favour, twelve playing in the West End at the end of 1983 and *The Mousetrap* celebrated its silver jubilee in 1977 and seemed well set for its golden. But it was the end of an era. Ralph Richardson and Redgrave died; Olivier, Gielgud, Scofield, even Alec Guinness were veterans whose time was running out. There were plenty of good younger actors coming on, but none seemed stamped with quite the authority of the old brigade.

To judge by figures of library lending, reading remained a popular sport though despairing publishers sometimes felt that nothing sold except perhaps books

Gregory's Girl was one of the best of the cheaply made and idiosyncratic minor masterpieces which redeemed the reputation of the British cinema. Written and directed by Bill Forsyth, it starred Gordon John Sinclair as the lovesick Gregory and Dee Hepburn as the girl who put football above the delights of dalliance.

British cinema scored a notable success with the Oscar-winning Chariots of Fire, *a gripping story of the motivation and ambitions of an Olympic runner. In this picture Ben Cross, playing the champion hurdler Harold Abrahams, is running around the quadrangle at Trinity College, Cambridge with the future Olympic hurdler Lord Burghley (Nigel Havers) beside him.*

Two of the most celebrated British pop stars whose earnings surpass those of ten prime ministers and archbishops lumped together. The resolutely diabolic Mick Jagger of The Rolling Stones is here seen in action at Roundhay Park in July 1982; another veteran is the clean-limbed and religiously inclined Cliff Richard. Both stars appear immortal.

Agatha Christie's The Mousetrap ran and ran, celebrating its silver jubilee and appearing to be well set for its golden. This picture is taken from the birthday celebrations of 1976. The current leading lady, Mary Law (on the right) is handing over the charge to her successor in the role Helen Weir.

associated with TV programmes or those by an Edwardian country lady. Fiction was bolstered by publicity for the Booker prize, which broke through in public esteem in 1980 when *Rites of Passage* by William Golding defeated Anthony Burgess's *Earthly Powers*. Next year the sales of Salman Rushdie's *Midnight's Children* – by no means readily accessible as novels go – showed that the British at last had a literary prize carrying some of the commercial weight of the Prix Goncourt in France. None of these authors, however, was among the leading recipients when the first tranche of Public Lending Right was paid out to authors in 1983; to write thrillers or better still, romances, and to produce a book a year over a long period were the criteria necessary to secure massive borrowings from the public libraries. Catherine Cookson far outstripped her rivals in the competition to be Britain's most borrowed, and probably most read author.

The rewards for successful novelists were considerable but as nothing compared to those of the pop star. In the 1980s there were half a dozen youngsters (or not-so-youngsters) who were among the best paid people in the country. David Bowie, Boy George, Elton John, the breezily Christian Cliff Richard and resolutely diabolic Mick Jagger, above all that survivor from the Beatles, Paul McCartney, measured their income in millions; a single hit like John's 'Your Song' or McCartney's 'Mull of Kintyre' earned their creators more than a school-teacher or coal-miner would accumulate in a lifetime.

The world of the newspapers was tempestuous. Lord Thomson was so enraged by the obduracy of his printers that he closed *The Times* and *Sunday Times* for a year, lost £40 million, reopened, and sold out to Rupert Murdoch, already proprietor of the *Sun*. David Astor, in 1975 sold the *Observer* to the American company Atlantic Richfield, which in due course passed it on to the controversial 'Tiny' Rowland. The *Star* introduced bingo for its readers, with weekly prizes worth £30,000. By mid 1981 it was putting on 100,000 sales a month and threatening the supremacy of the *Sun*. Murdoch retaliated with his own bingo and temporarily cut his price. The egregious Robert Maxwell, Murdoch's deadly rival, acquired The Mirror Group and joined in the circulation battle. Even *The Times* started its own up-market bingo related to movements

Ralph Richardson and Celia Johnson star in William Douglas-Home's The Kingfisher *in 1977. Both are now sadly dead and an era is ending in the British theatre.*

On the whole the National Trust and the great public collections did a good job of preserving
Britain's heritage, but there were some painful losses. Some of these arose when the former
Rothschild palace of Mentmore was sold to an obscure but rich religious sect and its contents of
jackdaw magnificence widely dispersed. This photograph shows the lavishly decorated
main hall.

on the stock exchange. The great proprietors merrily cut each others' throats, to the entertainment of the public if not themselves.

Those anxious to preserve Britain's heritage on the whole did well, with the National Trust recruiting its millionth member. They had their setbacks, though. The Rothschild palace of Mentmore was sold to a quaint if prosperous religious sect and its contents of jackdaw magnificence dispersed at auction. Warwick Castle went to Madame Tussaud's and some of its noblest furnishings, notably the Bellini altarpiece, were scattered. It was revealed that Lady Spencer-Churchill had burnt Graham Sutherland's portrait of her late husband, Sir Winston. A Saxon illuminated manuscript went to Germany for £8.14 million; and the bulk of a collection of drawings from Chatsworth, which were sold at auction for £19 million, and Kenneth Clark's Turner which fetched £7.4 million, also went abroad. But there were victories too. Many fine houses, notably Kedleston, Belton and Kingston Lacey, were acquired for the nation; Count Seilern's collection – conservatively valued at £30 million – was left to London University; and the Getty Foundation, which had to spend at least $2 million a week to maintain its charitable status, was foiled in its bid to buy Duccio's crucifixion for the Getty museum in the

Mrs Thatcher visits the Daily Mirror *in March 1985 and speaks to her socialist admirer, the new publisher of Mirror Group Newspapers, Robert Maxwell.*

The day of the tower block was over, and the cities began painfully and expensively to retrace their steps. Here two blocks in East London in 1981 are demolished after it was decided that the cost of repair would be prohibitive – even if the final result would have been socially acceptable.

The new Humber bridge was opened in June 1981. It was the world's longest single span suspension bridge and cost £91 million. Though motor vehicles were busily on the move when this photograph was taken, pedestrians and cyclists had to wait another few weeks until the Queen officially opened the bridge.

The hull of the Mary Rose, *a warship of Henry VIII's fleet, breaks surface on 11 October 1982 after some 450 years at the bottom of the sea.*

United States – largely through the private generosity of a member of the Getty family. The National Gallery at last unveiled the plans for its extension, but the Prince of Wales described the projected tower as 'a monstrous carbuncle'; others were equally unenthusiastic, and the project seemed likely to be indefinitely delayed till the three Sainsbury brothers offered to devote some of the profits from their vastly successful chain of grocery stores to an entirely new development free of commercial involvement.

Much else changed and sometimes progress was reversed. People stopped building tower blocks for dwellings and began to talk about pulling them down instead. Asbestos was found to represent a health hazard and began to be ripped expensively from Britain's buildings. Telegrams disappeared, as also did the old sixpenny or 2½p piece. Decimal coinage was first resented, then taken for granted, and the paper pound was finally withdrawn after much indignation. Litres co-existed uneasily with gallons and centigrade with fahrenheit, but the young knew only about the former and they were sure to win in the end. The Humber Bridge was opened in 1981, and the *Mary Rose*, a warship of Henry VIII's fleet, was salvaged after the best part of 500 years.

But it was the microchip that introduced the most conspicuous changes and offered the greatest potential for the future. Few people indeed had ever seen a chip or understood with any certainty what it did or how it did it, but it was known to inhabit watches and electronic toys, robots and computers, to maintain extraordinary amounts of information in its memory, to follow the most complicated instructions and to direct the activities of powerful and intricate machinery. With the aid of a microchip factory benches that had employed a hundred people could be controlled by a single technician or, more mysterious still, a robot. Much menial drudgery was spared as a result, productivity soared and goods became cheaper, yet also unemployment increased. The process was only just beginning yet the consequences seemed obvious. The microchip was added to world-wide recession and Mrs Thatcher's monetarist policies to swell the problem of unemployment which dominated the Britain of the 1980s.

Mrs Thatcher never considered unemployment to be a weapon with which to implement her policy; but she accepted that it was a price that might have to be paid if Britain was to be itself again. Her aims were vociferously proclaimed: to carry the banner of capitalism against the Luddites and vandals of the left; to restate the traditional values of Victorian England – thrift, self-help, diligence; to cut public spending and chop back swollen bureaucracy – even in 1984 there were 650,000 civil servants; to reduce taxes and increase incentives; to make the nationalised industries pay and, whenever practicable, restore them to the private sector. Her first budget showed the way she planned to go, indeed took what seemed to many an alarmingly precipitate step in that direction. The basic

The micro-chip was the vital element in the vast range of electronic toys and devices that flooded the market and began to take over factory assembly lines. There may well be one inside this robot dog, here demonstrating its talents outside St Paul's Cathedral.

A picture of a silicon chip – to look at just about as boring an object as one can imagine and one which few of us understand but which seems certain to transform the day-to-day life of the British citizen.

rate of income tax was cut from 33 per cent to 30 per cent, the top rate from 83 per cent to 60 per cent. When in due course the 15 per cent surcharge on unearned income was removed, the multi-millionaire, who had previously kept only £2 out of every £100 of his unearned income, now was left with twenty times as much.

Instead of occupying the middle ground that Mrs Thatcher was vacating, the Labour party obligingly edged towards the left. Tony Benn, prime mover in this process, based his campaign on populist appeal and the finding of common ground with Marxists and local activists. First capture the constituency parties, then dispossess the parliamentary party of its power or reform it by enforcing compulsory reselection of members and evicting the moderates and right-wingers. 'For God's sake stop arguing: the country is crying out for unity' appealed Callaghan in 1980, but the conference ignored him and voted overwhelmingly for unilateral disarmament and the immediate closure of American bases in Britain. When Callaghan resigned later that year, Healey was defeated for the leadership by Michael Foot. In 1981 the party agreed to choose its leader by electoral college, with 40 per cent of the votes going to the trades unions, 30 per cent to the constitu-

ency parties and 30 per cent to the members of parliament. As a result Denis Healey, once seen as Callaghan's certain successor, barely scraped in as deputy leader ahead of Benn.

It was this shift in the control of the party as much as the Labour party's hostility to Europe that led Shirley Williams, David Owen and Bill Rodgers – the gang of three – to break away and form their own centre grouping, the Social Democractic Party – SDP. Roy Jenkins joined them on his return from the European Commission and in 1981 an alliance was formed with the Liberal party. By the end of the year there were twenty-seven SDP members, all but one exiles from the Labour party, and Shirley Williams captured Crosby from the Tories, overturning a majority of 19,000. (At the same election 223 people voted for the Raving Loony Society; a feature of by-elections of the period was the number of eccentrics and exhibitionists who stood for various fanciful causes or – as with Screaming Lord Sutch – for themselves.) When Roy Jenkins won Hillhead, Glasgow, pushing Labour into third place, it seemed that the Alliance might become the principal party of opposition.

Opposition throve. Mrs Thatcher's dedication to the cause of monetarism, rigid control of the money supply,

A group of Labour notables join in a sponsored march that took them ten miles along the Thames and over the London bridges. Michael Foot and Denis Healey found sticks of use, Joan Lestor preferred a dog.

The 'gang of four', the leading Labour politicians who broke away to form their own centre grouping, the Social Democratic Party. From left to right are Bill Rodgers, David Owen, Shirley Williams and the first leader of the new party, Roy Jenkins.

caused dismay to some of her followers and to the man she had supplanted, Edward Heath. A distinction grew up between 'dries' and 'wets': dries who supported the prime minister in all her austerity and wets who bewailed the consequential cuts in education, public services and, in the last resort, employment. Her critics were driven from the cabinet or, like Jim Prior, shipped off to Northern Ireland. Mrs Thatcher scorned compromise; 'consensus,' she said, 'seems to be the process of abandoning all beliefs, principles, values and policies'. TINA, she was nicknamed – 'There Is No Alternative'. Not surprisingly, she made enemies, abroad as well as at home. '*Je ne l'aime, ni comme homme, ni comme femme*', remarked the French president, Giscard d'Estaing. The inner-city riots of July 1981 seemed to her critics to illustrate the perils of her course. Opposition grew, by-elections went badly; when Roy Jenkins won in Glasgow the government seemed in real, perhaps even terminal trouble. Then in April 1982 came the Falklands.

There had in fact been a mini-Falklands two years before, when terrorists has seized the Iranian embassy in London and held its occupants hostage. For a week of tension the embassy was besieged; then the SAS stormed the building, rescuing all the hostages who were still alive and killing five out of six of the defenders. It was a copy-book operation: adventurous, ruthless and successful. The public loved it, and some of the credit rubbed off on the government, who had kept their heads and given the experts a free hand.

The crisis and the credit were both immeasurably greater when the Argentinians occupied the Falkland Islands. The sovereignty of these islands had been in dispute for more than a century and everyone knew that the British government would have been delighted if the tiny population had opted for some sort of union with the Argentine. They consistently declined to be so obliging, however, and when the Argentinians had recourse to arms there was no doubt what the bulk of the British people felt the response should be. There were recriminations about the failure of the foreign office to foresee the invasion, and some argued that negotiations should be protracted almost indefinitely, but when an expeditionary force sailed to recapture the colony it did so with the support of almost everyone. This was no Suez which split the nation; there were doubts but in the main Britain was united.

The campaign that followed was dangerous, bloody and exceedingly expensive. Names that nobody had ever heard before were suddenly well known: Stanley, Goose Green, San Carlos Bay, Port Darwin. The sinking of the Argentinian battleship, the *Belgrano*, with heavy loss of life, brought reality into a conflict that had previously smacked of the pantomime (and was incidentally to plague the government for many months to come, with insistent complaints from the Labour MP, Tam Dalyell, that sinking had been ordered so as to sabotage a promising peace initiative). Almost immediately afterwards the British destroyer, HMS *Sheffield*, was sunk by an Exocet missile and the perils of

In 1980 the Iranian Embassy in London was captured by terrorists and its occupants held ransom. After a week of siege and the murder of one of the hostages the SAS stormed the building. They are here shown poised for the assault. The result was strikingly successful, all the surviving hostages were rescued alive and five out of six terrorists killed.

Southampton, 13 May 1982. A soldier bids a fond farewell to his girlfriend as the task force prepares to leave for the Falklands. No one really believed that it would come to fighting, yet the campaign that followed was dangerous, bloody and exceedingly expensive.

Lord Carrington, the foreign secretary, accepted responsibility for the foreign office's failure to foresee the Argentine invasion and resigned with dignity and grace. The government was the poorer for his loss.

this ambitious operation became painfully clear. When the Argentinian forces finally surrendered on 14 June, the nation experienced vast relief and justified pride. The return of each vessel of the expeditionary force was the occasion for tumultuous joy and a patriotic gala.

Mrs Thatcher's determination and calm in the face of great danger won the nation's admiration. The result was a tremendous upsurge of support for the government. The temptation to call a snap election and cash in on the victory was resisted, but when a general election was called in June 1983 the 'Falklands factor' was still a potent force. Labour helped to make things easier for the Tories by wrangling with all its customary venom over defence, policy towards Europe and other issues. The result was catastrophic for Labour rather than a triumph for the Tories. Traditional working-class support defected to the Conservatives or the SDP/Liberal Alliance. Labour was left with 8,500,000 with the Alliance only 700,000 behind and the Tories ahead with thirteen million. With 42.4 per cent of the votes, the Tories won 61 per cent of the seats.

One drawback about so striking a victory was that the Tory backbenchers, confident that their govern-

The converted cruise ship Canberra *arrives back in Southampton with 2,000 Royal Marines aboard. The return of each vessel of the expeditionary force was the occasion for a patriotic gala; a flotilla of yachts and dinghies is here bobbing around the liner to join in the welcome.*

ment was in no danger of defeat, allowed themselves the luxury of opposition. The government found itself assailed on a variety of issues, most notably the abolition of the Greater London Council and a proposal to make middle-class parents pay more for their children's education, on which Keith Joseph was beaten into a humiliating defeat. The cabinet was more united than ever behind its leader. Lord Carrington retired with dignity and grace in recognition of the foreign office's failure to foresee the Falklands crisis and only Peter Walker was left to represent the wets. Mrs Thatcher, however, lost a staunch supporter when Cecil Parkinson became involved in an unsavoury marital scandal and resigned from the government. The Labour party for its part replaced Michael Foot by the forty-one-year-old Neil Kinnock, representative of what had come to be known as the 'soft left', affable, energetic, and providing some hope that the party might be reunited behind a set of policies that would not immediately alienate a majority of the electors.

The Falkland Islands were not the only part of Britain's former empire to preoccupy the government. In 1976 another attempt at a Rhodesian settlement

Cecil Parkinson was one of Mrs Thatcher's staunchest supporters, in great part architect of the electoral victory and by many deemed most likely to succeed as leader. Then he became involved in an unsavoury marital scandal and departed from office.

Though Mrs Thatcher resisted the temptation to call an election in the immediate aftermath of the campaign, the 'Falklands factor' still proved a potent element in the general election of June 1983. Here, looking somewhat perplexed, she shops with her daughter Carol in Finchley during the election.

The Labour party found a new leader in Neil Kinnock, energetic, affable, and offering some hope that the party might once more be united. Here he is distributing free butter to old age pensioners as a protest against the ever-growing butter mountain accumulated by the Common Market.

Shortly before Christmas 1983 the IRA exploded a thirty-pound bomb outside Harrods in London's Knightsbridge. Two police and three passers-by were killed and there were many injured.

had foundered and the next two years were marked by increasing violence, the flight of many Europeans from the country and the progressive collapse of law and order. A moderate multiracial administration led by Bishop Muzorewa failed to win the confidence of the more extreme nationalists or independent Black Africa. A conference in London in September 1979 preceded the installation of Christopher Soames as governor during a fleeting return to colonial status, followed by elections which led to an extreme left-wing politician, Robert Mugabe, becoming the first ruler of a wholly independent Rhodesia, or Zimbabwe as it now became. Another colonial vestige was tidied up in 1984 when an agreement on the future of Hong Kong was initialled in Peking. The Chinese were to obtain full sovereignty over the colony when the lease on the mainland territories expired in 1997, but agreed that for fifty years thereafter the capitalist system would survive and the city be allowed a degree of autonomy. The value of the agreement depended on the readiness of the Chinese to execute it faithfully, but few doubted that it was the best solution that could be hoped for.

There was no similar progress to record from Northern Ireland. The years 1977 and 1978 seemed to offer some grounds for hope, with markedly less violence. A strike organised by Ian Paisley to obtain a return to self-government and an all-out attack on the IRA was conspicuously unsuccessful. There were 111 deaths through violence in 1977, more than enough, but with 352 Northern Irish killed on the roads in the same period such a toll seemed almost tolerable. But no progress was made towards a permanent settlement and 1979 was marked by the murders of Airey Neave in Westminster, the British ambassador in The Hague, eighteen soldiers in an ambush at Warrenpoint and, on the same day as that last, of Lord Mountbatten, cousin of the Queen and former viceroy of India, with two members of his family at his holiday home of Classiebawn Castle in the Republic of Ireland. Hunger strikes at the Maze prison; a mass breakout; more murders in London, with a Christmas bomb outside Harrods, and the blowing up of the Horse Guards as they rode towards Whitehall and of the Royal Green Jackets band in Regents Park: these were the milestones of the next few sombre years. In 1984 a bomb in the Grand Hotel at Brighton only just failed to obliterate half of the British cabinet. Several political figures staying in the hotel for the Conservative party conference were killed; Norman Tebbitt and his wife were buried in the rubble and badly injured. Mrs Thatcher, who missed

A still more dramatic atrocity occurred at about 3 am on 12 October 1984 when the IRA blew up part of the Grand Hotel in Brighton where many of the cabinet were staying during the Tory party conference. Norman Tebbitt, the trade and industry secretary, was among the seriously injured and Mrs Thatcher herself was lucky to escape.

In 1981 the Prince of Wales married Lady Diana Spencer in St Paul's Cathedral. An estimated 750 million people around the world watched the ceremony on television, another 250 million listened on radio. Here the newly married couple make obeisance to the Queen before they leave the cathedral.

By providing the nation with an heir to the throne Princess Diana embellished still further her already impeccable reputation. Prince Henry followed in 1984 and is here shown at the christening with his great-grandmother, grandmother and parents.

An exultant crowd waits to cheer the Queen as she drives through the London streets on the Prince of Wales's wedding day in July 1981. The people in the picture are obviously aware of the presence of the camera, but there can be no doubt about the reality of their enthusiasm.

Unemployment was the scourge of the age. More than 300,000 youngsters joined the dole queue for the first time in September 1982. For many of them it seemed unlikely that they would ever find employment. A group of teenagers here wait disconsolately outside the social security office in Brighton.

1984 was marked by the long drawn-out and fiercely fought coal miners' strike. Here at Askern Colliery in South Yorkshire police and pickets await the 4 am workers' bus. Too often such peaceful scenes were followed by bouts of frightening violence. The strike lasted for just under a year before the men returned to work.

injury or death by a hair's breadth, emerged with her reputation for courage and dignity under stress still further enhanced.

It was, however, the battle with the trade unions and the problem of unemployment that marked Mrs Thatcher's second administration. Under Labour governments the trade unions had become almost a wing of government, more powerful in some ways since they rarely had to worry about the dangers of a contested election. With Mrs Thatcher's accession, they found themselves left out of discussions of economic policy and treated with some disdain. Their standing in the public's estimation was already low, and the high level of unemployment put them in a weak bargaining position in any confrontation with employers or the government. When legislation was passed curbing their right to strike without first holding a ballot of their members – a battle that they had twice won before – they were hesitant in offering out-and-out defiance. Their membership dwindled – they lost half a million members in 1981 alone. But it would have been a foolhardy government that wrote them off as a force in national life. The trade unions still had something over ten million members and their blocking

power was enormous. The Conservatives might consult them rarely but they could not afford to ignore them.

The starkest confrontation came, as so often, with the miners. Arthur Scargill became President of the National Union of Mineworkers in 1982 and almost at once showed what might be expected of him by walking out of a meeting with the Coal Board after a mere four minutes. He tried to call a strike on pay and pit closures but in a ballot was rejected by 61 per cent of his miners. Undiscomfited he tried again, this time so arranging things that a ballot could be avoided. He did not get solid support, but most of the miners were on strike by March 1984.

A year later they were back at work again, having gained nothing. That round had been won by the government but only the most sanguine believed that as a result of it the war with organised labour had come to an end.

The striking miners swelled the already alarming unemployment figures. Month after month, as inflation fell, so the total of the unemployed rose inexorably. It was not just a British problem – by the end of 1981 there were twenty million unemployed in the fifteen

The People's March for Jobs took a procession of unemployed on a 280-mile trek from Liverpool to Trafalgar Square. Here the march passes through Hitchin on the day's stage from Letchworth to Luton.

The royal hat-maker, Freddie Fox, shows off a selection of his products. The Queen would be surprised, even dismayed, if she were described as smart; she has her own style and sticks to it with splendid indifference to the vagaries of fashion.

On the balcony of Buckingham Palace on the occasion of the Queen Mother's eightieth birthday.

Princess Diana quickly showed herself to be fashion conscious yet highly individual in her taste.
Here she attends a reception at Lancaster House for the London Fashion Week of 1985.

most industrialised nations. The British figures, though worse than those for most of the members of the EEC, were far better than those of the underdeveloped world. Nevertheless, when the total passed three million early in 1982, there were many Conservatives who felt that Mrs Thatcher's monetarist policies were making things worse and that a switch in policy was overdue. A particularly distressing feature was that whatever new jobs were created tended to go to those seeking work for the first time or only recently out of work. By the end of 1984 more than one million had been out of a job for over a year, half a million for two years. It seemed progressively less likely that more than a handful of these last would ever be employed again. The sum of human misery and degradation represented by such a statistic was incalculable.

In 1984, for the first time in its peacetime history, Britain imported more manufactured products than it exported. The value of the pound was sustained by the export of oil, and as the oil price slumped on the international markets, so the pound fell with it, closer and closer to parity with the dollar. Hopes that this drastic devaluation would lead to a recovery based on increased exports never seemed quite to be fulfilled. Britain's economy was in trouble, if not near disaster.

AGAINST SO bleak a background, it would not have been altogether surprising if the monarchy had been dismissed as extravagant, frivolous, or at least irrelevant to the needs of the nation. If such sentiment existed it was rarely voiced; even that champion of republicanism, Mr William Hamilton, seemed curiously muted. The monarchy for its part, after twenty-five years of relative quiescence since the coronation, now burst

The Silver Jubilee of 1977 showed that economic difficulties did nothing to tarnish the average Briton's affection for the monarchy and determination to have a good time if humanly possible. Eighty-year old Fred English of Manor Road, East Molesey, spent more than a week decorating his house with tinsel, flags, bunting and royal portraits in preparation for the great day.

forth with two great state occasions of splendour.

First was the Queen's silver jubilee in 1977. The build-up to this event followed the course of all such royal junketings. First there was apathy and some confusion. What did the jubilee commemorate? Some said D-Day, more the royal wedding, which to their surprise when they came to work out the dates seemed to render Prince Charles illegitimate. Once this was straightened out there were complaints about the expense and wasted effort. Early enthusiasm was patchy, though at Shelton in Oxfordshire on 5 February (the day of the *real* accession) sixty villagers gathered in heavy rain around the village pond to sing 'Land of Hope and Glory'. Gradually the people became interested, then involved, finally plunged into hectic turmoil as every village and street prepared to hold its private celebration.

Almost to the day itself it seemed that, without the stands or the foreign potentates, the procession to St Paul's would be only a shadow of the coronation. Instead it was a tumultuous and gigantic success. Most moving of all was the Queen's walk from St Paul's to the Guidhall, with the crowd surging forward to see, or better still to touch her. 'We have come here because we love you,' blurted out an office girl in her early twenties. 'I can feel it and it means so much to me,' replied the Queen. In her speech at the Guildhall she declared: *When I was twenty-one, I pledged my life to the service of our people and I asked for God's help to make good to them that vow. Although that vow was made in my salad days when I was green in judgment I do not regret nor retract one word of it.*

Then it was home to vast yet orderly crowds around the Palace and all the varieties of local celebration: more than 6,000 street parties in London and 139 in

After the thanksgiving service for the Silver Jubilee in St Paul's Cathedral the Queen walked from the north door to the Guildhall. The crowd responded to her presence with delirious enthusiasm, reaching out towards her as if there were some magic benefit to be gained by touching her.

Prince Andrew, the Queen's second son, was a helicopter pilot aboard HMS Invincible when the Falklands war began. Some people assumed he would be put in a place of safety, but neither he nor his parents would have accepted anything of the sort. he did his difficult and dangerous duty manfully and he and his shipmates returned in triumph to be greeted at Portsmouth by his mother.

President Reagan applauding an attentive, but restrained, Queen. The occasion was a State banquet at Windsor Castle in June 1982.

The Queen holds her only granddaughter, Zara Phillips, at the Windsor Horse Show in June 1984.

Exeter. Piano-smashing was a feature at Watton and Stone; for some reason newly minted traditional sports involving gumboots, such as 'welly-wanging', 'welly-throwing' and 'welly-hoying' were prominent all over the country.

As a tourist attraction, acclaimed around the world, the jubilee was a notable success. So too did it stimulate trade at home:

> *Oh to be in England*
> *Now that Spring is here,*
> *Oh to be in Skinner's (China and Glass)*
> *In Jubilee Year*

read a high street proclamation in Sutton, Surrey. The usual plethora of souvenirs, postcards and brochures adorned the shops. Robert Lacey's *Majesty*, a skilfully crafted exercise in making bricks with a minimum of straw, sold 200,000 copies by the end of jubilee year, and thirty-one other books on aspects of the subject achieved some measure of success.

Those who said that the monarchy was popular only in the prosperous south were confounded by the tumultuous welcome given the Queen in the great industrial cities of Scotland and the North of England.

Dour, socialist Glasgow in particular showed an enthusiasm that rivalled any reception in the south. In 1977 the Queen spent a hundred days on tour in the United Kingdom, travelled 8,000 miles, kept 800 engagements; and all this added to 56,000 miles of jubilee tours around the Commonwealth in the spring and autumn.

Four years later came the royal wedding. The Prince of Wales's putative brides had been a subject of speculation in the press for several years, even to the point when an official denial had to be made of reports that he was to marry Princess Marie Astrid of Luxembourg. The name of Lady Diana Spencer had been one of many mentioned among possible contestants, but it still came as a surprise when the engagement was announced in February 1981. Lady Diana was patently young, beautiful, well-born, British and Protestant and there was every reason to believe that she was high-spirited and benevolent as well. The chorus of approval was deafening.

It did not subside until the wedding, nor indeed afterwards. At least 600,000 people stood between the Palace and St Paul's to see the couple pass. More than 750 million around the world watched the proceedings

The Queen and the Duke visit a Scottish manufacturer of bottled and canned foods in Scotland in July 1982. The Duke's expression as he samples the product is admirably non-committal – a grimace might be worth many thousand pounds to a rival manufacturer.

on television, a further 250 million listened on radio. When Lady Diana fluffed her lines and got her fiancé's names wrong, the nation's heart went out to her. Her popularity has never faded. Eleven months later she added to her impeccable reputation by producing a royal heir, Prince William. 'I think it's a very lovely name,' said William Hamilton benignly, 'and I am sure they had me in mind when they chose it.'

The Prince of Wales was not the only royal hero. Prince Andrew had played a role as a helicopter pilot in the Falklands war, his Sea King helicopter hovering above HMS *Invincible* as a decoy to attract Exocet missiles from their true target. He performed and spoke of this unenviable task with characteristic insouciance. Otherwise he seemed intent on winning for himself the maverick reputation that had belonged in the previous generation to his aunt, Princess Margaret. She did not resign the title without a struggle. Her marriage broke up in 1976 – an operation handled with restraint and dignity; her divorce became final in 1978; and in that same year she incurred the disapproval of the Bishop of Truro, who described her holiday in the West Indies with the celebrated gardener, Roddy Llewellyn, as 'foolish' and urged her to withdraw from public life.

It was not necessary to go to the Falklands for members of the royal family to incur danger. Lord Mountbatten was murdered by the IRA in 1979 and two years later, shortly before her son's wedding, the Queen was shot at in the Mall on her way to the ceremony of Trooping the Colour. The Queen controlled her startled horse and quietly rode on; the gun turned out to be loaded only with blanks, but her vulnerability to attack by anyone who was prepared to take the risk had been made alarmingly obvious. That attempt at least was in a public street. In 1982 Michael Fagan, thirty-five years old, unemployed, and under the illusion that he was a son of Rudolph Hess, climbed into Buckingham Palace, evaded the police, reached the Queen's bedroom and sat on her bed for twenty minutes, or so, telling her about his problems. The Queen rang to summon help but the police were slow in coming and the conversation continued until a servant finally arrived. Fagan too was harmless, but the revelation that the Queen's innermost sanctum could be so easily breached caused dismay to all and much heart-searching among those responsible for her safety.

In July 1976 the Queen and the Duke of Edinburgh, in the royal yacht *Britannia*, sailed into Philadelphia

The Queen is greeted at Euston station by Peter Parker, Chairman of British Rail, before boarding the new Royal Train for her jubilee tour of Scotland in May 1977. In the background are wives of the workmen who ensured that the new 100 mph train was ready on time.

The Queen leaves St George's, Windsor, after the Garter ceremony. Of all the splendiferous fancy dress parades involving the royal family none can be more picturesque or more historic than this.

The royal wedding took place on 29 July 1981. The Prince and Princess of Wales are here leaving St Paul's in their open carriage. More than 600,000 people watched them along the way.

On the balcony of the Palace after their return from St Paul's the Prince of Wales kisses the hand of his new wife. The younger bridesmaid, Catherine Cameron, looks decidedly apprehensive but Lady Sarah Armstrong-Jones and Lord Nicholas Windsor plainly approve.

In June 1982 the Princess of Wales produced an heir to the throne. The gratified parents stand outside St Mary's Hospital in London where their child was born.

As the Queen rode down The Mall for the ceremony of Trooping the Colour a man fired several blanks at her from a replica pistol. The Queen calmed her horse and rode on without more ado. No harm was done but the incident showed how impossible it would be to protect any member of the royal family from attack by a desperate assassin.

where the Declaration of Independence had been signed 200 years before. 'I speak to you as the direct descendant of King George III,' said the Queen boldly, to the evident pleasure of her audience. No one can prove that this visit, or the many others that the Queen paid to foreign countries, made any direct contribution to British prestige or its good relationship with the countries visited. Nor can it be shown that exports rose or more favourable treaties were negotiated as a result of the royal tours. Nevertheless, all those best qualified to judge are satisfied that the Queen, by her trips abroad and reception of foreign grandees at home, makes an important contribution to Britain's foreign policy and its balance of payments. It is still more evident that the monarchy is the most important single feature in the complex of sights, scenery and ancient pageantry that draws tourists to the British Isles.

Any doll in a crown, wired to mouth the speeches written by its advisers, could have done as much. Queen Elizabeth II was much more than a doll. Suc-cessive prime ministers have testified to her acumen, her experience and her wisdom. Governments have come and gone, but she has continued, indifferent to party, above faction, uniquely able to view events in the longer term; to view them, too, as Queen not of the United Kingdom alone but as Head of the Common-wealth. In 1979 she visited Lusaka to open the Com-monwealth conference. Developments in Rhodesia had made Britain violently unpopular; the press was hos-tile; the auguries for a fruitful meeting could hardly have been worse. The Queen took the Zambian leader, Kenneth Kaunda, to one side. 'Kenneth,' she said, 'I've known you and Julius Nyerere longer than anyone else here. I don't want to get involved in the politics of Rhodesia. But do you want this conference to fail before it even starts? Don't you think it would only be fair to sit down?' The appeal worked; the press changed its tune; the conference was constructive and good-tempered. Nobody else could have done as much. Queen Eliz-abeth had shown once again that she was no mere figurehead but a potent force.

The Queen, seated between Presidents Kaunda and Nyerere at the Commonwealth Conference in Lusaka. The racial mix of the gathering is strikingly contrasted with what it was thirty years before (page 157, bottom).

By the mid-1980s motorways, with increasing frequency, seemed to be more like car parks.
In July 1982 this traffic jam near Bristol was twenty-five miles long.
Even this did not break the record.

A group of skinheads on the front at Southend taunt a policeman. Even if they have no respect
for the law they would surely be well advised to keep an eye on the law's dog.

The punk hair-do of the epicene youth in the centre of the picture contrasts strikingly with the skinheads at Southend. He/she is taking part in a demonstration in the City of London, aimed at a wide range of targets ranging from fur importers to firms trading with South Africa.

One of the worst disasters in British sporting history occurred at the Bradford City football stadium in May 1985 when a 77-year-old wooden stand caught fire and was quickly engulfed by flames. Fifty-three fans died immediately, many more were badly burned. In a year in which British football was banned from the Continent because of mob violence, it seemed as if soccer was destined to be a source of shame and tragedy for the nation.

*By the sixtieth year of the Queen's life Britain had undeniably become a multi-racial society.
Here two of her subjects study the form from the Royal Enclosure at Ascot.*

*The Notting Hill carnival annually produces an explosion of uninhibited fun. Although sometimes
marred by violence, convivial scenes such as this have become a symbol of inter-racial harmony.*

70,000 fans crowded Wembley Stadium for the Live Aid concert, the global rock show seen by an estimated 1500 million people in 160 countries, and believed to have raised some £50 million for famine relief in Africa.

Epilogue

Britain: Spring 1986

IF RIP VAN Smith or Jones had been laid to rest in 1926, then resurrected sixty years later and deposited at random somewhere in the British Isles, the chances are ninety-nine out of a hundred that he would see nothing to suggest he had had more than a fleeting doze. Most of the countryside remains as it was. In certain parts of the country he might see disconcertingly large plantations of conifers, in others miniprairies where he had been used to small, hedged fields, but the heaths, the moors, the downs, and the larger part of the cultivated land would show few marks of the passing of time.

It would be very different when he found his way to the nearest habitation, perhaps a cottage formerly lived in by some shepherd or farm labourer. This might well be derelict, roof half gone, garden a jungle; or garnished with the spruce and suburban elegance that suggested it had fallen prey to a week-ender from the city. If however it remained in the hands of an agricultural labourer the surprise for the visitor from the past would be no less striking. The cottage would almost certainly boast a metal contraption rearing above the chimney, sign that the miracle of television has bestowed its blessings on rural England. Inside there would be electric light and running water, if no central heating then at least a stove more efficient than anything known in the past, a refrigerator, a vacuum cleaner, possibly a deep-freeze and washing-machine. The standards of comfort would be immeasurably higher, the drudgery imposed on the housewife far less arduous. Her husband too would have had his work lightened by machines and be paid a wage which in real terms was princely compared with that earned by his father or grandfather sixty years before.

When he got to the nearest village there would be fresh shocks for Rip Van Smith. The village church would probably be locked; services would be held only every second Sunday; if he happened to coincide with one he would find a congregation far more scanty than that to which he had been used. The village school would be closed, transformed into a commodious retirement home; the children would depart every morning by bus to the nearest market-town a few miles away. The village shop might easily have closed as well, killed by the competition of the supermarkets, and the

local post office and smithy would have gone with it. The most conspicuous new development, apart from the additional names on the war memorial, would be a group of cottages on the outskirts of the village – less picturesque but considerably more weatherproof than their older neighbours. The pub might at first seem unchanged, but a venture inside would probably reveal that it had been acquired by one of the major breweries and now boasted an electrically powered 'log fire', a juke box, at least one electronic game and a system for piping music into every corner.

But it would not be until the revenant journeyed the few miles to the nearest market-town that the enormity of what had happened would begin to strike him. Particularly in the south-east of England, but to some extent everywhere in the British Isles, the town would have grown substantially, a welter of housing estates would sprawl over what had previously been farm land or the park of the local mansion. But it would be the proliferation of cars which would most amaze and daunt him. They would be everywhere, belching out fumes, roaring and hooting, jostling for parking space to the peril of the pedestrian. Either the high street would be rendered impassable, if not uninhabitable by their presence, or they would be exiled to some vast parking lot where they would line up in their hundreds awaiting their owners' return from shopping.

And the shops would belong to a different world. A few of the familiar names might survive, though their old windows would probably have been swept away to give space for plate glass showcases. Most of the small grocers, bakers, fruitshops, butchers, chemists would have been driven out of business by a supermarket, probably built beside the car park and catering for the motorist who stocked up with provisions once a week. In their place Rip Van Smith would find an extraordinary miscellany of emporia, whose purpose would seem to him either obscure or irrelevant to the needs of the society he had left sixty years before: Chinese takeaways, videos and home computers, betting shops and self-service launderettes, travel agencies, boutiques and health-food shops. His fellow countrymen would seem to have acquired a new range of desires and needs, and a new entrepreneurial class had sprung up to service them.

As he ventured towards London, or any other great conurbation, he would begin to think that nothing survived of the Britain he had known. It had been surrendered to the car; six track motorways blasting their way across a cowed countryside; endless petrol stations; garages, roadside shops and cafes, seeking to minister to the drivers. The suburbs would have swollen immeasurably; acre after acre that he had known as fields or woods now covered by a rash of council housing or the factories of whatever industry had seen fit to make camp there. Overhead, particularly if he approached London from the west, he would see, and still more, hear a stream of aircraft, all far larger than anything he had perhaps seen, more probably heard of before, stream-lined, mysteriously without propellers. By plane, by train, by car, by coach, the whole population would seem to be on the move, dashing perpetually from place to place in search of some unidentifiable holy grail.

And what a population he would see. In the summer, in central London or one of the other tourist centres, he would hardly hear English spoken, jostled as he would be by the milling crowds of Germans and Japanese, Arabs and Americans. Elsewhere, where once a black or brown face had been an exotic rarity, whole tracts of Britain's cities would seem to be populated predominantly by coloured immigrants, while in certain fields of employment, the London underground being a conspicuous example, the system would stop work instantly if the West Indian, in particular, withdrew his labour. The Rastafarian ringlets and Sikh turbans would startle the voyager from the past, but no more than the indigenous British punks, with hair in cockscomb or wild spikes, dyed green or pink or purple, striding through the streets with glazed expression as their portable transistors pumped pop music into the earphones they wore upon their heads. And above this polyglot bedlam would rear great tower blocks, soaring twenty or thirty storeys high, destroying the vistas that had delighted the inhabitants for centuries; some of them would be blocks of flats, some hotels, but most of them crammed with clerks and accountants busily making money so that more tower blocks could be built to keep them company.

One thing would have struck a familiar chord in the visitor from 1926: the monstrous regiment of the unemployed. Yet even here, though the proportions of workers to jobless might be roughly the same, the underlying realities would be very different. On the credit side, the unemployed in 1986 were far better off than their grandfathers in similar plight. The right-wing folklore of idle layabouts buying second cars and taking holidays abroad on the dole was demonstrably false, but everyone who claimed his rights was adequately if sparsely fed, clothed and housed. Yet the unemployed of 1926 at least felt greater confidence that when the economy picked up again their jobs would once more be available. The unemployed of 1986 faced the dread possibility that new technology might mean their jobs had gone for ever; a whole generation might be doomed to chronic under-employment or even worklessness.

THE STRUCTURE of society has changed and will continue to change at least as fast. Houses, clothes, foods, drinks, entertainments – all the bric à brac of contemporary life – have undergone a dramatic transformation. But has the human being changed? Superficially, the answer must be 'yes'. Today many more Britons have many more possessions. The dream of the enlightened capitalist – a property-owning democracy in which everyone who works gets and keeps a decent slice of the national cake – is closer to realisation than ever before. What people have, they value and wish to retain. The Briton today is more materialistic than in the past, and predisposed to elect a government that would allow him to keep what he has won and perhaps add to it rather than to vote in ministers who would pursue a more egalitarian and reformist policy. The values of the bourgeoisie have been adopted by millions who belong traditionally to the working classes. There is little comfort for the doctrinaire socialist in the frame of mind of a majority of the voters.

Yet this is only one side of the coin. The Briton today is more socially responsible than ever before. Cheeseparing governments may nibble at the edges of the National Health Service or the education budget, but no one challenges the basic assumption that it is the duty of society to provide for the nation's welfare and to ensure that its less fortunate members are spared the worst rigours of privation. The British today, under-privileged though they may sometimes feel they are in comparison with the Americans or the Arabs, are alive to their immense good luck in not being born into one of the famine- and plague-ridden areas of the world. Television periodically pricks the conscience of the affluent West with its portrayal of anguish in Bangladesh or Ethiopia, Cambodia or Central America, yet it cannot alone explain the sustained acceptance by the bulk of the population that it is the duty of the government to spend substantial sums each year on aid to the poorer parts of the world.

Nor can one doubt that in case of crisis the British would abandon their materialistic toys without undue dismay. They would meet disaster with the same fortitude and humour as in the past, just as surely as they would grumble and make life difficult for all concerned until the disaster was actually upon them. They would continue to view their neighbours with aloof suspicion until such time as their neighbours' house blew down, when they would work all night to dig them from the rubble and succour them afterwards. They would deplore chauvinistic gestures, shuffle their feet through 'God Save the Queen', reserve their patriotic fervour for the last night of the proms, yet, should need arise, would die for their country with the same resigned determination as in the past.

OF ALL THE facets of British society, the monarch has on the surface changed least of all. Buckingham Palace, Windsor Castle, Balmoral stand unblemished to show that the Queen is on her throne and all's right with the world. The pageantry continues undiminished, the paraphernalia of gold plate and gorgeous flunkeys adorns the royal occasion as it has always done. The helicopter may now be a preferred means of transport (by everyone except the Queen who detests the noisy beast), time-and-motion studies may be applied to the running of the royal households, but these are merely sophisticated means of achieving what has been done more laboriously in the past. Nor can such labour-saving devices be of more than limited value: the Rolls-Royce, far more efficient though it might be, can never replace the state coach; windows of bullet-proof glass, though more secure, are no substitute for the plumed glory of an escort from the Household Cavalry. 'Le style est l'homme même,' wrote De Buffon; and to a great extent the mystic pageantry with which the royal family surrounds itself *is* the royal family. The monarchy is not, cannot be, a modern institution. Today in 1986 it stands for essentially the same values as it stood for sixty years ago and as it will do sixty years ahead. It was an anachronism then and will be no more and no less of one in the year 2046.

But the paradox of the monarchy is that while it cannot afford to change too radically, it also must not ossify. Superficially the British nation has undergone a revolution, yet the essential stability of the nation has remained constant; superficially the British monarchy has shown itself immutable, yet it has evolved significantly in its attitudes and its nature. The British people have changed less than would at first appear, the monarchy more. The essential truth, which the Queen has understood and acted on, is that while the monarchy must respond to the movements and fashions of time, it must never ape them. A trendy monarch who sought to put the monarchy in the vanguard of radical experiment, who sent the royal princelings to communes and turned Buckingham Palace into a museum, would swiftly destroy the institution he sought to reform; yet a monarchy that failed wholly to adapt to the times would atrophy and perish. The Queen must walk a delicate path. She has done so with skill and authority since the moment of her accession. There is every reason to believe that she will continue to do so.

Index

Photographic acknowledgements

Colour. BBC Hulton Picture Library, London 82, 95, 118, 138-9, 166-7; Bridgeman Art Library (Guildhall Art Gallery), London 26-27; Camera Press, London 323 top; Camera Press/Patrick Lichfield 262-3; E.T. Archive, London 18, 19, (Tate Gallery) 30-31, 99; Geffreye Museum, London 30 left; Granda Television, Manchester 295 right; Milton Keynes Development Corporation 134-5; Photo Source, London 83, 91, 123, 175, 198, 199, 206-7, 242 top and bottom, 250-1, 263 right, 267 bottom, 302-3, 320 top; Popperfoto, London 86, 87, 90, 102 top and bottom, 106-7, 110, 122, 127, 130, 138 left, 142-3, 143 right, 162-3, 163 right, 170 left, 170-171, 194 left, 194-5, 214-15, 246-7, 247 right, 250 top, 258, 259; John Scott, Bracknell 219, 223; Syndication International, London 174, 218, 242-3, 250 bottom, 254-5, 255 right, 266-7, 270 left, 270-1, 290 left, 290-1, 294-5, 298-9, 303 top and bottom, 322-3, 323 bottom, 326 bottom, 327, 330 bottom, 331, 334-5; Judy Todd, London 298 left; Topham Picture Library, Edenbridge 326 top.

Black and white. Associated Press, London 316 right; BBC copyright photographs 264 top and bottom, 308 bottom; BBC Hulton Picture Library, London 9 bottom left, 11, 13 bottom, 16 top, 17 bottom, 20 bottom left, 21, 33 bottom, 35 bottom, 38 top and bottom, 39 top and bottom left, 40 top, 41, 43 top, 50 bottom, 51, 52 top, 53 top, 54 bottom, 59, 68, 71, 74 top, bottom left and bottom right, 98 top left, top right and bottom, 100 bottom, 103 bottom, 106 top, 115, 128 top, 133 bottom, 137 top and bottom, 145 bottom right, 147 bottom, 172 bottom, 178 bottom, 179 top, 181 bottom right, 200 bottom left; BIPNA, London 286, 336, 337 top; Birmingham Post and Mail 80; British Film Institute, London 50 top, 265 top; British Petroleum, London 281; Butlins Holiday, Bognor Regis 48 bottom; Camera Press, London/Karsh of Ottawa 2; Camera Press, London/Snowdon 186; Granada Television, Manchester 210; Gerald Howson, London 224 left; Illustrated London News 47 bottom; Imperial War Museum, London 81 bottom, 93 bottom, 97 bottom; Bill Kenwright Productions, London 265 bottom; Kobal Collection, London 141, 144 top and bottom left, 211 top, 309 top and bottom; The Raymond and Joe Mitchenson Collection, London 10, 34; The Mary Rose Trust, Portsmouth 314 bottom; Newnes Books, Feltham 8, 61 top right, 76 left, 112-13, 168 top, 178 top; Photo Source, London [Central Press] 148-9, 189 bottom, [Fox Photos] Front end paper, 29, 63 bottom, 66 top, 114, 117, 124 bottom, 157 bottom, 190 top, 274, [Keystone Press] 6, 9 top, 65, 153 bottom, 209 bottom, 211 bottom, 342 bottom; Popperfoto, London 20 top, 22, 23, 24, 25 top and bottom, 28 top, 36, 46 bottom, 56 bottom, 58, 60, 61 top left, 64 top and bottom, 72, 75 top, 81 top, 84, 85 bottom, 92 top right and bottom, 93 top, 94, 96 top and bottom, 97 top, 100 top, 101, 103 top, 104 top, 105, 108, 116, 119 left and right, 120 top and bottom, 121, 124 top, 136 bottom, 140 bottom, 146 top and bottom, 147 top, 155, 156, 158 top left and bottom left, 158-9, 160 bottom, 164, 168 bottom right, 184 bottom, 187, 190 bottom, 191 top, 208 top, 236, 239 bottom, 328, 333; Press Association, London 235 bottom, 237, 239 top, 245 bottom, 268 bottom right, 276 top, 287, 310 bottom, Back end paper; Rex Features, London 339; Houston Rogers, London 180 left; Rolls-Royce Motors, Crewe 241; Sotheby's, London 312; Syndication International, London 14 top and bottom, 16 bottom, 17 top, 28 bottom, 32, 33 top, 37 top and bottom, 47 top, 57 top, 61 bottom, 62, 63 top, 70 top, 73, 76 right, 77, 78 top, 79 top and bottom, 85 top, 88-9, 89 top and bottom, 92 top left, 104 bottom, 111, 128 bottom, 129 top and bottom, 132 bottom, 133 top, 150 top and bottom, 151 left and right, 153 top, 154, 157 top, 160 top, 161, 165, 168 bottom left, 181 top, 184 top, 185 bottom, 188 bottom, 189 top, 191 bottom, 193 bottom left and bottom right, 197 top, 200 bottom right, 204 top, 205 bottom, 208 bottom left and bottom right, 213, 216 top, 221 bottom left, 224 left and right, 226 top, bottom left and bottom right, 227, 229, 230 top, 231 top left, top right and bottom, 232, 233 top and bottom, 234, 238, 240, 244 top and bottom, 245 top, 248, 249 top, bottom left and bottom right, 252, 253 bottom, 256 top and bottom, 257 top left, top right and bottom, 260 top, 267 top, 268 top and bottom left, 269 top and bottom, 272, 275 right, 276 bottom, 277 top left, top right and bottom, 278, 279, 282 bottom, 283 bottom, 284, 288 top and bottom, 292 top and bottom, 293 top and bottom, 296, 297 top and bottom, 300 top left, top right and bottom, 301 top and bottom left, 306 top, 310 top left and top right, 313 top and bottom, 316 left, 317 top and bottom, 318 bottom, 319 bottom, 320 top and bottom, 321, 324 top, 329, 340 bottom, 341 bottom, 343; Topham Picture Library, Edenbridge 9 bottom right, 12, 13 top, 15 top and bottom, 20 bottom right, 35 top, 39 bottom right, 42, 43 bottom, 44-45, 46 top, 48 top, 49, 52 bottom, 53 bottom, 54 top, 55 left, 55 right, 56 top, 57 bottom, 66 bottom, 67 top and bottom, 69, 70 bottom, 75 bottom, 78 bottom, 106 bottom, 109, 125 top and bottom, 126 top and bottom, 131 top and bottom, 132 top, 136 top, 140 top, 144 bottom right, 145 top and bottom left, 152, 169 top and bottom, 172 top, 173 top and bottom, 176-7, 179 bottom, 180 right, 181 bottom left, 182 top and bottom, 183, 185 top, 188 top, 192, 193 top, 196 top and bottom, 197 bottom, 200 top, 201, 202-3, 204 bottom, 205 top, 209 top, 212 top and bottom, 216 bottom, 217, 220 left and right, 221 top and bottom right, 222 top left, top right and bottom, 225 right, 228, 230 bottom, 235 top, 260 bottom, 261, 273, 275 left, 280, 282 top, 283 top, 289 top and bottom, 301 bottom right, 304, 305, 306 bottom, 307, 308 top, 314 top, 315 top and bottom, 318 top, 319 top, 324 bottom, 325, 332, 337 bottom, 338, 340 top, 341 top, 342 top; Reg Wilson, London 311; Windsor Archives 7; F W Woolworth, London 40 bottom.